BREAKING THROUGH

Breaking Through

John B. McLendon,
Basketball Legend
and Civil Rights Pioneer

MILTON S. KATZ

The University of Arkansas Press
Fayetteville • 2007

ISBN-10: 1-55728-847-X
ISBN-13: 978-1-55728-847-9

11   10   09   08   07   5   4   3   2   1

Designed by Liz Lester

⊗ The paper used in this publication meets the minimum requirements of the American National Standard for Permanence of Paper
for Printed Library Materials Z39.48-1984.

LIBRARY OF CONGRESS CATALOGING-IN-PUBLICATION DATA

Katz, Milton S., 1945–
    Breaking through : John B. Mclendon, basketball legend,
and civil rights pioneer / Milton S. Katz.
      p.   cm.
    Includes bibliographical references and index.
    ISBN 1-55728-847-X (cloth : alk. paper)
    1. McLendon, John B. 2. Basketball coaches—United
States—Biography. 3. African American basketball coaches.
4. Discrimination in sports—United States. I. Title.
    GV884.M29K37   2007
    796.323'092—dc22
    [B]
                        2007016308

Frontispiece: John B. McLendon Jr. (Courtesy Joanna McLendon)

For my father, Sheldon Katz,
who always had a smile on his face
and, in his quiet, unassuming way,
instilled in me a love of sports and a
commitment to social justice and
human understanding.

CONTENTS

Contents

FOREWORD

By Billy Packer,
Emmy Award–Winning
CBS Basketball Analyst

After leading Georgetown to the national championship in 1984, John Thompson was asked if he was proud to be the first African American to coach a team to the crown. His answer was brilliant: "If I am a pioneer in 1984 it is only because men more qualified than I were wrongly denied the opportunity." While Hall of Famer Thompson's quote certainly relates to many, for me it refers to another Hall of Famer and one of basketball's truly great people, John McLendon Jr.

Much has been written about the historically significant National Collegiate Athletic Association's Final Four of 1966, when Texas Western, with five black starters, defeated the all-white team of the University of Kentucky. Some have written that the game's importance has been overstated, as black athletes had played in championships before 1966. Just three years earlier, Loyola of Chicago, with four black starters, had defeated top-ranked Cincinnati, which also started four black players. In my opinion, the 1966 game did—without question— have historical significance; however, with regard to racial breakthroughs in basketball, it pales in comparison to the firsts initiated by one man, Coach John McLendon.

John was the first black man to:

1. Graduate with a degree in physical education from the University of Kansas (1936);
2. Win three straight National Association of Intercollegiate Athletics (NAIA) national championships, coaching Tennessee A&I State University (1957–59);
3. Integrate Kansas City hotels and restaurants during the NAIA Tip-Off Tournament (1954);
4. Coach the Cleveland Pipers to a national Amateur Athletic Union championship (1961);
5. Coach a U.S. All-Star team overseas (1961);

6. Coach a now-professional team, the Cleveland Pipers, in the American Basketball League (1961–62);

7. Coach at the predominately white Cleveland State University (1966);

8. Coach and win a major international competition for the United States (1967);

9. Coach on the Olympic basketball staff (1968, 1972);

10. Write and publish a book on "fast-break" basketball (1965);

11. Be inducted into the Naismith Memorial Basketball Hall of Fame as a contributor to the game (1979).

When one considers the fact that in 2006, 25 percent of all coaches in the 334 Division-1 NCAA colleges were African Americans, one cannot deny the significance of the path that John McLendon laid.

History shows that John's overall record in thirty-four years of coaching at all levels includes 744 wins. He first made his mark at North Carolina College, as he led his team, without an all-conference player and with a starting lineup that included three players under five-seven, to the Central Intercollegiate Athletic Association championship —a championship his team won eight times in eleven years. His legendary team at Tennessee A&I State University, led by Dick Barnett and John Barnhill, won the NAIA national championship in 1957, 1958, and 1959, becoming the first in history to win three straight national crowns.

As John's legend grew in the basketball community, he had the opportunity in 1960 to put together an amateur team, the Cleveland Pipers, which defeated one of the United States' most acclaimed Olympic teams. Despite the fact that the Olympic team included the likes of future all-time Hall of Fame greats Oscar Robertson, Jerry West, and Jerry Lucas, McLendon's team prevailed in a great display of fast-break basketball, winning 103–96. It was the only loss the gold-medal team ever received, as John employed his four-second rule, requiring all five players to cross the ten-second line and be in position to score less than four seconds after any change of possession.

Coach McLendon was ahead of his time as a brilliant student of the game. He designed the two-corners offense, which later became the famous four-corners offense implemented so well by Coach Dean Smith of North Carolina. There is no question that John influenced the modern game—in regards to fast-break basketball, pressing defense, individual drill stations, the interim freelance delayed break, game preparation, and conditioning—as much as anyone who has ever coached the game.

John's book, *Fast Break Basketball,* is a must-read for anyone at any level who desires to coach the game. It covers all phases of coaching with great insight:

DISCIPLINE: Education is superior to enforcement as education yields cooperation. Enforcement yields acquiescence within the rules only.

FUNDAMENTALS: Plan every practice to carry over some aspects of the game. Do not practice unrelated skills. Add speed to the fundamentals after they have been mastered. Learning to execute fundamental skills properly at a faster pace is a player's problem and a coach's task. A coach never wastes time if he works on fundamentals, for he must always return to them whenever he gets into difficulty.

PLAYER RELATIONSHIPS: A coach must maintain the confidence of his players. Players play their hardest game for a coach whom they trust. Inspired games are never born in an atmosphere of distrust. Sell the game to your players to make them feel special. They are!

WINNING: There must be set forth an aim that is greater than winning but that carries winning within it. Winning should be considered not as a goal in itself but rather as something incorporated in the greater goal. Winning games in the process of attempting to reach a greater goal is a more worthwhile and meaningful experience than winning as an end in itself. The goal of striving for excellence in performance is a realistic one attainable only through persistence. It is thus possible to reach the goal while losing or to lose the goal while winning.

It was an honor to know John McLendon and to spend many hours with him discussing so many different subjects. His genius never failed to amaze me. He was a man of principle, a man of integrity, a man of brilliant intellect; a great coach, educator, ambassador, innovator, and consummate gentleman. John McLendon was an American treasure who made his game and his country a better place for all of us.

By Ian Naismith, Naismith International Basketball Foundation

I Miss My Big Brother

In 1999, I gave a eulogy for my adopted brother, John B. McLendon Jr. John's death was a tremendous loss to his family, his friends, the game of basketball, and myself. My grandfather Dr. James A. Naismith, the inventor of basketball, became John's mentor, advisor, and friend in the early 1930s at the University of Kansas.

When John called to tell me that he was seriously ill, I left Chicago within the next hour and drove to Cleveland Heights, Ohio, where John and his beautiful wife, Joanna, lived. Joanna had gone to get John some medication, and when I arrived at their home, John met me at the door. His small frame hugged me for a few minutes, and he said, "Brother, the enemy has pinned me down," referring to the cancer that had ravaged his body. He then showed me again the place where he kept the Naismith Good Sportsmanship Award that was given to him by the Naismith International Basketball Foundation in 1998 in Chicago. He was so proud of our family award, known as the most beautiful historic award in sports, that he and Joanna had purchased a special table for it.

I asked John to tell me once again the story of how he met my grandfather and how they had worked together to bend and break most of the racial rules at the University of Kansas. He was standing at the doorway of Dr. Naismith's office in Robinson Gym, he told me, the first day of his freshman year as a student at KU. Doc, sitting at the desk, looked at John and said, "Can I help you?" John answered that his dad had told him to find Dr. Naismith because he would look after him and because he was color-blind. Doc asked who he was, and he replied that he was John McLendon from Kansas City. Doc invited John to have a seat and said, "Well, dads are generally right."

Doc asked John if he knew his dad, and John said no, but that he had wanted to be a basketball coach since he watched a player shooting baskets the first time he saw an indoor gym as a young boy. He told Doc that his dad said he would find the money for him to go to college, but he had to go to the University of Kansas because the man that invented the game of basketball was a professor there. For a railroad man, John's dad had certainly done his research.

Dr. Naismith had a rule that if you were a student in the Athletic Department, you had to learn to swim. This was no problem for John, as he had been a lifeguard in Kansas City as a teenager. The next day he went for a swim in the KU pool. After showering and getting dressed, he walked past a maintenance man who was draining the pool. John asked if this was routine or if it was being done because he had just finished swimming. The man told him, "Use your own judgment." John replied that he hoped KU had a lot of money for water as he was going to swim every day. He then went to tell Dr. Naismith what had happened. The next day when John went swimming, Doc had his two biggest football players sitting on the edge of the pool to protect him. This got the message across very well. However, soon afterward, signs showed up on campus saying, "Do not swim with the Nigger." John gathered up some of these signs and gave them to his advisor. Doc had been in the Athletic Department for thirty-five years, but he took the signs to the chancellor and the president of the school and told them that if he ever saw another sign like this he would resign and go to another university. Dr. Naismith did not send mixed messages. The situation was resolved instantly.

Just before graduation, John went to Doc's office and said that he wanted to get his master's degree but didn't have the financial means to do so. Doc picked up the phone and called the chancellor at the University of Iowa to arrange a scholarship for his prize student. Within a year, John had completed his degree and commenced his legendary coaching career. It would culminate in 1979 with his induction into the Naismith Memorial Basketball Hall of Fame in Springfield, Massachusetts, where he would once again be united with his beloved mentor.

John died within days of my visit to Cleveland Heights, but he will live forever in the game of basketball, the Naismith family, and his little brother (me).

In the social history of the United States, it is widely recognized that sports has been one of the primary mediums for breaking down racial barriers in American society. For almost a century, African American leaders around the country have looked to sports as one path toward black advancement and racial reconciliation. In their book *Sport and the Color Line: Black Athletes and Race Relations in Twentieth-Century America*, Patrick B. Miller and David K. Wiggins point out that "since the civil rights era, historians have explored in detail the many ways African Americans deployed sporting achievement to inspire race pride and to prevail upon the dominant culture to fully abide by the doctrines of fair play and sportsmanship." Although most people recognize the pioneering role of Jackie Robinson in the integration of American sports, a diminutive, dignified African American coach named John B. McLendon Jr. played an equally important role. A legendary basketball coach, McLendon was also a pioneer, supreme innovator, teacher, and gentleman who waged a successful fight to break down barriers of segregation in college and professional athletics.[1]

On the evening of March 19, 1966, a national television audience and the 14,253 fans seated at the University of Maryland's Cole Field House witnessed, according to *Sports Illustrated* columnist Gene Menez, what many have since described as "the most important game in the history of college basketball"—Texas Western's 72–65 upset of the University of Kentucky in the National Collegiate Athletic Association (NCAA) championship final. This was the night the Miners' all-black starting lineup (a first in NCAA title-game history) and two reserves, also black, toppled legendary coach Adolph Rupp's all-white Wildcats. The story was so compelling it was made into the inspirational movie *Glory Road,* which opened to rave reviews nationwide over the 2006 Martin Luther King Jr. Day weekend. What the film leaves out, however, is that this glory road had been paved with grit and determination a decade earlier by the trailblazing efforts of John McLendon and the other founders of the National Athletic Steering Committee who worked alongside him.[2]

Nine years before Texas Western captured the NCAA championship, McLendon's black-college squads from Tennessee A&I State

University defeated more than a dozen white teams from all over the United States, including the South, to capture three consecutive National Association of Intercollegiate Athletics (NAIA) national championships, from 1957 to 1959. Of course, there was no national television audience for these NAIA basketball championships, and currently no movie celebrates these groundbreaking victories. Therefore, the glorious road of McLendon and his Tennessee A&I Tigers remains largely unknown, yet he and his superlative players, five of whom later played in the National Basketball Association (NBA), helped us get to where we are today.

I first met John B. McLendon in 1980, when I was conducting research on the integration of the NAIA basketball tournament, which took place in the 1950s. Although I had attended every NAIA basketball tournament since my family and I moved to Kansas City in 1974, I had never before been introduced to the man who was affectionately known as the "father of black basketball," the individual primarily responsible for integrating college basketball in Kansas City and around the nation. I was unaware at the time of the fact that McLendon had also broken through the color line in many other areas of athletics and society.

As I spent several days interviewing him, I came to understand the historic role he had played in the modern civil rights movement. This unassuming, gentle, soft-spoken man was a giant in the struggle for equal rights in American society. More than that, he was a writer, poet, historian, archivist, and teacher—indeed, a unique individual who, acting out of faith, courage, and compassion, had enhanced America's potential for integrity and justice. His faith in humankind and his ability to consistently do the right thing had given him superior judgment and the confidence to pursue a wise course of action in bringing about significant social change. John McLendon radiated a kind of fundamental decency that everyone admired and respected. We spent many days and evenings together watching basketball and talking about his life, the obstacles he had overcome, and the remarkable successes he had experienced over the years. He began to call me "little brother," and although I knew he treated everyone as if they were members of his family, I took immense satisfaction in knowing that he and I were becoming close friends. My wife and I visited him and Joanna at their home in Downers Grove, Illinois, and I saw the incredible archive he had amassed over the years. We authored a booklet together in 1988, "Breaking Through: The NAIA and the Integration of Intercollegiate Athletics in Post World War II America," and were the headliners at the 1989 conference of the North American Culture Association in Toronto, speaking on the role of sports in American popular culture. Based on extensive interviews conducted between 1987 and 1990, I authored the article "Coach John B. McLendon Jr. and the Integration of Intercollegiate and Professional Athletics in Post World War II America," which was published in the *Journal of American Culture* in December 1990.

With my encouragement, McLendon created a series of audiotapes for me as a historical record of his life in basketball and his contributions to the integration of American athletics. He entitled his work "Tales of the Hardwood" and sent the tapes to his daughter, Querida, for transcription. McLendon and I met annually at the NAIA tournament in Kansas City until it moved to Oklahoma in the mid-1990s. When I heard he had passed away in October 1999, I felt a personal loss but also, more important, the loss of a man who had never received the full credit he so richly deserved. Several years later, I traveled to Cleveland to meet with Joanna in order to look over his papers, scrapbooks, and photos. I was joyfully overwhelmed at what lay before me. I discussed with Joanna my intention of writing a biography of her husband, and she graciously agreed to give me complete access to anything I needed.

Along with the extensive material stored at the McLendon home in Cleveland, two other collections were highly beneficial in my research. The John B. McLendon Collection at the University of Kansas Spencer Research Library in Lawrence includes extensive letters, articles, scrapbooks, and photographs, and the archives at the Naismith Memorial Basketball Hall of Fame in Springfield, Massachusetts, houses a small collection relevant to McLendon's acceptance and induction into the Hall of Fame. After Joanna drew up an extensive list of her husband's closest colleagues and former players, I was set to begin researching the story of a man who had struggled his whole life to make American democracy a reality. This book is the result.

ACKNOWLEDGMENTS

In the course of researching and writing this book, I benefited from the help and cooperation of many individuals. Every one of the more than sixty people I interviewed not only spoke lovingly about John McLendon but also seemed genuinely grateful that he would finally be getting the credit he so richly deserved. One elderly man who had played on his CIAA tournament championship team in 1946 told me that he would gain further strength to live from the hope of reading my book about his beloved coach. Motivation like this was not uncommon, and it made the project immensely worthwhile.

Joanna McLendon not only provided complete access to her husband's collection but also gave me her time, encouragement, and inspiration, which made this book possible. My gratitude to her is immeasurable. A special note of thanks goes to Mike Cleary, executive director of the National Association of College Directors of Athletics (NACDA) and president of the John McLendon Minority Scholarship Fund, who provided invaluable insights and help with research and editing, rendering me additional aid through fellow NACDA employee Brian Horning. Not only did Deborah Dandridge, field archivist of the African-American Collections at the Spencer Research Library at the University of Kansas, help me navigate the McLendon Collection, but her excitement about my work was truly infectious. Matt Zeysing, historian and archivist at the Naismith Memorial Basketball Hall of Fame, also aided my research. At the National Association of Intercollegiate Athletics, past president and CEO Steven Baker, sports information director Dawn Harmon, and director of the Champions Character Initiatives Robert Miller were gracious in opening their archives to me and offering to help in any way necessary.

To everyone who gave me their time and insights during interviews, I offer my heartfelt thanks and appreciation, especially Richard Barnett, John Barnhill, Ken Denzel, Wayne Embry, Clarence Gaines, Dorothy Gaters, Ron Hamilton, Harold Hunter, Dennis Jackson, Sam Jones, Earl Lloyd, Richard Miller, George Parks, Alex Rivera, Jim Rodriquez, Dean Smith, Norm Sonju, Leroy Walker, and Thornton Williams. Sports information directors Kyle Serba from North Carolina Central and Kindell Stephens from Tennessee State University were especially helpful in providing insights and information. Photographs were graciously sent to me by Alex Rivera and Robert Lawson from North Carolina Central; Kindell Stephens from Tennessee State; Jim Rodriquez from Cleveland State; and Fred Whitted, historian and editor of the *Historic Black College and University Sports Encyclopedia* and CEO of the *Black Heritage Review*. I thank all of them for their time and effort. Marty Blake, Howie Evans, Ian Naismith, Billy Packer, and Bud Smith were especially generous in sharing their personal thoughts about McLendon, and I thank them all for their contributions.

I offer my sincere gratitude to Anne Canfield, vice president for communications at the Kansas City Art Institute, who edited the manuscript and offered helpful critical advice and encouragement. Illona Bernard and Bronwyn McLain provided secretarial and technical assistance with the text and photographs, and I thank them both for their patience and expertise. Several faculty development grants from the Kansas City Art Institute helped to make my research possible. Lawrence J. Malley, director and editor of the University of Arkansas Press, shared my enthusiasm for the book, guided it intelligently through production, and offered valuable critical suggestions that improved the work in substantial ways. The press staff was a pleasure to work with and first-rate in every way.

Finally, my deepest gratitude goes to my wife, Sharon; daughters, Stephanie and Tamara; son-in-law, Joshua; and grandsons, Asa and Eli, who expand my heart and nourish my soul. They always manage to keep me centered and whole, and with their love and encouragement, I find happiness and peace.

INTRODUCTION

On the morning of September 2, 1999, an impeccably dressed, diminutive, slender, eighty-four-year-old African American man sat on the stage poised to speak to the freshman class at the B. N. Duke Auditorium at North Carolina Central University in Durham. Although he was pleased to be here, he could not help thinking about how his wife, Joanna, back in Cleveland, had tried to keep him from going, for she feared her husband's health would be further jeopardized by the trip. John B. McLendon understood that Joanna's fears were real, for two and a half months earlier he had been diagnosed with pancreatic cancer. A month afterward, as the doctor at the Cleveland Clinic was preparing to operate, John and his wife found out that the cancer had spread so extensively throughout his body that an operation was inadvisable. The "Little Coach," who had spent his lifetime breaking through so many social barriers, could not break free of this physical one. He was dying, but a sense of purpose and a profound faith in the Almighty gave him the strength to carry on.

McLendon was introduced to the freshman class by Alex Rivera, the former director of public relations at the university and a close friend of his since 1939. Rivera talked about McLendon's numerous accomplishments, especially how, in 1941, he had given the school its first championship in any sport. "He was respected and genuinely loved by the students and the faculty at what was then North Carolina College for Negroes," said Rivera. "They called him 'Little Coach.' He is on a pinnacle by himself." Then it was McLendon's turn to speak. Although the lift in his voice was missing and the smile on his face a little less bright, those seated in the audience could not miss the strength of conviction behind his every word. His memory was still sharp as he spoke to the young students about his fifteen-year tenure at their school from 1937 to 1952 and how their grandparents' generation had been forced to fight the shackles of segregation every step of the way. He told them how he and his players had used courage, ingenuity, determination, and creative skill to overcome the obstacles that confronted them—and how hard they had worked to instill pride and dignity in themselves, their college, and so many others in doing so. As he had done many times before, McLendon shared with these young students reminders about how to live, about dealing with people, about respect for themselves and all human beings. He ended his talk with a plea that the students never sacrifice their morals or values to win. Always choose dignity and do your best, he said, and you will come out on top. The pride and humility of this legendary man evoked in the audience an appreciable response. This would turn out to be his last public appearance.[1]

After returning home, McLendon drove to Cleveland State University to meet his students on the first day of class for his course entitled "The History of Sports and the Role of Minorities in Its Development." Always the professor, McLendon loved teaching this class and felt it a privilege that the university invited him to return year after year. Dressed impressively in a double-breasted blue jacket, gold lapel pin, gray pants, and black buckled shoes, and with a white handkerchief in his jacket pocket, he introduced himself and handed out the course materials, which he had spent years developing. "Sports has been one of the most important agents for breaking down barriers in this country because it is so visible," he told his students. "We are going to learn in this class how the achievers in all these different sports became achievers. And to do that, you have to understand the context, the conditions under which they lived." He gave his students a few evocative examples of courageous men and women who had used sports as an important medium in the social revolution called the modern civil rights movement, stressing that all Americans were the beneficiaries of this democratic struggle. McLendon ended with a confession: "The reason I love to teach this course," he said with a smile, "is because I lived most of it."[2]

It would be the last class John McLendon would ever teach. His health deteriorated quickly, and he passed away a month later. On the day of his passing, he spoke to colleagues about his most recent passion, the Historically Black Colleges and Universities Heritage Museum and Hall of Fame. As Lut Williams, editor of the *Black Colleges Sports Page*, correctly noted, John B. McLendon's "contributions to the game of basketball and towards preserving for future generations the struggle to free America from the bonds of institutional racism in sports continued to his last breath."[3] He was a pioneer, supreme innovator, activist, historian, thinker, poet, and gentleman, whose remarkable courage, determination, and moral strength in the pursuit of human rights and social justice brought democracy in America a step closer to reality. This is his story.

CHAPTER 1

A Kansas Childhood and the Love of the Game, 1915–33

John B. McLendon Jr. was born April 5, 1915, in Hiawatha, Kansas, to Effie Kathryn Hunn and John B. McLendon. His father was born in 1882 in Ansonville, North Carolina, of mixed parentage. McLendon's grandparents on his father's side originally came from Washington, Georgia, where all the McLendons had been owned up until Emancipation by two brothers from Edinburgh, Scotland, named McLendon. His father left Ansonville after graduating from North Carolina A&T University, where he studied architecture and carpentry. Contracting work brought him west in 1905 to Boley, Oklahoma, an all-black town, where he oversaw the building of twenty-six homes. That same year, Booker T. Washington visited Boley and proclaimed it "the most enterprising and, in many ways, the most interesting of the Negro towns in the United States." A few years later, migration to Boley slowed down considerably, and in 1913, McLendon's father moved north to find new opportunities in Hiawatha, Kansas, ninety miles northwest of Kansas City.[1]

John's mother, Effie Kathryn Hunn, was a full-blooded Delaware Indian whose family, under Henry Baker, migrated from Kentucky to Kansas in 1879. The Bakers were among the approximately forty thousand "Exodusters" who fled the South between 1878 and 1880 after Reconstruction gave way to renewed racial oppression. The leader of the movement was a former slave, Benjamin "Pap" Singleton, a land speculator with a vision of establishing independent black communities across Kansas. The name "Exodusters" emerged when the emigrants compared themselves to the Biblical Jews leaving Egypt for the "Promised Land." McLendon later recalled that "Kansas was the only state in the Union that invited former slaves to come to their territory." The Exodusters thought of Kansas as "the Garden Spot of the Earth," the quintessential free state, the land of fiery abolitionist John Brown, where they would homestead their own land and find freedom. Once they arrived, however, this throng of mostly ragged and hungry ex-slaves was welcomed by some white settlers and spurned by others. Undaunted, many stayed on, including McLendon's great-grandparents, the Bakers, helping to build the American heartland. Upon arrival, the Bakers built a home in Kansas City, Kansas, the first stop inside the Kansas border, and then took up residence in the small town of Hiawatha. This town had been founded in 1857, named after the young Indian from Henry W. Longfellow's poem "Song of Hiawatha." Hiawatha's main street was designated Oregon Street after the Oregon Trail; parallel streets to the north of it were named after Indian tribes north of the trail, while streets to the south carried the names of tribes south of the trail. Located among the Kickapoo, Iowa, and Sac-Fox Indian reservations in northeast Kansas, the town had a population of approximately three thousand.[2]

Around 1912, McLendon's grandparents, James and Mariah Hunn, moved further west to homestead 320 acres that were shown in the tract books as "Indian Land" near Model, Colorado, twenty-two miles from Trinidad, on the Colorado–New Mexico border, on the banks of the Purgatorie River. The Homestead Act stipulated that if you stayed on a piece of land for five years, it was yours. President Woodrow Wilson signed the Hunns' original deed for their land, and it was passed to the McLendon children in 1955.

John B. McLendon Sr. met his future bride, Effie Hunn, at Washburn University in Topeka, Kansas, where he was teaching and she was a student. Their romance commenced when she wrote a poem for him based on his middle name, "Blanche." They were married in 1913 in Kansas City, Kansas, and purchased a modest home in Hiawatha. After John found employment with the Rock Island Railroad as a mail clerk in 1917, he and Effie moved to a comfortable, middle-class home on Haskell Street in Kansas City, Kansas, in an area called "Rattlebone Hollow."

The Wyandot Indians had settled the area at the confluence of the Kansas and Missouri rivers—what is now Kansas City, Kansas—in 1843, and the city was incorporated twenty-nine years later. Consolidated in 1886, this industrial and manufacturing center grew rapidly, its population just over 100,000 by 1920, with 14,405 African Americans living within its borders. "Rattlebone Hollow," located in the northernmost

Grandmother Mariah Hunn, mother Effie (Hunn) McLendon, John McLendon, and brother Arthur McLendon, Hiawatha, Kansas, 1917. (Courtesy Joanna McLendon)

part of the northeast section of the city, was originally the home of German and Slavic immigrants but became a largely African American enclave in the early years of the twentieth century. Although the exact origin of the area's name is not known, local historians offer at least two interesting theories. Some say it had to do with the large number of packinghouses in the area and the steel wagons on the clay roads

Father John B.
McLendon.
(Courtesy Joanna
McLendon)

"rattling dem bones," which meant a meat run. Others, however, relate
the name to the African Americans who arrived in the area in 1879. Their
only music came from men playing banjo or guitar and ladies and children with tambourines. Some of the men also played "bones"—ribs
scrapped from beef carcasses and well cured. They carried these bones
with them to church services; singing, they rattled the bones to the
music. Many expert bone rattlers lived in the area—thus the name
"Rattlebone."

Tragically, Effie died in the influenza epidemic of 1918, along with
a half a million other Americans, after her fourth child, Elsie, was born.
John Jr. and his brother, Arthur, went to live with their Indian grandparents, the Hunns, at their 5H ranch in Colorado, in a mud-and-straw-
block home on the prairie. Life was difficult there, as they had to walk

Mother Effie (Hunn) McLendon. (Courtesy Joanna McLendon)

more than five miles just to find fresh water. McLendon remembered that his grandfather was a horse wrangler, going out to catch wild horses and break them. His grandmother would wake the family up at 5 A.M. to read the Bible and insure they left the house in the proper frame of mind to tackle their work for the day. McLendon recalled how difficult it was for his grandparents to make a living, as "they were harassed all the time by the white folks out there." The first racial conflict he remembered came as he rode in a wagon with his grandfather, who always carried a gun in case there was trouble, as some men would regularly chase the wagon into the cornfields. "I didn't think of this as a black-white thing at the time, just that those men were bad guys," he later said. "Yes, I was scared. Some people later put up a sign, 'Colored Property,' on our

A Kansas Childhood and the Love of the Game

land and dynamited the well."[3] His older sister, Anita, went to live with some relatives and ended up on a ranch in Idaho. His younger sister, Elsie, stayed with one of his aunts in Omaha, Nebraska.

When John Jr. was six years old, his father married Minnie Jackson, a Kansas City schoolteacher, who became a second mother to the McLendon children. Although the McLendons had difficulty making ends meet, they were determined to one day send their children to college. One of Minnie Jackson's immediate goals was to reunite her husband's family, and she did so, bringing all the children back to Kansas City except for Anita, whose foster parents she could not locate. Forty-five years would pass before McLendon saw his sister again.[4]

The young McLendon was enrolled in Dunbar Elementary School at Sixth and Rowland Avenue, along with his brother and younger sister. The school was named after Paul Lawrence Dunbar, the first African American poet to garner national critical acclaim. All the primary and junior high schools in Kansas at the time were segregated, and as a young boy, McLendon didn't give this much thought. "We weren't led to think about it, in our house," he recalled years later. McLendon, an exceptional student, would finish his elementary education in four years. In the meantime, he and his brother enjoyed playing basketball in the peach basket they put up in their backyard and at Dunbar Elementary, which had a basketball hoop outside but no ball. "So," he recalled, "we'd throw rocks and socks in the hoop and everything else." McLendon fell thoroughly in love with the game during a sixth-grade class trip to Kansas City's new Northeast Junior High School. The door to the gym swung open, and he saw a polished basketball floor and a man sinking shots one after another. The man was P. L. Jacobs, the new physical training instructor. "I was spellbound," McLendon recalled. "I ran home to tell my mother I was going to be a physical training teacher and a basketball coach. She told me I was going to be a doctor, and my brother was going to be a lawyer, and my sister was going to be a teacher." Just as his mother predicted, Arthur did become a lawyer and Elsie a teacher. McLendon, however, chose a different path from the one his mother proscribed for him.[5]

Basketball consumed McLendon from this point on. He tried out for the team at Northeast and at Sumner High School three times beginning in the seventh grade but was cut every time, instead serving as the team's manager. Always sitting on the bench next to his first coach, A. T. Edwards, McLendon "was introduced to an emphasis on superior conditioning combined with lightning thrusts at the opponent's goal from the old center jump." His one high school letter came in gymnastics. When his mother saw her son's burning desire, she tempered her comments and laid down some objectives for him. He could no longer drink coffee or tea or touch any strong drink. He could no longer sleep on a pillow because old wives' tales said this would make his shoulders rounded. He had to observe a strict curfew and never stay up late. Also, along with his brothers and sisters, he was required to attend services with her at the Eighth Street Christian Church. His mentor, Dr. James Naismith, would later back up this principled approach to life, declaring that a coach must always observe the rules he sets for his players. McLendon would willingly follow the highly disciplined moral and social code set by his mother and his beloved mentor for the rest of his life.[6]

At five feet, eight inches, and weighing 160 pounds, McLendon did finally make a basketball team at Sumner's branch of Kansas City Junior College, under Coach Beltron Orme. Although he had a less than stellar career playing on this undefeated team, he fondly recalled that through the generosity of his teammates, he was able to score a point or two. "I didn't contribute much," he later admitted. "I was the tenth man on a 17–0 championship team. I was a running guard. What that meant was when we got the ball, I ran. I never developed any basketball skills. Only mental ones." While he ached to get in the game, the sideline became his home, and from there, sitting next to the coach, he studied his competition's every move. He learned what it took to be a champion, how to motivate players, and how to create team chemistry. According to Darin David, "He [McLendon] was more a researcher than a player." Still, McLendon was fast, and he later remembered that "the bigger guys would get the ball to me at the other end of the court. It was easy to make baskets that way." Significantly, as Carl Skiff would write years later, "The seeds of fast-break basketball . . . had been planted." They would blossom in the years to come in college and professional championship teams from Durham, North Carolina, to Nashville, Tennessee, and ultimately Cleveland, Ohio.[7]

In the Kansas of McLendon's youth, segregation was both institutionally and socially ingrained in almost very aspect of everyday life. Although Kansas had never been a Jim Crow state, an 1879 law did provide for segregation at the primary level, with local governments mandated to establish integrated high schools. Therefore, until 1904, the high school in Kansas City was racially integrated. However, in the spring of that year, an altercation very nearly resulted in the mob execution of an African American teenager named Louis Gregory. After an argument in Kerr's Park with two white boys, Gregory had fired his rifle several times. One of the boys, William Martin, was hit and died soon after. Following this incident, there was anger, hostility, and community agitation for separate schools from white patrons of the district. As a result, 1905 legislation was passed that authorized segregation in Kansas City high schools, but not the rest of Kansas.[8]

Sumner High School opened at Ninth and Washington Boulevard in the fall of that year as the only African American high school in Kansas. All the McLendon children attended this school, which was named after Charles Sumner, a U.S. senator from Massachusetts and an ardent abolitionist. John Hodge became principal in 1908 and remained in that capacity for forty years. He brought an exceptionally high caliber of education to Sumner, and the school gained acceptance from the North Central Association of Secondary Schools and Colleges. This certification was difficult to obtain, especially for African American schools, and it greatly facilitated the graduates' acceptance into college. As a result, Sumner turned out a large share of college graduates. Sumner had a very positive lasting influence on McLendon. According to historian Susan Greenbaum, "It developed into a place where students and teachers expressed the belief that they were working together to overcome the handicaps of racism, and to dispel the myths upon which this pernicious doctrine was founded."[9]

As a youngster, McLendon had been shielded from much of the harshness of a racially divided society by his stepmother, who assiduously kept him and his siblings out of establishments that refused service to blacks. "We were kind of protected from the ignominious side of segregation by just avoiding it," he later recalled. Indeed, McLendon never thought much about segregation until he grew older and a black schoolmate won an airplane-flying contest held at Memorial Hall but was denied first place because of his color.

McLendon's father had passed on a philosophy for dealing with racial discrimination, and his son often proudly referenced its practicality and wisdom. "He just told us that race was something we had to deal

A Kansas Childhood and the Love of the Game

with," McLendon recalled. "He encouraged us not to get angry. 'Get your emotions mixed up in a situation like this, you might not make the correct judgment,' he would say. 'You got to beat it some way, but not from an emotional standpoint.'" McLendon's father, who called John "the wizard" and Arthur "the lawpiece," urged his children to fight discrimination whenever they could "and be on the right side of the battle." When McLendon was preparing to leave for college, his father told him, "Go up there and do whatever anybody else does. And try to do it in a way that won't have you getting hurt. If you happen to get hurt, let me know. I'll be up there with my .44." In those days, railway mail clerks carried .44 Colt revolvers, and McLendon understood that his father would protect him if necessary. According to McLendon, the values instilled by his father helped give him the confidence to break down any barriers that stood in his way.[10]

CHAPTER 2

The University of Kansas and Dr. James Naismith, 1933–36

Although McLendon wished to enroll at Springfield College in Massachusetts, where Dr. James Naismith had invented the game of basketball in 1891, this was the Depression, and his family did not have the money to send him there. McLendon had saved what he earned at Cudahays Packing Co., muscling salt-cured cowhides from a cold cellar into sweltering railroad cars, and working as a lifeguard at the Edgerton Park swimming pool in his neighborhood, but there still wasn't enough money for him to go far away to college. While he was studying at Kansas City Junior College, however, his father discovered that Dr. Naismith was just forty miles away, in Lawrence, so McLendon headed to the University of Kansas. McLendon came to call this fortunate coincidence "providential placement."[1]

In the fall of 1933, his father drove him to the university in the family DeSoto and instructed him to go find Dr. James Naismith. The legendary inventor of basketball, now in his seventies, was employed at the university teaching in the physical education program. The state legislature had passed a special act stating that he could teach at the university as long as he desired. Although McLendon was concerned that he would be the first black student enrolled in the Athletic Department, his father quickly erased his son's doubts, telling him, "I'm a taxpayer, and you are entitled to do anything you want." One of McLendon's favorite stories was about the first time he walked into Dr. Naismith's office in Robinson Gymnasium as a young freshman, announcing to this famous man that he was going to major in physical education, that he wanted to learn how to coach basketball, and that he understood Dr. Naismith would be his advisor. "Who told you this?" Naismith inquired. "My father," answered McLendon. "Come on in. Fathers are always right," Naismith declared. The elderly professor and his student quickly forged a relationship that would change the young man's life.[2]

Dr. Naismith treated McLendon courteously, attentively, and with a kindness that enabled the young man to be reasonably comfortable in his new surroundings. The first class Dr. Naismith assigned him to was Economics 101, where McLendon encountered his first white teacher. The professor opened the class with an ethnic joke, and McLendon promptly walked out. He went directly to Dr. Naismith and told him he could not take the class. According to McLendon, Naismith replied, "'By all means,' and he commented from time to time that some people were ignorant and don't let that stop you."[3]

Dr. Naismith was not only McLendon's advisor but also his favorite teacher, instructing students in health, physical education, and anatomy and kinesiology, McLendon's favorite subject, which dealt with the analysis of motion and its application. McLendon frequently recalled that he learned a lot more from Naismith than could be found in textbooks: "Naismith didn't draw any plays. He talked about the essence of the game." He taught his students lessons about life, and his coaching philosophy would have a lasting, significant effect upon McLendon throughout his career. "I loved Dr. Naismith's classes," McLendon recalled. "He was a theologian, too, a man of wide knowledge, a philosopher. I used to go over to his house at night to talk about basketball and life. Even used to mow his lawn."[4]

McLendon took great pride in stating that the coaching principles he observed came almost directly from Dr. Naismith, who felt that all coaches should be teachers first, skilled in physical education, sociology, physiology, psychology, physical therapy, and kinesiology. McLendon learned from Naismith that sports were a means of influencing behavior under the stress and striving of competition. "Naismith believed you can do as much toward helping people become better people, teaching them the lessons of life through athletics, than you can through preaching," said McLendon. "So he had that in the back of his mind, that a coach is supposed to make a difference between what a person is and what he ought to be. Use interest in athletics as a sort of captive-audience-type thing, you've got him, now you have to do something with him." McLendon stated that Naismith "felt every athletic situation should be an education, and experience, in developing the whole man, and I've made it my coaching philosophy." Dr. Naismith told him that

Dr. James Naismith, professor of physical education, University of Kansas.
(Courtesy Spencer Research Library, University of Kansas Libraries)

"an athletic coach has as much influence on people as a minister." "How right he was," exclaimed McLendon.[5]

It soon became apparent to the youthful McLendon that his legendary advisor had dedicated his life to serving his fellow man, combining strong moral and religious underpinnings with the positive aspects of sports to advance the movement known as "muscular Christianity." This idea had been brought to America through the popularity of British author Thomas Hughes's blockbuster novel *Tom Brown's Schooldays* (1857) and its sequel, *Tom Brown at Oxford* (1860). The name "Tom Brown" itself soon became a metaphor for a prescription for healthy living, fitness, and Christian morality. Labeled "an American Tom Brown" by authors Tony Ladd and James A. Mathisen, Naismith firmly believed that physical activity and sports, especially team sports, developed character, fostered patriotism, and instilled ethical values that would serve participants well in later life.[6]

College sports, muscular Christians argued, should be the training ground for youths' spirits and consciences, as well as their bodies. At the nexus of muscular Christianity and college education stood the Young Men's Christian Association (YMCA). Indeed, it was in 1891, while working as a gym teacher at the YMCA's International Training School in Springfield, Massachusetts, under director Luther Hasley Gulick, that Naismith invented the game of basketball as a way to keep young men involved in healthy activity between the football and baseball seasons—and to inculcate in them the Christian values for which the YMCA stood. Appearing at the eighth annual convention of the NCAA in 1914, Naismith echoed the manly faithfulness of Tom Brown, insisting that college basketball, along with every other sport, should be put "on such a basis that it will be a factor in the molding of character, as well as . . . a recreative and competitive sport." According to Ladd and Mathisen, "For Naismith, basketball was more than a new game. It was a means to evangelize people about morality and Christian values, the essence of American muscular Christianity."[7]

Although the popularity of muscular Christianity was less overt when McLendon commenced his career, he was deeply influenced by Naismith and, like his beloved mentor, strongly believed that participation in sports could contribute to character development, instill moral values, and shape better people. McLendon often explained the philosophy he had received from Dr. Naismith simply and directly. "Athletics is supposed to be a teaching tool," he declared. "One is supposed to improve on the lives of young people through athletics—through the trials of making the team and through the discipline. If you don't improve lives, then you are not doing your job. That is my philosophy."[8]

As for player-coach relationships, the coach should be a person who demonstrates at all times his character and leadership, before his players and other students. Naismith believed that if you elected to be a coach, it was also your responsibility to be an advisor, counselor, and father figure and to act at all times as an example to the athletes in your care. A coach must teach athletes how to live a clean life—how to be free of harmful substances, such as tobacco, alcohol, and caffeine, and keep regular hours of rest, relaxation, and sleep.

Naismith, intrigued by the constant development of his game, fascinated McLendon. He absorbed every kernel of wisdom from his advisor, including his belief in the effectiveness of what has come to be known as fast-break basketball. "Dr. Naismith and I were watching some little kids play basketball one day," McLendon recalled, "and they were chasing the ball. Dr. Naismith told me that was the ultimate game. He said the ultimate game is to attack wherever the ball is and let your offense begin wherever you get the ball. He told me the game is patterned to be played with a full-court offense and full-court defense. I patterned my whole game after that philosophy."[9]

Naismith wanted his men not only to be "he-men," as he liked to call them, but to also be gentlemen, and he modeled this behavior in everything he engaged in. "We'd ask all sorts of questions and never did consider ourselves bold to do so, because he was open to just about everything," McLendon noted to *Sports Illustrated* writer Alexander Wolff. "Basically [he] told us, 'Keep your pants zipped.' But he shared that kind of stuff—facts of life. We thought we were really something, hearing about all that. We thought, 'Doc's all right.'"[10]

According to McLendon, Naismith deplored any form of discrimination, segregation, or prejudice. The professor treated all his students equally. "Dr. Naismith didn't know anything about color or nationality," said McLendon. "He was so unconscious about your economic or religious background. He just saw everyone as potential. There wasn't anything in his body that responded to anything racist."[11]

In the summer of 1936, Naismith received an invitation to attend the Berlin Olympics to celebrate basketball's official inclusion as part of the medal program, a goal toward which he had worked for more than thirty years. Understanding the high cost of travel overseas, members of the K Club at the University of Kansas took it upon themselves to raise funds to make Dr. Naismith's dream possible. Living on thirty-five cents a day, McLendon wanted to contribute but needed to raise some funds to do so. Deciding not to tell Naismith what he was up to, he asked his professor if he needed any help around the house. Naismith replied that his grass needed cutting. Grateful for the opportunity, McLendon went to work on what turned out to be an all-day job. For his efforts, Naismith paid him fifty cents, which McLendon returned to the professor as a contribution toward his Olympic journey.[12]

Eventually, the K Club raised enough funds for Dr. Naismith and his wife to attend the Olympics, and this became one of the most memorable events of his life. After the honor ceremonies, Naismith tossed up the ball between Estonia and France in the first basketball game in Olympic history. According to Bernice Larson Webb, "Naismith said that his happiest moment occurred when he saw his game played in the Olympics." Just after he returned from the highly politicized Olympics, where Jesse Owens had won several gold medals, someone asked him why the black man was apparently superior in track. "It's not any measurable physical difference," the professor replied. "It's all psychological, all in the minds of the competitors. You have people who have been put down, so they practice longer, they have more incentive, because they want to demonstrate that they shouldn't be discriminated against." McLendon remembered this lesson and applied it in his coaching philosophy. He also fondly recalled that in the same conversation a white student asked, "When will we catch up?" And Doc said, "The day everyone is treated equal. Then everyone will have an equal chance to be first."[13]

Naismith's attention and guidance helped McLendon surmount glaring institutional discriminatory practices during his junior and senior years. The university athletic administration barred black students from participation in intercollegiate athletics on the grounds that some schools would refuse to play Kansas if it had an integrated team. McLendon, then, suited up for tryouts for the basketball team, but his name was never called. He watched Coach Forrest "Phog" Allen's practices anyway, studying the game. It was not until 1947 that an African American student was allowed to play on the KU basketball team. Ironically, his name was Stanley Burt, and McLendon had coached him at North Carolina College in 1945.

McLendon did make the varsity boxing team in the 123-pound class. He had learned to box in a Kansas City recreation program run by a former prizefighter. "You would go to Edgerton Park at night, put on the gloves, and get in the ring with anybody you wanted to fight or who wanted to fight you," remembered McLendon. "I learned how to protect myself by fighting the worst hoodlums in town. I hid my gloves in the weeds near home so Mother wouldn't know I was boxing." Nevertheless, his tenure on the KU team turned out to be brief. When a Southern school refused to box Kansas with McLendon on the team, he wasn't allowed to compete. His teammates, however, backed him up, and the university's entire boxing program was cancelled as a result.[14]

Dr. Naismith was aware of McLendon's boxing skill. "One day," McLendon recalled, "he got me after class and said, 'There's a boy here that needs to be taught a lesson. I told him I knew a little guy—you—who could whip him!'" McLendon and the white boy went to the school's gym and laced on gloves. Although his competitor outweighed him by about forty pounds, McLendon's second punch caught his adversary flush in the face, and he was counted out in a sitting position. McLendon proudly recalled that he beat the white bully handily and that Naismith was very pleased to hear of this result. Unfortunately, McLendon also broke a bone in his wrist during the match, and although his wrist healed, the scar remained. Pointing to the scar years later, McLendon smiled, stating, "It always reminded me of the imprint Dr. Naismith had upon my life."[15]

McLendon, as the first black physical education student enrolled in the university, was told that no provision would be made for him in swimming and that he would be excused from practice teaching. These were both degree requirements, however, and McLendon would not accept this stipulation. Eventually, the story of his triumph at the swimming pool would become legendary on the KU campus. Although the university was integrated, the pool at Robinson Gymnasium was not. School officials reasoned that they could waive the swimming and water safety test for McLendon, a former lifeguard, but he had other ideas. Black students were usually given an automatic A in swimming, McLendon recalled, but he would not accept the grade without doing the work. Going to take the swimming test one day, he found the pool empty and was told it was being drained. When he asked the attendant for details, he was told, "We drain the pool every Wednesday." But McLendon knew better. He told the attendant that "he was going to have a big water bill because I was going swimming every day." McLendon came back the next day, and the pool was drained again. He was told not to return. Word quickly spread that a student in the

Athletic Department was trying to start "mixed swimming." Several of McLendon's friends on the basketball and football teams openly supported his efforts. A few joined him in the pool, and one, Jack Lovelace, circulated a petition simply stating that "we do not object to swimming with colored students," collecting one thousand signatures.[16]

Finally, Dr. Naismith sent his two biggest football players to stand guard while McLendon swam, but the tension remained. According to Ian Naismith, signs showed up on campus saying, "Do not swim with the Nigger." McLendon immediately gathered them up and gave them to his advisor. Dr. Naismith then took them to the chancellor and the school's president, telling them that if he ever saw another such sign he would resign and go to another university. McLendon then cut a deal with "Phog" Allen, head of the Athletic Department. "Dr. Allen had said the only reason I couldn't go swimming is that he was afraid for my safety," McLendon later wrote. "I asked him to keep the pool open for two weeks [for everybody]. If there's no incident, then open the pool for the colored. He went to Dr. Naismith, and they agreed."[17]

McLendon then called a meeting of the sixty black students enrolled at the university, explained what was going on, and asked them not to go swimming for the next two weeks. The fifty or so students who showed up for the meeting agreed to go along with McLendon's plan. All Naismith and Allen knew was that no incidents occurred. Although McLendon remembered Dr. Allen calling him "a smart-aleck," the athletic director did consent to integrated swimming when Dr. Naismith reminded him of the agreement he had made. Later, Allen explained that it was not his rule but university policy that denied open swimming. In any case, McLendon, who had cleverly integrated the pool, became the first black student at Kansas to earn a degree in physical education. In 1979, the university would award him its highest alumni citation, the Citation of Merit, which states, "This man, more than anyone else, was responsible for the integration of swimming and swimming pool programs at the University of Kansas." At the time, McLendon's efforts led to his nomination for a seat on the student council. Although he never campaigned, he was elected as a representative for the School of Education, thus becoming, in 1936, the first black student to serve on the student council at the University of Kansas.[18]

While serving on the student council, McLendon decided to challenge other discriminatory practices at the university. For example,

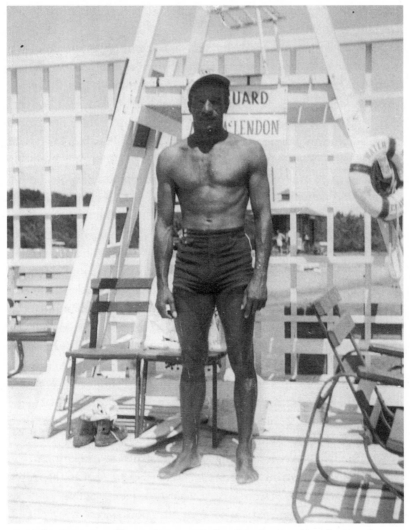

McLendon was an excellent swimmer and often found summer employment as a lifeguard. (Courtesy Joanna McLendon)

although black students paid extracurricular fees to the university like everyone else, they were denied equal access to facilities and events in the student union, particularly the annual spring dance. McLendon and his girlfriend, Alice, decided they would go to the dance anyway. When they reached the entrance, the puzzled young man serving as a security guard hesitated but allowed them to enter. Years later, with a broad smile on his face, McLendon related how he and Alice had

The University of Kansas and Dr. James Naismith

danced the night away to one of the swing era's essential bands: "Andy Kirk and the Twelve Clouds of Joy."[19]

By this time, McLendon had Dr. Naismith firmly on his side, and together the two would also find a way around the university's ban on black students teaching white students. The plan that Naismith created involved McLendon beginning his practice teaching as a junior, instead of waiting for his senior year like everyone else. Thus, McLendon would have two years of practice teaching, which would allow him to teach at three different levels—elementary, junior high, and senior high—in both segregated and integrated physical education classes. McLendon initially taught gymnastics at segregated Lincoln Elementary School part of the week and at integrated Lawrence Junior High School the rest of the week. After Thanksgiving, he attended basketball practice as an assistant coach at Lawrence Memorial Senior High School, an integrated school with separate white and black athletic teams. Although McLendon never even saw the white team at Lawrence Memorial, during his senior year, at age twenty, he was made head coach of the black team when the present coach became ill. "First game I ever coached was against my alma mater, Kansas City Northeast," he loved to say. "My father won a box of El Productos betting on my team."[20]

McLendon's Lawrence Memorial "Promoters" continued to win, and he eventually led his squad to the all-black Kansas-Missouri Athletic Conference championship. At the time, a center jump was still required after each basket, but McLendon employed his celebrated running game as best he could. "We were trying to fast break off the center jump," he recalled. More often than not, his team was successful. Naismith, deeply impressed with McLendon's maiden coaching experience, told his young protégé: "Whatever you do, continue your interest in basketball. I feel you have a good understanding of the game. Johnny, you're on your way. Basketball is your calling."[21]

"My grandfather was seventy-two, and John was eighteen," related Ian Naismith, the inventor's grandson and founding director of the Naismith International Basketball Foundation. "John wanted to be a coach, but there were no black coaches then coming out of the University of Kansas. James Naismith didn't know McLendon, but he was color-blind in an era poisoned by prejudice, and he took McLendon under his wing." Although Naismith was an extremely busy man, he always found time for his students. He genuinely liked McLendon and

McLendon with his first championship team, the Lawrence Memorial High School Promoters, 1936. (Courtesy Joanna McLendon)

gave him some extra pointers and insights. "I learned my philosophy of coaching from those sessions," recalled McLendon. "He told me never to put Xs and Os on a chalkboard. It was more important to instill positive thinking and goal orientation, to let your players know their long- and short-range objectives and to build your program step by step." "He was *the* man in my life," McLendon told Mike Walker. "He taught me everything I know about basketball and physical education. Everything I ever did when I was coaching, I can trace back to learning from him."[22]

Looking back on these formative years in 1996 as the NBA unveiled its fiftieth-anniversary season, McLendon stated that his life would have been far different if Dr. Naismith had not been his advisor. "This remarkable man never looked at life as black and white," wrote McLendon. "One thing he taught in the adjustment to adversity is that no matter what kind of problem you had, never let it defeat you. Even though you may not think that something is fair or just, you can't let that stop you. You just try to get around it. His philosophy was that adversity is just

21

another opportunity." McLendon took these words to heart as a student and put them into practice throughout his adult life.[23]

McLendon attended the final class Dr. Naismith taught in 1936, making him the last link to basketball's peach-basket era. Having assimilated everything he could from his beloved teacher, he felt confident he was now ready to conquer the game of basketball and life in a racially divided society. At the Naismith Memorial Gardens in Lawrence, Kansas, benches near the monument to Naismith are dedicated to some legendary coaches, including Adolph Rupp, Dean Smith, "Phog" Allen, and Ralph Miller. The third bench to the left of the monument is the one honoring John B. McLendon Jr.

After McLendon graduated from Kansas in 1936, Naismith helped him obtain a scholarship to earn a master's degree at the University of Iowa, a school whose physical education program had earned an excellent reputation for research. There was only one other black student in the program, William F. Burghardt, and he and McLendon became great friends. At Iowa, like Kansas, African Americans were not allowed to stay in student dormitories, and McLendon, with Burghardt, took up residence at a private boarding house run specifically for black students, paying ten dollars a month. McLendon worked diligently at his research job, participating in a breakthrough project under Charles H. McCloy, a pioneer in physical education. "My study was to prove that blacks and whites didn't need a separate age-weight-height scale," McLendon said. "Like they say, you're twenty years old and you're five feet, eight inches, you're supposed to weigh so much. Well, are there enough differences in the bony structure of blacks and whites to require a separate scale?" Many theories current at the time tried to explain the purported differences in the athletic achievements of the two races, especially after Jesse Owens's remarkable performance. "For instance," stated McLendon, "they used to say that blacks have a longer heel bone, and the femur was a different shape, and it caused them to have more jumping ability. We found out it wasn't so." In fact, McLendon's part of the study concluded that no measurable physiological differences exist across racial lines. There were, of course, variations among individuals, "but there wasn't enough difference in the total measurement to need a different scale," he said. "They balance." McLendon, an exemplary student, completed his degree with a major in health, physical education, and recreation in just nine months. "I had to, in that short time," he said, "because that's all the money I had."[24]

John B. McLendon Jr., University of Kansas graduation photograph, 1936. (Courtesy Joanna McLendon)

While studying at Iowa, McLendon married the petite, pretty, outgoing coed Alice Hultz, whom he had taken to the annual spring dance while both were students at the University of Kansas. Years later, their daughter, Querida, recalled the story of how her father had followed Alice home across large cornfields to what turned out to be her aunt's house. After introducing himself to her aunt, he asked permission to call on Alice, and her cousins showed him how to get back to town on their bicycles. From that day on, the two were constantly together, and they became engaged shortly after McLendon's college graduation. They remained married for sixteen years and had two children together, John III in 1939 and Querida two years later.

CHAPTER 3

Establishing a Tradition of Excellence
North Carolina College, 1937–52

Upon graduation from the master's program at Iowa, McLendon was offered his first full-time coaching job at Kansas Vocational School near Topeka. After his first month as basketball coach, he went to the principal with a request for a contract. Although the principal wanted to retain McLendon, he refused to give him a contract, stating that his word was good enough. Thus, when his University of Iowa roommate and friend William F. Burghardt requested that McLendon join him at Durham's North Carolina College for Negroes (later North Carolina Central), where he had been made head of the Physical Education Department, McLendon joyfully consented. Ironically, this was the same state McLendon's father had left for the Midwest years ago. Although his mother had misgivings about her son moving to the South, and his wife preferred to remain close to her parents' home in Kansas, McLendon took off for North Carolina by train in August 1937. It didn't take long, however, for the twenty-two-year-old Kansan to be introduced to the ugly world of institutionalized segregation in the American South, which his father had warned him about. "The first time I ever saw a Jim Crow sign was on the way to North Carolina," he recalled. "Although I'd been through a lot of racial situations in Kansas, I'd never seen colored and white fountains until I got to North Carolina."[1]

North Carolina College for Negroes was founded in 1910 by James E. Shepard, who served as its president for thirty-seven years. Although largely undistinguishable from other historically black colleges in the South founded around the turn of the century, it earned the distinction of being the nation's first state-supported liberal arts college for African American students. When McLendon joined Burghardt at the college in 1937, becoming his assistant and the assistant coach in football, basketball, and track, his salary was sixty dollars a month, plus room and board. McLendon would eventually organize the college's graduate program in physical education, the first of its kind in North Carolina, and coach boxing, wrestling, and swimming. But basketball was where he would make his mark, transforming programs across the nation.

Students at America's traditionally black colleges had been playing basketball since 1910. The competition among these colleges was organized into more than a half dozen athletic conferences, but the teams were largely ignored by white fans and the mainstream media. "Arguably, black-college basketball in the 1930s, 40s, and 50s was among the best competition in the country. But in 1937 when McLendon arrived in North Carolina, that notion was highly questionable," Billy Packer and Roland Lazenby note in *The Golden Game,* their comprehensive history celebrating the one hundredth anniversary of basketball. McLendon and other black coaches "knew in their hearts" that their teams were good, but before they could convince whites of this, they had to convince their fellow blacks. "Even the black population didn't know it and didn't believe it," McLendon recalled. "They had succumbed to the one-sided propaganda."[2]

In 1940, Burghardt split football and basketball at the college into separate programs, naming the idealistic and energetic McLendon as head basketball coach and director of athletics. Coach McLendon brought a new seriousness to black-college basketball; his tenure at North Carolina College revolutionized the sport, commencing its trajectory upward to the elevated status it enjoys today. Because football season ended in early December, basketball did not begin until after Christmas, lasting until baseball season. McLendon wanted to get ahead of the competition, however, so he began the custom of keeping his players in town so they could practice and be ready to play immediately after Christmas. To work this out with the administration, he and his players resurfaced the gym floor over the holidays, offsetting the expense for the school. In turn, this allowed the college enough money to feed and house the players while it was closed. "Mop and broom scholarships," McLendon loved to call this arrangement, which not only provided many a player the financial opportunity to stay in school but also drove home the work ethic that McLendon wanted to instill. His philosophy was simple and direct: as coach, he

Assistant Coach McLendon with William F. Burghardt, North Carolina College for Negroes, 1939. (Courtesy Alex Rivera, North Carolina College)

would work harder than his players would, and his players would work harder than all their opponents.[3]

Known as a strict but fair disciplinarian, McLendon quickly conveyed to his players what was required of them and what behaviors would not be tolerated. They were expected to study, attend all classes, go to the church of their choice on Sundays, and always conduct themselves as gentlemen. At five feet, eight inches, McLendon looked up to most of his players when he spoke to them and never raised his voice. "Still, whatever he said, you could believe he would do it," said Sam Jones, who played for him at North Carolina and later starred in the NBA with championship teams for the Boston Celtics. According to another one of McLendon's star athletes, Harold Hunter, Coach McLendon would tell his players, "Fellas, you can have the whole alphabet to play around with, but just leave the three W's alone—wine, weed, and women." With their coach as a role model, his players understood the value of getting a college education, and most of them earned their undergraduate degree.[4]

McLendon's Kansas roots helped him recruit numerous players from the Midwest, especially from his hometown of Kansas City. Many of his best and most loyal players—Richard Miller, Marland Buckner, Harold Hunter, and Ron Hamilton—came to the South from Kansas City to play for Coach McLendon. Each of them fondly recalled how McLendon personally brought them down to North Carolina and cared for them as if they were members of his family. McLendon quickly established himself as an able recruiter, observed Alex Rivera, longtime head of the school's news bureau and public relations department, "because he had a charisma that mothers liked." It certainly helped to persuade parents to send their sons to play for McLendon when they were told that the coach was a person of high character who didn't drink, smoke, or curse and who attended church on a regular basis. McLendon believed that character and integrity were essential to the success of his students and athletes, and he taught by example. According to Rivera, "You could bring your wife or daughter out to any of his practices without fear of hearing any foul language whatsoever."[5]

Selected as a member of the All National Team from Armstrong High School in Richmond, Virginia, and honored as its Most Valuable Player, Thornton Williams remembered Coach McLendon as a very persistent and effective recruiter. According to Williams, "McLendon kidnapped me to play for North Carolina College." Williams recalled how McLendon was so persuasive in convincing his mother that North Carolina College was the right place for her son that she gave him all his clothes to take back to the Durham campus. McLendon then left her money for her son to take the bus to Durham and a taxi to campus. Williams recalled angrily confronting McLendon in the college gym, but to his surprise, no apology from the coach was forthcoming. McLendon simply allowed Williams to calm down, then told him that he was the player the team needed for a national championship season. Williams decided to stay. Laughing about the incident years later, he remarked on how much he had learned to respect and love McLendon. Playing for McLendon, he said, changed his life.[6]

According to historian Pamela Grundy, McLendon remembered the free-flowing form of play taught to him by Dr. Naismith, and the attack element of fast-break basketball, but he took the approach one step further than his mentor suggested. "He developed," wrote Grundy, "conditioning drills, complex plays, and a wide-ranging strategic philosophy." He was acutely aware early on in his career that a number of coaches and athletic directors had voiced the opinion that his undisciplined, playground, street-style basketball had no place on a collegiate basketball floor: this was just not how the game was supposed to be played. McLendon chose to answer these critics not only on the court but also in his groundbreaking 1965 book, *Fast Break Basketball: Fine Points and Fundamentals,* the first book published by an African American coach. "Contrary to its reputation," he explained in the book's introduction, "the fast break is not an 'aimless,' 'helter- skelter,' 'run and shoot,' 'fire horse' game except in the appearance of its rapid, often demoralizing action. It is a planned attack with multiple applications; it is a designed offense which can be utilized in one or more of its several phases each time a team gains possession of the ball." McLendon argued that "the break away from the stereotyped game of 'set offense first and fast break when you can,' to 'fast break first and set offense when you have to' has added a new dimension to the game which multiplies the coach's repertoire of scoring possibilities and, equally important, allows the use of limited-ability personnel in important team-play positions, a great morale factor." In conclusion, he maintained that "the fast break as a primary offense is the recommended game for coaches searching for increased stature in their profession and added victories for their record."[7]

McLendon outlined fifteen reasons why the fast-break game could consistently put any team with even mediocre ability into the scoring column:

1. It can successfully employ players who have limited all-around talent but who have one or two special abilities.

2. It offsets the lack of sufficiently trained defensive personnel.

3. It can break an opposing team physically and decrease their advantage of skill and size.

4. It is the best answer to opponents who force your team to run.

5. It creates the need for excellent conditioning and health practices that insure this status.

6. It serves as a detector of physical unreadiness and physical limitation.

7. It inspires teamwork basketball.

8. It is the best game for consistent performance since it utilizes the close shooting attack in the "optimum scoring area."

9. It is an exciting, entertaining game to the player, coach, and spectator.

10. It is the most versatile offense.

11. It complements more defenses than any other offense.

12. It has been used most successfully by many teams in all areas of competition; is a winner by record.

13. It allows for ease of team organization.

14. It is a high-pressure offense designed to disorganize opposing team defense and limit opposing team offense.

15. It is basic to continued preparedness for international competition.[8]

McLendon, then, maintained not only that the fast break produced maximum victories but that it also made the game more exciting and fun to watch. As Grundy later observed, "In McLendon's estimation the style also influenced its practitioners in ways that raised versatility to an art." While fast-break basketball was "a winner at the turnstiles," McLendon wrote, "more importantly, it is a game of increased challenge to the young contestant. The challenge lies in the player's learning to make the most of the many choices confronting him. The high speed game requires quick sound reactions, lightning-quick decisions, and corresponding physical and mechanical adjustments to meet the ever-changing situations." The fast-breaking game would not only test the players' endurance but also force them "to adjust to a rapidly-forming defense counteraction. All of these factors," he concluded, "make this kind of game interesting, entertaining, and educational to the participant and onlookers alike."[9]

McLendon became legendary for his emphasis on conditioning. To get his players ready for the season, he would have them run two miles, from the gym to the track and back again, and run a mile around the track every day in less than six minutes—"championship miles," he called them. If they failed to make the grade, he would give them a few days to get in shape. "He gave us a certain amount of time to get up there and back," remembered several of his players. "If you didn't, you couldn't be on his team." John Brown, who played on three championship teams for McLendon at North Carolina, recalled how the players would be woken up at 4:30 to commence their morning run. A strict disciplinarian, McLendon also had his players run three miles if they broke curfew or had another infraction. "Coach would run you to death," said Brown. "And most of the time he would run with us with a smile on his face."[10]

Back in the gym, McLendon had his team play three-on-three full-court basketball—a grueling form of competition that required players to play defense from baseline to baseline and get the ball across half-court within four seconds. If you lost, you had to continue playing. If a player didn't execute properly in practice, he stayed on the court until he did. McLendon had his players wear low-cut Converse shoes, for he wanted the team to be associated with speed. "Fatigue is purely psychological," he stated. "It's impossible to get tired if you want to win badly enough." Ultimately, to be successful, McLendon later wrote, the coach and the players "must believe that the personnel of a fast breaking team is unique in terms of *conditioning, determination,* and *stamina,* and that only the *dedicated* athlete can find a place in this basketball system."[11]

"Superior conditioning," McLendon wrote, "achieved through cross-country running which precedes the season's opening by three to four weeks is a *must.* Some games, we plan to beat teams with better players by running them into errors and misjudgments solely caused by fast-break-induced fatigue. Our team cannot admit fatigue as a factor in their own performance. It is nonexistent as long as the desire to excel is uppermost in the player's mind." McLendon's conditioning objective for every team he coached was to have each player in such a state of physical readiness that he could play forty minutes of full-court offense and defense. "When the player can manage this performance," concluded McLendon, "he is ready for any game, since all other games are less demanding."[12]

"EACH PLAYER ON THE SQUAD MUST CONDITION HIMSELF AS IF THERE WOULD BE NO SUBSTITUTION IN HIS POSITION!" McLendon declared, and tournament time was no exception. During their fifth consecutive night of play in the 1958 NAIA Championship Tournament in Kansas City, his Tennessee A&I Tigers scored over 100 points against a seeded opponent in a game without a single substitution. In 1959, in another NAIA Championship Tournament, on the fourth successive night of play, his team engaged in another high-scoring battle (115–85) without a substitution until the final two or three minutes.[13]

McLendon put his philosophy into practice from the very beginning of his illustrious coaching career. From his first days at Durham, he aimed to blend an aggressive defensive press with a high-speed offense that utilized specific lines of attack. Furthermore, he stressed what seemed at the time a revolutionary idea: filling three lanes on a break to secure a manpower advantage in the frontcourt. To accomplish this, McLendon crafted highly conditioned athletes who would wear down the opposition.

From 1940 to 1954, his fast-breaking teams led the Colored Intercollegiate Athletic Association (renamed the Central Intercollegiate Athletic Association [CIAA] in 1950) in scoring ten times. And when McLendon moved to Tennessee A&I State University, his teams continued to run opponents off the floor. They employed the full-court press so relentlessly that opposing coaches tried to slow them down by tightening the nets so the ball would get stuck. McLendon, unphased, learned to bring a pair of scissors on the road. To create what he considered a winning balance, he created a platoon system, with a short team he used for pressing, called the "Mighty Mites," and a tall team he used for power. "I would use the small team to get out on the court and run, run, run and press, press, press," McLendon recalled to Packer and Lazenby. "Then I'd put in the tall team and have them stretch out their arms in a zone." His 1940–41 roster included a seven-foot center, Norbert Downing, and a six-eight forward, Harold Colbert, both from the same Indiana high school. There were no goal-tending rules at the time, and McLendon instructed Downing to take maximum advantage of his height. "Anything that came down the court, he'd jump and knock it away," McLendon said with unusual satisfaction.[14]

Establishing a Tradition of Excellence

Alex Rivera took great delight in remembering that the "Mighty Mites" ran so much against Shaw University one night that the exhausted officials called time-out to catch their breath. "These kids are gonna kill somebody," Rivera recalled one official saying. "There's no need to run down there with them," the second official responded. "They'll be right back in a second." McLendon's initial college squad ran past most of its opponents to an easy victory, captured the college's first conference-visitation or regular-season championship, and entered the inaugural Negro National College Championship Tournament over the weekend of March 21, 1941, at the Freeman Avenue Armory in Cincinnati. Here, teams and champions from six conferences would compete to determine the best black basketball team in the nation.[15]

Although McLendon was short of funds for the trip, he was convinced that his Eagles had matured into something special and was eager to challenge the other black schools for the first national title. So he took his team on the twenty-seven-hour bus ride, stopping in Roanoke, Virginia, to play an exhibition game against North Carolina A&T College to raise the necessary funds for the rest of the trip. The A&T coach, Roland Bernard, agreed to the game with one extraordinary condition: he could name any two of McLendon's players to sit out. McLendon agreed, and Bernard strode into the locker room minutes before tip-off and pointed to North Carolina's two tallest players, Downing and Colbert. As a result, "Slim" and "Slam," as they were affectionately known, sat on the bench during the entire game. The Eagles won the game anyway, earning $150, enough money to get to Cincinnati. "But the tournament was a bust; they ran short of money," Rivera later explained. "Finances were so tight that there was no money to pay for food, lodging, and incidentals. The Cordelia Hotel evicted the Eagles and set their belongings on the street. The team relocated under the stairs of the Armory," where they would be playing the following day.[16]

Originally scheduled to be played over three days, the event, because of financial constraints, was crammed into thirty-six hours. McLendon's team played four games on Saturday, at 10 A.M., 2 P.M., 7 P.M., and 9 P.M. Curiously, the tournament promotional material identified McLendon's school as North Carolina State, instead of North Carolina College, and his players had the word STATE displayed across their jerseys. The Eagles beat three conference champions that day: Clark College (61–54), West Virginia State College (61–39), and Kentucky State College (43–37); they were scheduled to play Southern University, which had defeated them on Friday, at 9:00 that night. Since the tournament was "double-elimination," McLendon, who knew that the city's blue laws forbade Sunday games, asked the event's promoter what would happen if his team won the first game. After the promoter assured him that he didn't have to worry about this, McLendon was surprised to see that he was the referee for the game. Whether this was a factor in its outcome is debatable, but—interestingly—all of McLendon's starters fouled out, and his team bowed to Southern, 48–42.[17]

Even with the loss, however, the Associated Negro Press voted the North Carolina College Eagles—with a 19–5 record under their twenty-five-year-old coach, John McLendon—the true "Negro National Champions." A number of sports enthusiasts today believe that the basketball played by the traditionally black colleges in the 1940s was the best in the country. Looking back on those teams, Rivera proudly declared: "We could have beaten Duke and Carolina in the same day. One in the morning and one at night." In spite of the acclaim, however, the Eagles had to make the long trip home without a meal, for the trip money was totally exhausted. "The players ate crackers and peanuts and didn't complain. They would have walked on water and gone through fire for McLendon," Rivera explained.[18]

According to Packer and Lazenby, "These black college teams performed on a shoestring budget along with the hindrance and danger of segregation. Every athletic trip was viewed as 'campus to campus,' particularly throughout the Deep South, where a routine stop at a gas station could lead to a racial confrontation and serious trouble." Black teams like McLendon's packed their food along and slept on the campuses of other black schools. Most of the time, the players slept in a campus dorm room set aside for visiting teams, and sometimes a guest house was set aside for coaches. However, a few times the Eagles slept on beds brought into the locker room, and once they had to spend the night in a boiler room, where the heat almost made them ill.[19]

"You had to plot your ways," McLendon recalled, "and always plan every detail in advance. A simple trip from one school to another was like plotting your way through a minefield in a war." McLendon's solution was to steer around problems as much as humanly possible. "I was fortunate to avoid a situation where I'd have to lose my self-respect," he explained to Packer and Lazenby. "You do not want to get into a situation where your dignity would be destroyed right in front of your team."[20]

Establishing a Tradition of Excellence

McLendon with his first North Carolina State College Eagles captain, Reginald Ennis, 1941. (Courtesy Joanna McLendon)

McLendon's strategy for dealing with racism was severely tested in Georgia in 1941 and a few years later on a trip with his team through West Virginia. After playing in the first Peach Bowl postseason game, losing in the last few minutes to Morris Brown College, the North Carolina College football team was returning to Durham from Columbus, Georgia, in a private Southern Railway coach, when a large group of white men boarded the train. When these men realized that the all-black team had its own private car, they became highly agitated and demanded that if the two coaches and their team did not get off the train at the next depot, they would not let it proceed. The situation grew very tense as Head Coach Burghardt and Assistant Coach McLendon tried to avoid an ugly confrontation. Just as the train pulled up to the station, however, they heard a kid with newspapers in his hand running up and down the platform yelling, "Pearl Harbor Bombed by Japan." The angry white men rushed out to buy the newspaper, and the confrontation was averted.[21]

McLendon's with his first North Carolina College Eagles team, the 1941 "Negro National Champions." *Seated, left to right:* James Hardy, Richard Mack, Floyd Brown, George Mack, Leo Fine, Walter Womack, William Peerman. *Back row, left to right:* John B. McLendon, Rudolph Roberson, Reginald Ennis, John Brown, Norbert Downing, Harold Colbert, Lee Smith, Buford Allen, Monroe Collins, Albert Johnson. (Courtesy Alex Rivera, North Carolina College)

Some years later, in the mid-1940s, as McLendon related in rich detail to Pamela Grundy, his North Carolina College team caught the bus in Charleston, West Virginia, after a game with the Yellow Jackets of West Virginia State, and headed to another in Bluefield. The bus was crowded that evening, and the only seat left for one of the team's seven players, Henry "Big Dog" Thomas, was next to a white woman cradling a baby in her arms. As was the custom in the South, blacks had gone to the back of the bus, and whites had been seated from the front; the open seat was right in the middle, on what would prove to be dangerous ground.[22]

McLendon politely asked the young woman if Thomas could sit next to her. When she responded affirmatively, McLendon told his center to sit down. The other players and McLendon himself continued to stand, McLendon reasoning that since Thomas was the team's leading scorer, he needed to rest more than the others. Everything was fine until

Establishing a Tradition of Excellence

the bus driver saw Thomas and the white woman in the rearview mirror. He stopped the bus midroute, angrily bolted down the aisle, and confronted McLendon. "He has to get up," the bus driver barked. Thomas did not say anything, as his coach had earlier instructed; he just looked at McLendon, pleading for guidance. The coach composed himself and stood his ground. "He doesn't have to get up," he declared. "The law says we seat from the back, they seat from the front. It's the last seat on the bus, and he can sit in it if he wants to."[23]

As the men stood confronting one another, McLendon was pleased to find that he had developed some support. The other passengers just wanted to reach their destinations, and it appeared that even the white riders did not blame him for this inconvenience. "Go sit down and drive the bus," he recalled many of them saying. "We've got to get to where we're going. Get on, let's get out of here." McLendon watched the driver's rapidly reddening face and realized that he might be gambling with his life. "I knew he had a gun under his front seat," he later explained. "But more was at stake than survival." The bus driver sat down for a few minutes, but once the bus moved into the mountains outside of Charleston, he pulled off the road and returned to the back. "He can't sit there," he repeated. "I'm not moving this bus until he gets up."[24]

As a representative of his team, his college, and perhaps his race, McLendon knew that if he gave in, his players would never forget it. Racism was based not only on relegating black people to second-class status but also on humiliating its victims. Given the values passed down from his mother and father, McLendon was not about to relent. Assessing the potentially dangerous situation, he quickly made the decision to enact a strategic retreat while keeping his dignity intact. "It's a matter really of learning how to maintain a position of respect. And to do this you do try to avoid confrontation. Because if you're made to lose your dignity, stripped of your manhood in front of your players," he said, "you can't be in a position to tell them to be a man, about life, about anything." McLendon looked calmly at the driver and then at the passengers. "Since this is such a big problem for you, and these people have to get where they're going, I'll tell you what we are going to do," he declared. "We're going to get off the bus."[25]

The players followed their coach off the bus and stood beside the mountain road. As they waited for another bus, it soon became apparent that McLendon's strategy had worked. "They laughed about it," he said. "They really thought we had won. Because you can see what kind of position you can put that kind of person in. That you're better than he is—if that's what the problem is. He's not making any points by doing that." Another bus came along within the hour, and the team went on to Bluefield in time for the next game.[26]

According to writer Pamela Grundy, "McLendon's strategic retreat had made his point, preserved the team's dignity, and averted violence." "He focused," she wrote, "not on his own courage, but on his broader goal—helping his players become the kind of men who could negotiate not only an opposing team's defense, but also the many challenges they would face after they left his care." Indeed, the coach used every possible situation to teach his players dignity, respect, and what it took to be proud, resourceful men. "That's what you're trying to make of them," he declared. "Men who can handle life well. You might have to almost be ready to sacrifice your life to maintain that position in their respect."[27]

During such difficult situations, encountered all too often in a deeply racist society, McLendon found it helpful to heed the advice Dr. Naismith had given him years before. He tried his best to keep his players focused on their goals rather than on the ignorance of others. "We had little ways," McLendon recalled to author Ron Thomas. "We would say, 'I wonder what these people are going to do next.' We tried to make them a butt of the joke and imitate them. Young people can adjust. We always put people that treated us like that in a lower class. They were showing how ignorant they were and how mean they were. You had to have some kind of rationale to have fellas keep focused on other things than being constantly put down, and had to do the same for yourself."[28]

McLendon explained to Grundy his philosophy of self-discipline, self-awareness, and how to insure your dignity in a racist society. "What it meant: you have to maintain yourself, all you are capable of, at all times," he said to his players. "You can't lower yourself to be a marginal playing team, dirty tactics. If you are in the right, well, you are going to prevail, even though the system appears to be against you. It's really not you being any less, it's because somebody's worried about you already being much more than they want you to be. You play the game of life the way you play this situation."[29]

Thus, while U.S. troops were fighting racial hatred and injustice overseas during World War II, McLendon tackled it at home in several creative ways. Like most African American coaches who practiced what Patrick B. Miller and David W. Wiggins identify as "muscular assimilationism," McLendon set out to use the discipline and strategy of competitive athletics to prepare young people for the challenges of adult life. Obtaining racial respect and overcoming the obstacles of Jim Crow society became the guiding principles of the young coach's life, and he created opportunities to put these principles into action.[30]

In 1942, McLendon had another powerhouse team, led by captain Reginald Ennis from Smithfield, North Carolina, a complete player "who could do it all," McLendon recalled, as solid in the classroom as he was on the court. With a 14–0 record, McLendon challenged half a dozen teams in the North and Midwest to play his team in Washington, D.C., since this was neutral ground where integrated play was not against the law. The only team to respond favorably was Brooklyn College, which had beaten every other school in the New York area. This led to the first integrated game in our nation's capitol. To underscore its historic significance, McLendon invited First Lady Eleanor Roosevelt, hoping to prove that the administration supported his efforts. Sympathetic to the cause but unable to attend, she sent Interior Secretary Harold Ickes, a strong civil rights supporter, as her personal representative.

McLendon wished to instill confidence and a sense of pride in his players and validate his own coaching methods and abilities. "Because of the exclusion of blacks in sports, if you were practicing the games that other people were playing, you really had no way to decide whether you were really playing it well," he later explained to Grundy. "The white teams were the ones you read about in the newspapers. You read about our teams once a week in the weeklies. . . . I was kind of a hard taskmaster, tried to do it tough-love style, that's what they call it these days. And get my fellows to achieve. But they weren't sure that they were coming up to the standard that I had set. . . . It's almost like you're in another world and you don't know whether you are doing what you are supposed to do or not. So the only way to prove it is to play them." When the Eagles, then, in their first integrated game, earned an emotionally satisfying, hard-fought victory over Brooklyn College, 37–34, McLendon saw immediate results. "When we played that game," he said, "and our guys won the game, they felt like, 'Well, we're really playing basketball. Coach is a real coach here. He's not just coaching a game that only we play, but he's coaching a game that they play, and all these pictures we see on Sunday—we're better than they are.'"[31]

The Secret Game

McLendon wanted his 1944 CIAA champion Eagles to have the same learning experience. "I had taught them that the game we played was equal to or superior to the game they read about in the newspaper," McLendon told Bud Shaw of the *Cleveland Plain Dealer* in 1997. "We wanted to make the point that, 'If you play the game the way it's supposed to be played, all this stuff in the paper is nice for somebody else, but it doesn't demean you. It doesn't mean you can't do it. It means the [social] system isn't going to highlight it, that's all." Although Durham was like all Southern cities at the time—a town with rigidly enforced segregation—attitudes on college campuses were slightly better. Still, college sports in the American South "did not exist in a social and cultural vacuum," as noted by historian Charles H. Martin. "The region's pervasive system of white supremacy and racial segregation controlled athletic policy as tightly as it did university admissions." McLendon's reputation as a winning coach earned him invitations to come watch Duke University play, but always with a stipulation. "I was invited, but they told me I would have to sit on the end of the bench in a waiter's coat," he remembered. "I wasn't about to do that." Thus, when a challenge to break through racial barriers came from the Duke University campus, he seized the opportunity.[32]

The Duke Blue Devils had won the Southern Conference Championship, but there was an intramural team on the Duke campus, based at the medical school, that many believed was even better, as it was stocked with former college athletes who had been sent to Duke as part of army and navy training programs. Indeed, the boys from Duke were feeling so good about their team that they commissioned an article in the local paper declaring themselves state champions. Exactly how the secret game between this Duke Medical School team and North Carolina College came about is still laced with ambiguity. McLendon once recalled that his student trainer, Vivian Henderson, who later would become a nationally recognized economist and president of Clark College in

Atlanta, had read the newspaper article and called Duke's unofficial coach, Jack Burgess, to issue the challenge. There's one team you haven't played, Henderson reportedly said. This was McLendon's Eagles, whose fast-break, pressing defense style had resulted in a 19–1 record. The Eagles had just concluded their schedule, falling 57–52 to unbeaten Lincoln University of Pennsylvania in a game played at the Renaissance Ballroom in Harlem. Billed as the "Negro National Championship," this game was their only loss of the season.[33]

Eagle George Parks, however, the only surviving North Carolina player, provided a more common explanation. There was some ongoing contact, he said, between a few students from Duke and North Carolina College, who met occasionally through YMCA programs—at considerable risk—to discuss racial issues. "We had fruitful discussions," Parks remembered. "We talked about things in general, a lot about race and ethnicity, and basketball came into the discussions." At one meeting, Parks overheard an idle boast that the Duke Medical School basketball team was the best in the state. Taking exception, he issued a challenge. According to Mike Potter, the subsequent brainstorming session among the students eventually led to the notion that a team from Duke could play the Eagles, the game determining which team really was the best. When McLendon heard about this plan, he eagerly endorsed it, and he and Jack Burgess, who had earlier competed against black players at the University of Montana, set up the contest.[34]

Whoever laid the groundwork for the game, both teams were ready for the challenge, with a couple of conditions. No one was to be told about the game, and no spectators would be allowed. The game would be played in the North Carolina College gymnasium, since there was no way to sneak the Eagles onto the completely segregated Duke campus. It would be a regulation contest, complete with referee and a game clock. "There wasn't any way the school was going to survive if they were integrationists," McLendon recalled. "We quickly made the rule this would be a nonpublic affair." Thus the interracial pickup game was set—twenty-one years before the color barrier would be broken in the Atlantic Coast Conference. However, as historian Scott Ellsworth noted, in spite of the precautions, "it was still an endeavor fraught with peril—especially for McLendon. If word of what was to happen reached the newspapers, or the state legislature, he would surely lose his job. And if the police happened upon the game while

The North Carolina College Eagles' CIAA Visitation champions, 1944. *Left to right:* John B. McLendon, George Parks, George Samuels, Billy Williams, James Hardy, Aubrey Stanley, Floyd Brown, Henry Thomas, Edward Boyd (trainer). (Courtesy Alex Rivera, North Carolina College)

it was in progress, he might lose a great deal more." The Ku Klux Klan had held a public meeting in Durham just one week before. And earlier in the year, when a black GI failed to move quickly to the back of the bus, the bus driver shot and killed him. An all-white jury took just twenty minutes to exonerate the driver for his action.[35]

Nevertheless, shortly before 11 A.M. on Sunday, March 12, 1944, the Duke players piled into two rented cars for the trip to the North Carolina College campus. McLendon picked this time because he knew the entire city of Durham, black and white, would be occupied with Sunday church services. The Duke players took a circuitous route to satisfy themselves that they weren't being followed. When they entered what was referred to as "the colored section" of town, they covered their car windows with quilts, so as to avoid drawing attention to a group of young white men driving down Fayetteville Street in broad daylight. They pulled up to the steps of the gymnasium and got out with jackets over their heads. "I remember when we got out of the cars, heads popped out of the dormitories across the street," remembered David Hubbell, who grew up in Durham and played for the Duke team. Edward "Pee Wee" Boyd, the North Carolina team manager and Coach McLendon's right-hand man, told Ellsworth that "Coach Mac brought them in through the women's dressing room side

Establishing a Tradition of Excellence

of the gym. When we saw these white faces being uncovered, nobody said anything." The gym was then locked, and no spectators were allowed in.[36]

McLendon's five-year-old son, John, and three-year-old daughter, Querida, were crouched in the corner, watching. Querida remembered her father having the children shake hands with the Duke coach—the first time they had ever been that close to a white man. She was so scared that she initially hid behind her mother's skirt, but her father had always told her and her brother not to be afraid of anyone, so they responded accordingly. Although Alice thought that she and the children should be in church instead of at a basketball game, McLendon had convinced her that this was a historic occasion, and he wanted their children to witness it.[37]

McLendon welcomed the Duke players, who seemed a bit startled to find a gym floor painted black with white stripes. At the other end of the court stood the North Carolina Eagles, dressed in their maroon jerseys, satin shorts, kneepads, striped wool socks, and high-top sneakers. Treating the game as no big deal with his own players, some of whom had been raised not to look a white person in the eyes, McLendon instructed them to go out and play the way they always played. In spite of all the precautions, a number of students had heard about the game and climbed up on boxes, barrels, crates, and ladders to look through the windows, six feet off the ground, to witness white and black players on the same court. Many of the players on both sides were understandably apprehensive about what would happen next. None of the Duke players had ever competed against a black team. "The thoughts running through my mind would be, 'Well, this just isn't done,'" Duke player Hubbell recalled on ABC's *Nightline* in 1997. "Not only were we breaking the law," sixteen-year-old North Carolina College player Aubrey Stanley recalled to Ellsworth, "we were breaking tradition. I don't know which one was worse in the South at that time. Had it been up to me, no, I would not have done it."[38]

Both teams played very tentatively at the beginning. Most of the black players had never touched a white person before. "For the first five minutes, you felt like you were the biggest sinner in the world," Boyd told Ellsworth. "But then we found out that the black wouldn't rub off and the white wouldn't rub off." Hubbell recalled his teammates also being initially somewhat apprehensive, "but once we got into the flow of the game it really didn't matter." Duke took an early lead, but after a few minutes the Eagles began running their fast breaks and employing a pressure defense, forcing turnovers and errant shots. Eagles player Stanley told Ellsworth that it suddenly occurred to him about midway through the first half "that these men weren't supermen. They were just men and we could beat them." Henry "Big Dog" Thomas was a top scorer for the host team, and Parks was superlative under the boards, snagging rebound after rebound. James "Boogie" Hardy and Floyd "Cootie" Brown ran down the court perfectly, executing their patented fast break, leading to easy baskets for them and their teammates. McLendon's Eagles eventually trounced the Duke Medical School team, 88–44. Eagles manager Boyd remembered that the victory went beyond basketball. "We represented every black soul in Durham, whether they knew it or not," he said, "and when we got a lead, we wanted a bigger one." "It was obvious that our challenge was taken very well and we deserved the trouncing we got. Those guys were exceptionally good ballplayers," said Duke player Jack Burgess on *Nightline*.[39]

After the rout, McLendon instructed half the players from each team to switch sides and play in integrated groups. "It is one of the best ways for people to learn about each other and get to respect one another," he said later. Years afterward, North Carolina player George Parks would refer to this as "just God's children horsing around with a basketball." Considering the times, however, it was much more than that: it was a courageous act of civil disobedience against an unjust system, a well-crafted conspiracy to break down a long-standing social barrier.[40]

Following the games, all the participants shook hands and walked to the North Carolina players' dormitory, where they got to know one another and had refreshments. "We called it a bull session," Hubbell said. "Our students and their students just talking about the way things were." After an hour or so, the Duke players got into their cars and drove back to their campus. Everyone understood that they were never to talk about their interracial experience. As Duke player Lloyd Taylor declared to Ellsworth, "I think they would have been castigated" if they had done so. "Not enough credit is given to the Duke players," McLendon recalled. "They were in a bad position. They would have been considered bad people, even called Communists at that time." The teams would never compete against one another again, but many years later several of them remembered that from this day on they saw themselves and their

Establishing a Tradition of Excellence

world in a new way. "I didn't ever tell my classmates abut it," Duke's Dave Hubbell told Potter. "But what we learned then was that at least in a certain area, in a game that had rules, blacks and whites could get along with no real problems."[41]

As for McLendon, he understood the substantial risk to himself, his players, and his college, but he believed that what he was doing was worthwhile. As he later recalled, "I knew it was against the law, but I believed the law was stupid and didn't pay much attention to it. All you try to do is avoid detection." The Durham police never found out about the game, nor did the white newspaper. A reporter for the *Carolina Times,* Durham's black weekly, heard about the game but, after an appeal from McLendon, decided not to publish anything. Even in interviews years after he retired from coaching, McLendon steered clear of talking about the game. Interviewed by Bud Shaw in 1997, McLendon stated, "I just wanted to further the idea that we all played basketball, that we all played it well, and that we should be playing it together. Only later did I realize the hazardous position I put our school president in."[42]

Although the clandestine event was kept secret for over half a century, McLendon was proud of what he and all the players had accomplished that day and was confident that the lessons learned were worth the effort. Interviewed on *Nightline,* he declared, "You try to make a contribution in your life to something that is worthwhile. Although I did not go out and march in a parade and protest, there are ways you can get towards where you should be in relationships."[43]

Sixty years after the secret game, a historic exhibition basketball contest took place on the Duke campus, in Cameron Indoor Stadium. On November 11, 2004, the North Carolina Central University Eagles took the court in the first official basketball game between Durham's two universities. This time the Eagles were no match for the boys from Duke, and they bowed to the Blue Devils, 95–58. "Sixty years after the secret game, the teams reunited for all the world—and more importantly—for all of Durham—to see," Bryan Strickland wrote in the *Herald-Sun*. Duke University coach Mike Krzyzewski understood the historic significance of the event. "I love the fact it's the 60th anniversary of the secret game, and one of the reasons we played this this year is because we're celebrating the 100th anniversary of Duke basketball," he said. "And certainly 60 years ago in this town with Coach McLendon and his team and the medical students, that's a big part of our history. It just shows how basketball has been an amazing vehicle to bring about good change, effective change." One could imagine Coach McLendon proudly declaring, "I couldn't have said it better."[44]

The CIAA Tournament

During the 1940s, McLendon's fast-break style and pressure defense were revolutionizing college play, and the North Carolina Eagles were setting scoring records that many people found difficult to believe. One of McLendon's early superstars, Rudolph "Rocky" Roberson, of Atchinson, Kansas, scored 58 points against Shaw University in February 1943 to break the single-game scoring record of 50 points, held by Angelo "Hank" Luisetti, the Stanford All-American and future Hall of Famer who developed the running one-hand shot, which few players had ever seen before. To set the record, Roberson hit on twenty-five of thirty-two field goals and netted eight out of ten free throws. Equally important, McLendon's cagers subsequently finally received attention beyond the black community, as Bill Stern, a well-known radio personality, announced the news of Roberson's performance on his nationwide show: "And it happened at a little school in North Carolina." A year later, in another game against Shaw, the Eagles racked up 67 points during the second half, another national record.

"Most of the teams played the slow, bring-it-down-the-court style," said Aubrey Stanley, who played for McLendon from 1943 until 1947 and was captain of the first CIAA championship team in 1946. "With him it was get the ball to the center, hit the wing man and go. We were always looking for the two-on-one, three-on-one, and we often got it."[45]

McLendon's 1944 team recorded nineteen victories and only one loss, and the following year his record was 18–2. The team began to draw enormous crowds. Since the Eagles gym held only twelve hundred people, fans quickly learned that they had to arrive three hours early if they wanted to get in. "The black citizens would bring games and food and have a party while waiting for the game to start," recalled McLendon. In the fall of 1952, North Carolina College proudly unveiled a forty-three-hundred-seat gymnasium with a million-dollar price tag. Interest in the team was so great that college officials announced they would begin radio broadcasts for fans unable to secure seats. Although McLendon was grateful for the strong support, he understood that all the excitement had to be put into perspective. "In 1950," Grundy notes, "competitive fever at North Carolina College games ran so high that the coach issued a written admonition to his fans." "For the emotional basketball fan whose feelings of loyalty and rivalry and elation and depression are so pronounced during the game, I prescribe H. R. Peterson's Tenets," McLendon wrote in the *Carolina Times*. He went on to expand on his philosophy of coaching and life: "Basketball is a game—not a battle or a fight. Basketball is for the fun and enjoyment it produces—not to provoke bitterness and sorrow. A basketball game is not a matter of life and death. Basketball is a game from which there must emerge a victor and a loser. In general, only a few points separate the two. The victors deserve congratulations: the losers respect. Victory should develop a spirit of tempered elation mixed with tolerance."[46]

Self-control was a mark of honor for McLendon and his teams. McLendon understood that a coach is the one person who most influences player, fan, and student behavior during competition and that it is imperative that he respect authority, which in the game is represented by the officials. "It's a very worthwhile discipline," McLendon explained in 1961 to *Cleveland Press* sportswriter Jack Clowser. "Many years ago, I learned that if a coach pops off, throws towels around and stomps on the floor, he's creating a bad example for the student body. They often react with a storm of booing for the officials or the other team. In my early years, I went to the microphone more than once to request order from the students. When they started to call us the 'House of Sportsmanship,' I was extremely proud."[47]

Along with tremendous local interest in CIAA basketball, McLendon always dreamed of showcasing his talented squads before a wider public. At the close of World War II, he joined with Talmadge Hill of Morgan State College, John Burr of Howard University, and Harry Jefferson of Virginia State College to revive a prewar plan for an end-of-season basketball tournament as "a grand way of celebrating the season by bringing the best teams together." Such an event, supporters argued, would serve many purposes, making possible "a time for fellowship with those from other member institutions, a great social occasion, a time for some presidents to show off their best athletes and coaches . . . a time for students and alumni to brag about their team, a time to crown the best tournament team, a time for the big pro scouts to see most top athletes together, a time to make the necessary money to operate the association, and finally the time for the news media to extol the merits of the occasion and let the fans in other parts of the country know what the association has achieved." William Bell of North Carolina A&T College appointed Talmadge Hill as chairman of the committee. According to McLendon, it was largely due to Hill's leadership and dogged determination that the proposed tournament became a reality.[48]

In 1946, with a five-hundred-dollar budget, the inaugural CIAA basketball tournament opened at Turner Arena in Washington, D.C. Since the money that had been allocated was not immediately available, each of the committee members—along with George Singleton from Virginia State, who served as secretary-treasurer—personally contributed one hundred dollars to get the tournament off the ground. The arena was really nothing more than a boxing gymnasium near Howard University that could barely seat two thousand people, but it was all they could get, since the venues in most Southern cities would not welcome a black-college conference tournament. "It was a dank, dark, cold, smoke-filled place," West Virginia State's All-American center Earl Lloyd later said of the building that held the early CIAA tournaments. "But to us, it was Madison Square Garden." Legendary Winston-Salem Teachers College coach Clarence "Big House" Gaines remembered that players had to sleep on bunk beds set up in an empty gymnasium because they weren't allowed in the area hotels.[49]

In spite of all these limitations, the tournament succeeded beyond expectations. At the conclusion of an incredibly exciting week of superlative basketball, the championship game went into triple overtime, as McLendon's unseeded, fifth-ranked Eagles were pitted against the second-seeded Virginia Union Panthers, who had dropped only one conference game the entire season. The Eagles, who were once again known affectionately as the "Mighty Mites," had no player over six-two, their average height five-nine. In many a game, fans saw four rapid little players tearing up the court. Of these four, the tallest was Richard "Mice" Miller, at five-seven; Marland "Buck" Buckner was only five-four. "We were not the best team there, talent-wise," team captain Aubrey "Stinky" Stanley later said. "We were the best conditioned.

Coach McLendon always felt that if you had two teams of equal ability, the better-conditioned would win."[50]

North Carolina guard Richard Miller remembered that during pregame preparation, Coach McLendon invented a new offensive pattern that would prove very useful during the tournament. Miller called this the "open offense" because it placed men around the perimeter of the front court. "We opened up the middle by placing two forwards on the side near the corners, allowing the three guards to handle the ball," he recalled. "It was due to our exceptional speed and ball handling that we could drive the middle and take shots from a closer range and also outmaneuver our taller opponents." "We couldn't beat Virginia Union with their superior big men, and we were having problems in the middle," said McLendon. "So I just took our big men and put them in the corner. The effect was to spread the offense and minimize a height advantage." This offense later became Tennessee State's "two-in-the-corners" freeze offense, for McLendon's national championship teams of the 1950s, and North Carolina's "four-corners" offense during the 1970s, under Dean Smith.[51]

Describing his unique two-corners offense in 1957, McLendon wrote, "Its purpose is, first, to protect our lead, second, to extend our lead, and third, to end the game in our favor. Underlying these purposes is the basic idea of creating the illusion that the ball is to be withheld but at the same time offering a constant threat and effort to score." Coach Smith saw McLendon diagram this strategy when they were together at a Christian Athletes Conference in Estes Park, Colorado, in 1970. Smith was so impressed by what McLendon was outlining that he asked him to repeat it so he could write it down. McLendon, frequently asked about this, would later laugh and say, "They called it four corners. I always say they took my two corners and made it a victim of inflation." In Smith's autobiography, he states that he was "wrongly credited as the sole creator of the Four Corners," naming McLendon as one of several coaches who applied a delay game similar to his.[52]

"Obviously, John did use that defense," recalled Billy Packer, former Wake Forest University player and longtime CBS broadcaster. "The perception is that Dean Smith had to invent it because it was modern times and it happened on television. I'm not sure about the origins of it, but I can tell you that if John McLendon makes a statement, you can be sure it's an honest statement. He's one of the class guys in the history of basketball."[53]

McLendon's team was not given much consideration going into the three-day 1946 tournament. But beginning with the first game, in which the Eagles defeated the fourth-ranked West Virginia State team 60–56, tournament fans began to take notice of this scrappy little team of speedsters. By the time they had soundly beaten the top-seeded—and previously undefeated—Lincoln University Lions 55–46 in the semifinal game, sportswriters and fans began to take them seriously. "We made a pact to win it all," recalled Stanley. "Every team we played in the tournament had beaten us in the regular season, so we were highly motivated."[54]

The triple-overtime championship game between North Carolina and second-seeded Virginia Union was a college basketball classic. The game saw fourteen lead changes and was tied ten times. With less than a minute and a half left to play in the regulation ball game, the Eagles were six points behind. Then five-seven Robert "Skull" Herring cut in sharply for a layup, and E. Parker "Daddy Mac" McDougal followed with a shot from the circle. With thirty seconds to go, the Eagles stole the ball from the Panthers, and Stanley, the top performer for the North Carolina team, drifted into the right-hand corner and calmly let fly with a set shot that hit the bottom of the strings, ending regulation play at 48–all.

In the second overtime, the Panthers led by four points with less than a minute left. But the smaller, quicker Eagles rallied once again off their patented fast break, as Herring raced down the court and hit the mark with a layup. After the Eagles stole the ball on the Panthers' throw-in, Stanley made good with another spectacular set shot with five seconds to go, and the game was sent into its third overtime. Once it began, McLendon's superbly conditioned squad took over the game. Stanley sensed that Virginia Union was through. "I could see their chests heaving," he said. "I could see them trying to catch their breath. They'd never played that all-out, up-and-down style and weren't used to it." Coach McLendon remembered Stanley telling him "to straighten up his coat and tie and get ready for the big trophy. They are worn out, and we are just getting ready to play."[55]

"After a third resting period, play was resumed, but the courage and stamina displayed by the little fellows from Carolina had sapped the

Establishing a Tradition of Excellence

energy of the Union Club. In the final five minutes of overtime play, the 'whiz kids' romped and cavorted just like it was the first half of the tournament game," reported *Norfolk Journal and Guide* sports editor Lem Graves Jr., who called the game his "all time sports 'thrill-of-a-lifetime,'" despite his home state team's loss. "Passing with lightning precision, and cutting into the basket in magnificent form," Graves continued, "they [the Eagles] dropped in four baskets in succession and then put on an 'ice' show to run the time out. Richmond's Thornton Williams contributed the first and last of these four baskets to the Carolina total while Stanley sandwiched two field goals in between." It was during this game that McLendon first used the "corners" offense. "I had been experimenting with it," McLendon recalled, "and when we went into the third overtime period we went into the 'corners.'"[56]

During the third overtime, all the players and fans and Virginia Union's coach were standing, understandably exhausted yet screaming for their team to triumph. According to Richard Miller, the atmosphere was so intense that some fans fainted. Both McLendon and his assistant, LeRoy Walker, remembered Virginia Union coach Henry Hucles becoming so excited that he ended up briefly sitting at the end of North Carolina's bench. North Carolina player Thornton "Fatbread" Williams, however, remembered Coach McLendon "sitting very relaxed as though nothing was happening around him." Williams later stated that in all his life playing basketball, from the playground through high school and college, he "never witnessed a coach as cool as McLendon was under great pressure." McLendon's composure under pressure, and his team's, paid off, as the Eagles triumphed 64–56. Although everyone on the team had contributed, playmakers Stanley and Miller and forward-center Williams had paced the Eagles to victory.[57]

Tournament MVP James Dilworth from Virginia Union remembered that his team had played extremely well for Coach Hucles but lost to a better team that evening. "It is my opinion," he said, "that the cohesion of the N.C.C. Eagles, and their determination, led to their victory, and it was this fact that I attribute to a man who stood along and above his coaching colleagues, Coach John McLendon." Dilworth continued to praise Coach McLendon: "The man exhibited sensitivity, positivity, in addition to a unique quality and quantity of basketball 'know how.' As a result of these assets, it gave vent to maximum effort and performance by his charges."[58]

Years later, McLendon wrote that "the greatest testimonial to the teamwork and outstanding ability of this North Carolina team was the failure of the sportswriters to place a single player on the all-conference team. It was not only the startling speed, dexterity, and endless stamina which marked the undersized players, but their thoroughly team-oriented approach to the game which made them so remarkably success-ful." He went on to explain that "the fast break system which they played inspired, in fact required, the team play they so completely exemplified."[59]

W. N. Rivers, of the Capital Classic Association, presented the first-place trophy to McLendon and moments later handed him a handsome trophy for team sportsmanship, making the moment even sweeter. "Whenever I think of dedication, extreme determination, team unity, splendid school spirit, sportsmanship and strong friendship between players, I think of these great little men before I think of any others," McLendon later said.[60]

Interestingly, John E. Brown, a member of North Carolina College's first championship team, was returning to the college after serving in the army, by way of Washington, D.C. He went to the tournament and, arguably, played a decisive role in the Eagles' victory. Brown was seated at the top of the arena, in back of the Eagles' goal, for the final half of play. Behind him was a circular shutter-ventilator that opened and closed when affected by wind drafts. The afternoon sunlight intermittently shone directly through the glass backboard on the North Carolina team, and Brown became convinced that this distracted and bothered the play-ers when they attempted shots. "I became so infuriated at the sun," Brown remembered, "I took my recently acquired topcoat and threw it into the blades of the ventilator, which immediately shredded my coat, but the sun was stopped for good. Stanley made four of four in putting N.C.C. into overtime. I felt I had helped my team."[61]

North Carolina assistant coach LeRoy Walker, who would go on to worldwide renown as a U.S. Olympic track and field coach and interna-tional ambassador of sports, later explained that the championship "rep-resented a triumph over great odds." Walker stated that he had never seen, before or since, "any basketball to equal the drama and excitement of these two expert teams . . . dueling to a super-climactic finish. . . . I remember thinking that a better script for continuing growth and inter-est in CIAA sports couldn't have been written by Hollywood." "It was

Establishing a Tradition of Excellence

McLendon's first CIAA Basketball Tournament championship team, 1946. *Back row, left to right:* Marland Buckner, Frank Galbreath, Willie Williams, Richard Miller, Robert Herring. *Front row, left to right:* John B. McLendon, Aubrey Stanley, E. Parker McDougal, Frank Harvey, Thornton Williams. (Courtesy Alex Rivera, North Carolina Central)

a great time for the tournament to begin," McLendon said. "It was the end of the war and people were in a state of restlessness. It gave them an outlet."[62]

Years later, after McLendon's Eagles trounced Clarence Gaines's Winston-Salem College Rams 119–65 in 1949, the two future Naismith Hall of Fame coaches became close friends. Gaines saw "Little Mac" as a role model and tried to absorb everything McLendon told him. "He helped my development and also all the black coaches he came into contact with," Gaines later stated. "He had no secrets. You could ask him any question and he had a logical answer. He showed you how to recruit and train people." The two coaches even went on recruiting trips together to save money on gas and talk basketball strategy on and off the court. Gaines's territory was western Kentucky and southern Illinois, whereas McLendon's was Chicago, northern Indiana, and Kansas City. They never tried to recruit each other's prospects, developing a friendship that endured for more than fifty-five years. Explaining the difficulty he and McLendon had on recruiting trips in a segregated society, Gaines recalled: "We couldn't stop at hotels so we had to sleep in the car. He'd sleep in the front, I'd have the back." To Gaines, McLendon "was a pioneer, an innovator, a teacher, an educator, and an excellent clinician. He was the first in everything as far as we were concerned.

For basketball, he had a level of competence that anyone would have a tough time meeting. His whole life was devoted to basketball."[63]

Indeed, with his unique philosophy and strategy, McLendon produced exceptionally successful teams at North Carolina College. Perhaps he succeeded so well because he kept his larger objective always in mind. "My goal was to keep a team ready if integration ever came," McLendon told Packer and Lazenby. "In that sense, we were always working for a goal beyond the present competition. Our players were playing beyond what it took to beat other black teams. I wanted them to be ready. If the door ever opened, we could show the world that we could play basketball." As many African Americans returned home after serving their country in World War II and became more assertive in fighting for their rights, racial attitudes began slowly to change. Always one to capitalize on an opportunity for racial justice, McLendon seized the moment. In 1949, High Point College athletic director Jim Hamilton helped McLendon schedule one of the first public interracial games in the South, a contest between North Carolina College and a solid Camp LeJeune Marine team, led by University of Washington All-American center Jack Nichols, a first-round draft choice who ended up playing ten seasons in the NBA. The Eagles emerged victorious, and their coach became even more convinced that his teams could not only compete but prevail over integrated competition.[64]

Commenting on McLendon's "will to win," All-CIAA Conference guard Harold Hunter, who played for McLendon in 1950 and then served as his assistant coach at Tennessee A&I State University almost a decade later, talked of how he and the other players respected McLendon not only as a tireless tactician and masterful strategist but also as an exemplary role model. "Coach is everything to the fellows," said Hunter. "He's just got something that makes you want to do your best for him. He's just the kind of man the fellows would like to be."[65]

McLendon's Eagles went on to win eight CIAA visitation tournament championships, and he produced a 264–60 record from 1940 to 1952, an astounding .812 winning percentage. He was honored as CIAA Coach of the Year in 1948 and CIAA Coach of the Decade for 1946–55. In 1950, however, a new president, Alfonso Elder, took over North Carolina College and made an unpopular decision to deemphasize athletics. Around this same time, the North Carolina General Assembly ruled that state money was not to be used for athletic programs. While

Establishing a Tradition of Excellence

this decision was a hardship for large schools, it was devastating for smaller ones. At the end of the spring semester in 1952, President Elder announced that all athletic scholarships were voided. If scholarship students returned in the fall, they would be required to pay full tuition, at the time more than three hundred dollars. "That wrecked my team," recalled McLendon, "and they waited until the kids went home for the summer to tell them." The coach was devastated, mainly for his athletes, and it seemed to him that the school had not looked at enough alternatives. "In those days we couldn't write up an athletic scholarship agreement as you can today," said McLendon. "All the kids had to go on was your word without a written agreement, and in terms of recruiting, that was the essence of your program."[66]

In the student newspaper, McLendon voiced his disappointment that the school would no longer be committed to supporting a "first rate athletic program." To make the situation even more untenable, the responsibility of directing athletics at the college fell to McLendon's office, while all the authority resided in the president's. As the school's athletic director, McLendon was saddened by what he considered to be a harmful change, and he decided to resign. McLendon recalled that LeRoy Walker immediately came to him and expressed his intention to resign in support, but McLendon told Walker to stay on because he was bringing tremendous prestige to the college and only one of them was needed to make the point. When the students and townspeople heard the news, more than two hundred staged a demonstration protesting the administration's new policies and pleading with their popular coach to stay. The students agreed to a nonviolent protest that resulted in a sit-down strike they vowed would last until the coach returned to campus. McLendon released a seventeen-point manifesto that, he said, would need to be signed by Elder before he would return. The enormous pressure to retain Coach McLendon was further intensified by the actions of a group of one hundred students who circled the president's home in their cars all day and night.[67]

McLendon subsequently decided that because of "philosophical differences" with Elder, he would not return to the campus under any circumstances, and Hampton Institute in Virginia quickly hired him. An editorial in the Durham newspaper stated that no practical man could have long endured the kind of treatment McLendon was subjected to at North Carolina College, concluding with these words: "He will be sorely missed but never forgotten by the students and alumni who saw in him that rare specimen of a human seldom found on Negro college campuses—a highly trained but practical instructor." In 1991, the college honored McLendon by renaming its campus arena the McLendon-McDougald Gymnasium.[68]

In 1952, then, McLendon moved to Hampton Institute, which had begun the first black-college basketball program in 1909. One of McLendon's best friends was the athletic director at Hampton, and another was head coach. Although Hampton prided itself on academic rigor and awarded no scholarships, which made recruiting somewhat difficult, McLendon won 70 percent of his games in his two years there (thirty-two of forty-six). His team's 18–5 record in 1952–53 was the school's best in twenty-seven years, impressively reversing the previous season's record.

Before he left North Carolina for Virginia, McLendon also went through a personal transition, as he and Alice, who had been separated, finally divorced. According to his daughter, Querida, McLendon was both a devoted father and a loving husband, although he was constantly in the gym or his office, or coaching his team, or on the road watching basketball games and recruiting new players. In order to spend time with their father, Querida and Johnny would come to the gym, put out the basketballs, and sweep the floor if necessary. They even learned to keep statistics during games, so they could share in their father's life as much as possible. Everyone in the family understood, however, that basketball came first, and Alice and the children would have to adjust accordingly. For Alice, especially, this was difficult. McLendon later admitted the marriage failed "largely because I was so wrapped up in basketball I had little time for my family." His wife never felt comfortable in the segregated South and would have been happy if her husband had coached high school basketball in Kansas the rest of his life. After waiting for her father to come home from one lengthy recruiting trip, Querida remembered, she told him, "You are the only man I know who shouldn't be married."[69]

During his separation from his wife, McLendon had met Ethel Richards, then a student at North Carolina College. After her graduation in 1946 with a degree in sociology, she moved to New York, where she was employed as a social worker. Years later, she and McLendon got

Establishing a Tradition of Excellence

One of McLendon's last recruits at North Carolina College, Sam Jones, played with the Boston Celtics and was later chosen as one of the fifty greatest players in NBA history. (Courtesy Fred Whitted, Black Heritage Review Photo Library)

together on one of his recruiting trips to the city. They fell in love and were married in 1954. Ethel attended her husband's basketball games; she was there to celebrate his national championships at the NAIA tournaments in Kansas City. According to Ethel, John McLendon was a good and attentive husband, but stability was lacking in their lives. In the next thirteen years, the family would move from Virginia, to Tennessee, to Cleveland, back to Tennessee, and then to Kentucky, where they purchased their first home. In 1966, when McLendon accepted the offer to coach at Cleveland State University, Ethel declared her unwillingness to pick up roots once again. She had just received tenure as a professor of sociology and social work at Kentucky State University and did not want to give it up. The two were divorced soon thereafter.[70]

CHAPTER 4

A Pioneer for Integration

The National Basketball Association and the National Athletic Steering Committee, 1950–53

Extensive scholarship by social historians documents how World War II acted as a catalyst for social change in American life. Among the most important changes brought on by the war was the push toward an integrated society, which inspired the civil rights movement of the 1950s and 1960s. This push for integration had an impact in the world of sports. In the summer of 1949, six teams from the National Basketball League were absorbed into the Basketball Association of America. The two merged professional leagues were immediately renamed the National Basketball Association, which began its inaugural season with twelve teams and no black players. Black players had returned to the National Football League in 1946, after a twelve-year absence, and history was made in "the national pastime" the following year, when Jackie Robinson broke the color barrier in professional baseball, playing for the Brooklyn Dodgers

Although black players were not officially banned from the NBA, there seemed to be "an understanding" that blacks were not welcome in the league. In his illuminating book *They Cleared the Lane*, Ron Thomas offers two explanations for this. First, in those days, Thomas writes, black players never received recognition in the white press; therefore, very few appreciated the caliber of basketball they were playing. Second, professional basketball owners chose not to integrate to avoid upsetting Abe Sapperstein, the owner of the Harlem Globetrotters, whose frequent appearances before NBA games kept several teams from going under. In spite of these obstacles, a number of farsighted men felt that change was necessary and would not be denied.[1]

In 1948, the *Washington Post* announced that for the first time in the seven-year existence of the District of Columbia's Uline Arena, blacks would be allowed to attend all events. The article also stated that local high school and college athletic teams and organizations could rent the arena, starting immediately. The CIAA, looking for a larger venue for its popular annual basketball tournament, became one of the first black organizations to book an event at Uline. In 1949, its tournament moved from Turner Arena, with its two-thousand-seat capacity, to seven-thousand-seat Uline, home of the NBA's Washington Capitols, and quickly evolved into a major athletic and social event. After watching the CIAA tournament, showcasing the talent that Coach McLendon and his colleagues had talked and written about over the years, NBA owners like Ned Irish of the New York Knicks and Walter Brown of the Boston Celtics began to take notice. Irish wanted to sign former Globetrotter star Nat "Sweetwater" Clifton and threatened to withdraw from the league if he was unable to complete this transaction. As the 1950 NBA draft was about to begin at the Bismarck Hotel in Chicago, the owners voted six to five to allow black players to be drafted by teams in their association.[2]

Although Charles Cooper of Duquesne University was the first black player to be drafted by an NBA team—the Boston Celtics, on April 25, 1950—All-Star guard Harold Hunter of John McLendon's North Carolina College team became the first black player to sign an NBA contract, with the Washington Capitols. The Capitols had earlier chosen two-time black-college All-American Earl "Moon Fixer" Lloyd, of West Virginia State, in the ninth round of the draft. They selected Hunter in the following round. Lloyd's team and Coach McLendon's squad had played in the 1950 CIAA tournament's championship game, North Carolina winning, 74–70, and Hunter named the tournament's Most Outstanding Player, with Lloyd a worthy runner-up. "The management and coaches of the Washington Capitols were in the stands," McLendon later told Thomas, "and shortly after the game they told me 'we will notify you and just might give your players a tryout.'" Capitols owner Mike Uline was among those watching Lloyd and Hunter in the tournament, and he was duly impressed. [3]

"A number of us coaches had tried to get the NBA to look at black players," recalled McLendon, even though most of his players had never considered professional basketball a realistic option. Sports columnists like Sam Lacy of the *Baltimore Afro-American* and Wendell Smith of the *Pittsburgh Courier* had also championed the cause continuously, asking how the NBA could pass up all the talent from black

A Pioneer for Integration

schools. McLendon wrote articles for the *Pittsburgh Courier* and the *Carolina Times* to increase interest in black-college athletics. At the same time, as Thomas points out, Uline was under considerable pressure to integrate his team, as the Capitols were suffering from low attendance and it was believed that Washington's growing black population might be more supportive if they had one or two black players to cheer for.[4]

Obviously impressed by what he saw at the tournament, Caps owner Uline contacted McLendon at the end of March, formally inviting Hunter and Lloyd to a tryout. Hunter, originally a schoolboy sensation in Kansas City, Kansas, said that when he was in college, playing in the NBA "was the farthest thing from my mind." But when McLendon told him about the impending tryout, Hunter was confident that he would match up against the pros. He had competed against major white college players serving in the army for eighteen months before completing his college career and had always measured up. "So, I didn't take a back seat to any of them," he said. "I figured I was as good as them, better than most."[5]

For his part, Lloyd had captured All-State honors at Parker-Gray High School in Alexandria, Virginia, and had twice been named an All-American by the *Pittsburgh Courier* for his stellar play at West Virginia State University. However, he had never competed against white players before and was understandably apprehensive. Although he and a teammate, Bob Wilson, had traveled with the Harlem Globetrotters for a week after graduation, assuming that was the only postcollege option available to them, Lloyd was unhappy with the grind of the team's demanding schedule and with its treatment in segregated cities. McLendon often remarked that the West Virginia State star was one of the most promising big men in basketball, but Lloyd was thinking of becoming a schoolteacher when he got the call from the Capitols inviting him to their NBA tryout in Washington, D.C.[6]

The tryout was scheduled for April 6, 1950. McLendon and Hunter drove up together from North Carolina to Washington, D.C., then picked up Lloyd at his parents' home in Alexandria, Virginia, a Washington suburb. Both Hunter and Lloyd remembered that McLendon drove them to Howard University so they could work out for a short time in the gym and get loosened up before the tryout. "We ran through a little two-man stuff just to get the ball in their hands, for about a half hour," McLendon explained. "We started down to Uline and on the way down the hill, Earl said, 'Wait a minute. I don't know how to switch.'" Having seen Lloyd play many times in CIAA competition, McLendon recalled that Lloyd's coach didn't allow his players to switch defensive assignments if their path was blocked by an offensive player's pick set. West Virginia State coach Mark Cardwell instead instructed his players to fight through the pick. "As soon as he said it, I started looking for a playground," McLendon told Thomas. "I turned off Georgia Avenue and the first street happened to be a dead end street." They got out of his car to review how to switch on defense, with McLendon pretending to be a third player. A passerby walking across campus joined in as a fourth so they could go two-on-two. "We worked for about ten minutes so Earl could go to the tryout with a degree of confidence," said McLendon.[7]

At the Capitols tryout, McLendon and the two players were met by McLendon's assistant coach from North Carolina College, LeRoy Walker. Both Walker and McLendon advised the players not to overdo it, to stay calm, to play within themselves. "One thing we were saying was this is not the time to do anything different than what got you this invitation," Walker said. "Somebody has seen you with your skills and ability to play basketball. Don't try to do anything different or special or more than you are capable of. Do what got you here." Other members of the Capitols were already in Uline Arena when McLendon, Walker, and the two players walked in. "We didn't know what to expect," McLendon explained to Thomas. "Twenty-four players froze, because it was the first time black players were in a camp." The Caps, however, had been told that some black players would be coming for a tryout, and everything went smoothly during the session. McLendon watched intently as the players went through numerous three-on-three drills, later relating to Thomas that he was pleased to see that the combination of Lloyd, Hunter, and Johnny Norlander, from Minnesota's Hamline College, was unbeatable.[8]

Walker recalled that Coach Bones McKinney and his companions, whom he assumed were the team owners or upper management, "were impressed with Lloyd because he handled the ball very well, had good speed, and could put the ball on the floor, which for them was unusual for a big man." As for Hunter, Walker declared, they were impressed with his speed. "Harold had something that's unusual even now,"

Walker later told Thomas. "He would create one-on-zero fast breaks. Because he had speed, he would throw the ball several feet ahead of him and had the speed to catch up with it in the middle of the dribble. He would just run by people for lay-ups." According to Lloyd, Hunter was the best-conditioned athlete he had ever seen, and the other players and coaches had also never seen anyone quite like him. Lloyd recalled thinking that everyone present seemed to be impressed with him and Hunter but somewhat surprised at how easily they fit in with the other players. "They [the Caps officials] were absolutely flabbergasted," Walker recalled. "Mac and I were looking at each other—how skillful these young men were from historically black institutions."[9]

The two black players did indeed apparently do very well, for after the tryout the coaches and players were asked to come upstairs to the Capitols' office. "Both players were offered contracts," wrote Thomas, "and because Hunter was one of his players, McLendon remembers having Hunter sign first so he could be the first black player to sign a NBA contract." "I decided I should get something out of this," he often said. "Harold was five-eleven, Earl was six-six, so I said, 'Harold, you sign first because you're the shortest.'" So Hunter beat out Lloyd for a historic first "by about ten seconds," as McLendon loved saying with a grin.[10]

"They took us to the office and I sat behind a desk and went through the motions of signing," Hunter told Thomas. "They told McLendon what they would pay me and they put it in the contract, $4,000, and I signed it. Teachers were starting at $1,000 or $800 a year, so $4,000 was a heck of a salary for me." Hunter remembered that back then there was not much ambition among blacks to play professional ball: "The only thing you looked to as a pro was to go to the Globetrotters, and they only picked a few. . . . I hadn't given much thought to it, but McLendon was ahead of us." Since Lloyd was the coveted big man, his salary was a little more than Hunter's, which "felt like a fortune at the time." While the money offered the two black players was apparently less than the average white player was being paid at the time, McLendon was proud to witness the standout black cagers finally being given a chance to play professional ball, taking great satisfaction in watching them sign. Although he had only competed against Coach McLendon in the past, Lloyd remembered being in awe of him, not only for his exemplary coaching abilities but also for his immense wisdom and the professional manner in which he handled everything concerning the contracts. McLendon understood the historic importance of breaking through this barrier. When the Washington Capitols actually selected the two players in the draft on April 25, 1950, making Lloyd their ninth pick and Hunter their eleventh, another milestone in integration had been reached. McLendon often took pride in noting that all six of the first blacks in the NBA came from traditionally black schools, a talent base that could no longer be ignored.[11]

In an article in the *Washington Post,* reporter Jack Walsh wrote, "Washington's Caps, who sagged artistically and financially last season, made some momentous draft choices at the NBA meetings in Chicago yesterday. They drafted Ohio State's Dick Schnittker and Southern California's Bill Sharman, two of the nation's outstanding collegians. They also selected their first Negro basketball players—West Virginia State's Earl Lloyd . . . and Harold Hunter, captain of North Carolina College, CIAA champion." Although Lloyd had a successful nine-year NBA career with Washington, the Syracuse Nationals, and the Detroit Pistons, five-eleven Hunter was cut before the season began, for in the end the Capitols decided to look for height to replace six-eleven center Don Otten. Further, according to Lloyd, it was obvious that the owner of the Caps would keep only one black player, and a big man met the team's needs better than another guard would.[12]

Upon leaving the Capitols, Hunter played in the semipro Eastern League and the following season tried to latch onto an NBA team with the Baltimore Bullets, later fondly recalling playing in an exhibition game against Celtics great Bob Cousy. Although Hunter impressed the Bullets staff, the team cut him for what he believed to be racial reasons. Ironically, Baltimore was the only NBA team at that time to already have more than one black player on its roster, topping off with two. Hunter then went back to play in the Eastern League for one more season. Expressing a modicum of regret, Hunter remembered how he never got to play in a regular-season NBA game. After turning down an offer from the Globetrotters, he began a teaching and coaching career, later assisting Coach McLendon during his national championship years at Tennessee A&I State University. When McLendon resigned in 1959, Hunter succeeded his mentor and became the Tigers' head coach. In his first year, he led his team to the NAIA national tournament, progressing to the semifinals, where the Tigers lost to Westminster College of

A Pioneer for Integration

Pennsylvania in a 39–38 cliffhanger. Over nine years, Hunter went on to have considerable success at Tennessee State, and in 1963 his team earned the school's first bid to participate in the NCAA College Division Tournament, the result of a long struggle that gave McLendon great satisfaction. As McLendon noted, however, all black schools, no matter their size, were confined to the "college" division until 1970, when the NCAA began admitting them into Division 1.[13]

As for Lloyd, he enjoyed a solid nine-year NBA career. On October 31, 1950, he made history when he became the first African American to take the court in an NBA game, one day ahead of Charles Cooper of the Boston Celtics and four days before Nat "Sweetwater" Clifton of the New York Knicks. On that historic day, the Rochester Royals defeated his Washington Capitols, 78–70, Lloyd contributing 6 points to his team's effort. During Syracuse's championship season in 1955, Lloyd averaged 10.2 points and 7.7 rebounds per game, becoming, alongside teammate Jim Tucker, the first African American to win an NBA title. In 1968, Lloyd became the NBA's first black assistant coach, joining the staff of the Detroit Pistons. Three years later, he became the second African American head coach, again with Detroit. Joining his longtime friend John McLendon, who had helped him reach the NBA, Lloyd was enshrined in the Naismith Memorial Basketball Hall of Fame in 2003. Although he never played for Coach McLendon, looking back on his basketball career, Lloyd clearly remembered the positive influence the older man had on him, recalling how his admiration and respect for the little coach from rival North Carolina College had grown over time. "If you can find anybody on this earth that was a finer person than him," Lloyd said in 2005, "I'd like to meet him."[14]

Integrating Collegiate Basketball: The National Athletic Steering Committee

On July 26, 1948, President Harry Truman issued Executive Order 9981, abolishing segregation in the U.S. armed forces and ordering full integration of all the services. Although he was inspired by this historic action, McLendon, as usual, was already in motion, playing the first public integrated basketball game in the state of North Carolina, against the Camp LeJeune Marines, and founding and organizing the National Basketball Committee to address racial inequities in college

Earl Lloyd, the first African American to take the court in an NBA game. (Courtesy Fred Whitted, Black Heritage Review Photo Library)

sports programs. He later stated that "these 1940 basketball experiences [trials] had me believe more strongly that sports was the best vehicle for interracial understanding—for the players and coaches, surely, but also inclusive of the fans and spectators."[15]

McLendon formed the National Basketball Committee, representing the Colored Conferences, as they were then called, in 1948, at the New York meeting of the National Association of Basketball Coaches (NABC), an umbrella organization including coaches from the NCAA and the National Association of Intercollegiate Basketball (NAIB). McLendon's committee submitted a request that "the Colored Colleges of the U.S. be integrated into the National Basketball program in such a way that there would be an opportunity to take part in the N.C.A.A.

A Pioneer for Integration

Playoffs and Tournament." Although the NABC discussed this request, the minutes reflect that no action was taken: "While the Board was favorably inclined toward the proposal, it had no authority to act. The application was referred to the N.C.A.A."[16]

McLendon's committee then submitted a detailed integration plan on February 26, 1949, to Kenneth L. Wilson, executive secretary of the NCAA, whereby colored colleges might take part in the association's play-offs and championships. Along with McLendon, the committee included the following coaches: E. A. Adams, from Tuskegee Institute, in Alabama; J. H. Cooper, from Wilberforce University, in Ohio; T. L. Hill, from Morgan State College, in Maryland; E. L. Jackson, from Howard University, in Washington, D.C.; H. R. Jefferson, from Virginia State College; Vernon McCain, from Maryland State College; A. W. Mumford, from Southern University, in Louisiana; and H. A. Kean, from Tennessee A&I State University. Wilson placed their request before the tournament committee in Seattle during the NCAA championships in March. He wrote McLendon on March 29 that, "after careful consideration, it was their feeling that it would be impractical to recommend your request to the Executive Committee [of the NCAA]."[17]

Wilson reminded McLendon that currently the basketball tournament was run according to district representation; if it was to change, "this would mean that if a colored team were selected from a district, there would be no other representation." Furthermore, the letter stated, "It was their feeling judged from the records of one of your good teams that played on the Coast this year that the quality of competition at the present time is not equal to tournament caliber." Although Wilson promised he would take the request to the executive committee, he recommended that a more practical strategy would be to engage in as much competition against NCAA members as possible and try to get into the small-college tournament in Kansas City, sponsored by the NAIB.[18]

McLendon wrote back to Wilson on May 17, strongly stating his disappointment. Since all the colleges affiliated with the CIAA fell into the all-Southern District 3, according to the NCAA, ongoing prohibitions against integrated basketball made intradistrict competition impossible. "In all other NCAA areas of sports there is not such a door shut in our faces as in Basketball," McLendon declared. "We feel that this is not your aim and that an opportunity will be given us when all the facts are known."[19]

On April 18, 1950, McLendon condemned this undemocratic policy in what historian Pamela Grundy calls "an uncharacteristically emotional column that reflected both his frustration at the NCAA's recalcitrance and his confidence in his team's ability." "A few teams in the East will play CIAA opponents," McLendon wrote in the *Carolina Times*. "However, there is not a single team in District Three which has the nerve, spine, backbone, or guts to play a CIAA opponent. Not a single institution in District Three will play a CIAA opponent on any terms since every one of them is bound by the chains of negative interracial practice. Some that are not so steeped in the phenomenal stupidity are afraid of the loss of athletic prestige, which would naturally result after the CIAA prowess on the court enacted its inevitable toll." He concluded with a statement clearly illustrating the depth of his disappointment: "The NCAA may mean *NATIONAL COLLEGIATE ATHLETIC ASSOCIATION* to some people, but to us it means *NO COLORED ATHLETES ALLOWED.*"[20]

Not one to be easily discouraged, McLendon was already planning a pragmatic strategy to accomplish his goal. A year later, he joined forces with two other coaches from the CIAA, Howard University's Eddie Jackson and Virginia State College's Harry Jefferson, to travel to New York City for the NABC's annual convention to petition that black schools be allowed to enter national tournaments. According to McLendon, John Lawther of Pennsylvania State University, president of the NABC, agreed to place the question before the executive committee. When he returned, he told the three coaches: "Our committee has approved your petition unanimously. We feel that such a step is long overdue and your schools must be included if basketball in America is to become truly American."[21]

The next step was to advise the black coaches of this significant support, then make an official request to the two national collegiate championship sponsoring organizations, the NCAA and the NAIB. The NCAA, however, dealt the campaign for justice in college athletics an abrupt setback when it decided to hold its 1951 convention in Dallas, Texas. When it was announced that the NCAA convention hotel would abide by its policy of segregated facilities, thus systematically excluding black members from full participation, black coaches and athletic directors met and decided to boycott the convention. Some representatives expressed their regret that the petition could not be presented personally, but they added that they could not see any advantage to suffering indignities to do so. As McLendon explained, "Our thinking was why should we go there to ask for equality and be treated unequally in the process?" Mack Greene, director of athletics at Central State University in Ohio, speaking for the black representatives, made his point clearly in a long, passionate letter to Hugh C. Willet and Kenneth L. Wilson, president and secretary-treasurer of the NCAA: "The luxury of racial prejudice is much too costly in delusions, dollars, and warped lives on both sides of the color line. The NCAA must stop giving comfort to the enemies of democracy by the tacit admission that, even at our so-called level of enlightenment, democracy is impractical."[22]

A few weeks after the Dallas meeting was announced, McLendon received letters from A. C. Lonborg, chairman of the NCAA tournament committee, and Walter Byers, NCAA executive assistant, stating that the petition for inclusion had been denied by the executive committee, which had voted to keep the basic tournament structure in place. Byers also informed McLendon that, under the present rules, all member institutions were considered impartially on the basis of their season records. "You may rest assured that our selection committee will watch the performance of teams of the four major colored conferences," wrote Byers. "When one of your schools has an outstanding basketball team, it will be considered for a member-at-large berth in the tournament field on the same basis as the other member schools of this association."[23]

On January 24, 1951, McLendon requested that all National Basketball Committee members send him "the full expression of their feelings" regarding the recent letters from NCAA representatives. He cautioned his associates that their comments might be published in leading black newspapers; if they did not wish to have their names and letters so used, they should say so. As for McLendon, his thoughts and feelings on the matter were obvious. "It seems to me our fight begins now," he declared to his colleagues, and he began to work on creating new avenues to break through the obstacles they faced.[24]

As a result, an official forum was created to bring about an organizational focus for the nation's black colleges. Accordingly, the National Athletic Steering Committee (NASC) was officially formed when twenty-one representatives from black colleges met on August 15, 1951, at Chicago's Washington Park YMCA. Initially, the representatives planned to call their organization the Negro Athletic Steering Committee, but

McLendon and Greene persuaded them that "since negotiation was their base instead of publicity for the Negro cause, it would be more advantageous to use the title *National* Athletic Steering Committee instead." The committee's purpose was to study the problems of segregation and discrimination in intercollegiate athletics and to suggest ways to change it. To implement this program, NASC leadership decided that their primary goal would be to get a black team into the NCAA and/or the NAIB national championships.[25]

Harry Jefferson was elected president of the NASC, and Mack Greene became executive secretary. Over the next two years, Greene attended innumerable meetings of both the NCAA and the NAIB, requesting that black colleges be allowed to enter the national tournaments. Although Walter Byers, by then executive director of the NCAA, congratulated the NASC on its forward-looking program and considered securing certain NCAA members to work with the organization, the NCAA was not about to take these black colleges into its tournament. According to McLendon, the NCAA "declared that it had no championship apparatus which accommodated black colleges." "In fact," wrote McLendon, "the organization argued that it had no way to include 'small' colleges at all, as it arbitrarily regulated all black schools to 'small college' status." Along with this, the NCAA "voiced the fear," McLendon stated, that "fans may not accept or appreciate the kind of game you play," and "your coaches may not be competent enough."[26]

Fortunately for the NASC, the NAIB, under the leadership of Al Duer, was far more receptive. Theoretically, the NAIB was open to any team good enough to qualify, although, as noted by historian Francis Hoover, "the organization preferred that the participants be white only." The NAIB bylaws did not include any discriminatory provisions, but the tournament committee had essentially implemented an informal rule against black participation when the organization was established back in 1940. Indeed, segregation was firmly entrenched in Missouri, a former slave state. "Thus the NAIB functioned in an environment that was at best indifferent and at worst actively hostile to racial integration," remarked historian John R. M. Wilson. "Besides that, a substantial proportion of the NAIB colleges were in the South, making any progressive racial ideas very difficult to voice even if one subscribed to them." Although Duer had been executive director of the NAIB for less than two years in 1951, as a devout Christian who believed in human equality, he insisted that democracy could work in sports and took the opportunity to try to implement it. Back in 1946, when he was athletic director of church-affiliated George Pepperdine College in California, Duer had witnessed a black player, Rosamond Wilson, a forward from Morningside College in Iowa, forced to sit on a bench, acting as team manager, and watch his team be defeated in NAIB tournament play, a humiliation compounded by its taking place on his nineteenth birthday. Duer wrote to then–NAIB executive secretary, Emil S. Liston, that this "deplorable action was undemocratic and I definitely feel we should take it off the constitution." Furthermore, he stated, he was "ashamed we hold an attitude of that kind in a national tournament." Liston wrote back that he agreed "100%" with Duer on this matter but added, "How soon the NAIB will be strong enough to rescind this rule I do not know." He suggested that Duer meet privately with association leaders from the South to discuss this issue during the 1947 tournament. Duer acted accordingly but met with such resistance that little was accomplished.[27]

The NAIB would be forced to deal with this issue the following year, when New York's Manhattan College was invited to play in Kansas City but informed tournament officials that the team could not accept because of racial bars prohibiting black players. Manhattan had no black players on its team that year, but accepting an invitation under this condition, the administration believed, would condone racial prejudice. The day after Liston wrote back to Manhattan, asking that it to reconsider its position and pointing out that the NAIB's executive committee would be addressing this issue during the tournament, he received a letter from Louis G. Wilke, chairman of the 1948 Olympic Basketball Committee, protesting the fact that blacks were not allowed to play in the tournament. Wilke furthermore stated that because of this policy NAIB participation in the upcoming Olympic trials would be in jeopardy. Since this missive came just two days before the tournament was to begin, Liston immediately polled the executive committee by wire, asking its members to vote on admitting black participants to the tournament. By a vote of seven to two, the committee announced the lifting of the ban on black players.[28]

On March 10, 1948, Clarence Walker, a reserve guard from John Wooden's Indiana State University team, became the first black player to step onto the court in the Kansas City tournament. When Walker came out on the court, he was shaking so hard he could hardly move, but he

Al Duer and John B. McLendon Jr. were pioneers in the integration of college athletics. (Courtesy NAIA)

was greeted with applause, indicating that many white spectators approved of his participation. "I refused to go to the tournament if Clarence couldn't go," Coach Wooden told the *Kansas City Star* in 2002. "He was part of the team, and that was that." Indiana State made it all the way to the championship game that year, losing to the Louisville Cardinals, 82–70, but Walker could not stay at the team hotel in downtown Kansas City. A local minister housed him across the river in Kansas City, Kansas.[29]

The following year, black players arrived from San Jose State College, Portland University, and Lawrence Tech of Detroit to participate in the national tournament. Although Liston received a few angry letters as a result, he and the NAIB executive committee also won the admiration and respect of many. Among those who applauded the development was a group of farsighted men from the nation's black colleges who were diligently working to bring about black-college participation in national tournament competition. But the process of inte-

A Pioneer for Integration

grating the black schools in the NAIB was considerably more challenging than gaining recognition for the talents of individual black players, only coming about because of the persistent and patient efforts of a number of courageous men. Segregation was a way of life in Kansas City and the state of Missouri, and Duer, now serving as executive director of the NAIB, felt it was imperative that he proceed cautiously, since this was a potentially volatile situation.[30]

Greene responded in an emotional letter to Duer on November 6, 1951, stating that the issues regarding the participation of the black colleges "do not reside in the narrow prejudices and provincialism of Kansas City." Duer and the executive committee, Greene wrote, should work to apply the NAIB's code of ethics, which incorporated a clause against all prejudice, and actively "oppose pettiness and bigotry where we find it in our daily lives and most certainly in the conduct of our sports programs. We have no fears about the fans of Kansas City," concluded Greene. "Some few may be lacking in the training for tolerance and decency, but we believe they have a conscience and we know their conscience is on our side."[31]

Finally, on March 12, 1952, Duer phoned Mack Greene from the Phillips Hotel in Kansas City, "talking with a voice husky with fatigue but full of enthusiasm," to inform him that the executive committee of the NAIB had unanimously approved a motion that "all colleges for Negroes that meet required standards are eligible for NAIB membership," that "the national tournament of the NASC will be sponsored by the NAIB in 1953," and that "the winning team of the NASC tournament will be eligible for participation in the Kansas City national tournament." Further, Central State College would be eligible for the Ohio district playoffs, and therefore ineligible for the NASC Tournament; as district patterns changed, other Negro colleges would be granted full participation in their districts and might also reach the Kansas City tournament. Greene elatedly wrote in the NASC newsletter: "The door is now open to all colleges for Negroes to world competition in basketball. Let's prepare ourselves for all that it means!" He then urged all NASC colleges to send in ten dollars for their membership in what was now officially called the National Association of Intercollegiate Athletics (NAIA). Within weeks, thirty-six black colleges had officially joined the organization. As a result, both the nature and the tempo of college basketball would be changed forever.[32]

CHAPTER 5

Groundbreaking Championship Years at Tennessee A&I State University, 1954–59

The NAIA intercollegiate basketball tournament is the world's oldest and largest. According to Dick Mackey of the *Kansas City Star,* it began in Kansas City's newly completed Municipal Auditorium in 1937, when Emil Liston, athletic director of Baker University in Baldwin, Kansas, and James Naismith "joined with prominent Kansas Citians and conceived the idea of a tournament to decide a small-college national championship." The Amateur Athletic Union (AAU) basketball tournament had just left Kansas City for Denver, because of a more lucrative financial contract, and "there were those," wrote Mackey, "who wanted the void to be filled." With civic support and Liston's enthusiasm, the first all-college basketball tournament became a reality in March 1937. An invitational eight-team meet of Midwestern champions, this opening tournament was the forerunner of the thirty-two-team NAIB tournament, now sponsored by the NAIA.[1]

Although attendance was sparse the first year, and the event took in less than seven hundred dollars at the gate, "this pilot tournament," wrote Kansas City columnist Bill Richardson on its twenty-fifth anniversary, "set the stage for the longest continuous national collegiate tournament in any sport in the nation." With the exception of the war year of 1944, when travel restrictions were put in place by the federal government, the thirty-two-team, thirty-two-game weeklong basketball marathon has been adopted by Kansas City–area sports fans, each year attracting basketball devotees from across the United States and throughout the world. And in 1953, thanks to the persistent and courageous efforts of John B. McLendon, Mack Greene, Harry Jefferson, and the other men of the National Athletic Steering Committee, historically black colleges and universities would finally be able to participate in this well-established American sports classic.[2]

In March 1952, the executive committee of the NAIA approved a "District-at-Large" (29), in which all NASC colleges whose membership was approved by the organization would be eligible for NAIA national meets and tournaments. B. T. Harvey, a professor at Morehouse College in Atlanta, Georgia, was elected the first chairman of the district. "In effect," wrote McLendon, "what was equal to a black-college national championship was agreed upon as a structure for filling the NAIA berth from that district." Henry Arthur Kean, athletic director of Tennessee A&I State University (later Tennessee State University), and Walter Davis, the school's president, immediately offered their facilities as the tournament site. Of the approximately eighty-six black colleges eligible for the national tournament, only one would be able to go to Kansas City. Although this wasn't total integration, as McLendon declared: "It was the first foot-in-the-door thing that we could deal with. Furthermore, it created within us a great spirit of competition, which improved our team because you had to win the Negro National Championship to get into the NAIA tournament in Kansas City."[3]

The District 29 playoff, held at the end of February 1953 in the newly finished "Kean's little garden," was won by the host team over favored North Carolina College—ironically, the school that McLendon had coached for the previous fifteen years. Thus, on March 10, 1953— one year before the landmark Supreme Court decision in *Brown v. Board of Education,* a case rooted in Topeka, Kansas, emphatically declared that "separate but equal is inherently unequal"—Tennessee A&I, coached by Clarence Cash, whom McLendon fondly called the "diminutive dynamo," became the first black-college team to take the floor in a national tournament.

Mack Greene described what happened when the Tennessee A&I Tigers came up to the national tournament in Kansas City:

> The scene was the Kansas City, Missouri Municipal Auditorium on March 10, 1953. I sat with ten thousand other fans to watch a basketball game that was about to start. This is normal behavior for the average present-day American citizen. But to me, this was not a normal event. I was about to witness a dream come true. A hush came over the crowd as if in response to my own emotional tension as the door in the far end of the huge arena opened and ten good looking college boys dressed in white warm-ups trotted onto the floor. I watched with intense interest every overt mani-

festation of the unusually large first round audiences. I recalled I had warned two years earlier that I did not know the Kansas City spectator. As the team dribbled the length of the floor, the crowd gave them a rousing cheer which equaled in enthusiasm the welcome given any of the other thirty-one teams from all parts of the United States entered in this National Intercollegiate Basketball Tournament of the NAIA. The ten boys, all with extra protective cutaneous pigmentation, had come to Kansas City to represent the District-at-Large of the NAIA. They were the team from Tennessee A&I State University in Nashville.[4]

The *Kansas City Star* reported the next day that "history was made as Tennessee A&I State University, the first team from an all Negro college to participate in a national tournament, advanced to the second round, defeating Geneva College of Beaver Falls, Pennsylvania, 89 to 88." The Tigers were called the surprise team of the tournament the following day, as they moved into the quarterfinals with a decisive victory over St. Benedict College of Atchison, Kansas, 79–56. In their third appearance, they were eliminated by East Texas State College, 72–67. Although the Tigers' ability was a source of great pride, as Greene pointed out, this was not the most important consideration: "The fact that a team was entered into the national tournament from a college for Negroes, located in a section of the United States where state law prohibits inter-racial competition among colleges, is the salient and dramatic aspect."[5]

The following March, Cash coached Tennessee A&I to another District 29 championship, only to be ousted in the first round at Kansas City before ten thousand spectators by Regis College of Colorado, 60–58. However, of greater importance, the basketball committee gave added recognition to black-college teams by inviting the Tigers to participate in the 1954 NAIA Christmas Tip-Off Invitational Tournament in Kansas City. Eight teams were annually invited to this prestigious tournament, usually the previous year's champion and runner-up, along with selected teams that had shown their superior talent in the NAIA national ranks.

In July 1954, Clarence Cash resigned abruptly as head basketball coach of Tennessee A&I, choosing not to go along with the administration's proposed plan to accelerate the university's athletic programs. While McLendon was still at Hampton, Tennessee A&I's athletic director, Henry A. Kean, and Walter S. Davis, its president, contacted him, believing him to be the best basketball coach in the country. They told McLendon: "If this is going to be the mission of your life, you better come out here, because we have the athletes and the government behind us. Here you can manage this on a national level, and this is the place for you to be." Underscoring the Tennessee A&I motto, "A+ Performance in Deluxe Fashion," Kean and Davis put their considerable energies into recruiting superb athletes as a way to increase the school's enrollment, enhance its reputation, and build an athletic program equal to those at white universities.[6]

With little deliberation, the Tennessee A&I administration went on to hire John McLendon as the men's head basketball coach. Although, McLendon stated, "I regret leaving Hampton and the CIAA, the offer at Tennessee State presented opportunities that I could not resist." "I was brought to Tennessee State to continue the process of integration," he said, and he eagerly accepted the challenge before him. Upon McLendon's signing, Sam Lacy, veteran sports editor of the *Baltimore Afro-American,* wrote, "Plans at Tennessee call for the setting up of a virtual empire, out of which is to be fashioned the finest (they hope) cage material the collegiate world has ever known."[7]

Tennessee A&I State University had assumed a powerful presence in college basketball, having begun sponsoring the black national high school basketball tournament in 1945, which helped it recruit the best players. McLendon had plans to take the program even further, aided by the fact that he had turned out dozens of young coaches from his former college in North Carolina, and they were loyal in helping him recruit the most accomplished athletes for his new assignment.

Having the most gifted athletes, however, would not necessarily result in team success. McLendon understood from the beginning that it was imperative to get his players to believe in his system both mentally and physically. As he had stressed at North Carolina, conditioning would be the key to victory. "I started a conditioning program for the players," McLendon proudly recalled. "We ran three miles a day in less than twenty minutes for twenty-one days in a row. Our team goal was that no other team would enter into a game with us in better condition than we were." "When I got down to Tennessee State, we trained hard, practiced hard, and played hard," recalled stellar guard Ron Hamilton. "We wanted to live up to the school's winning tradition."[8]

McLendon made it clear to both Kean and Davis that he intended to win his first season and bring a national championship home to the university as soon as possible. He fulfilled the first part of his promise, amassing a remarkable 29–4 record. When NAIA executive director Al Duer called him to extend an invitation to the 1954 Tip-Off Tournament in Kansas City, McLendon stated that "he was extremely happy, not only because he recognized this as history-making, but because of the implied progress in race relations via the NAIA and the apparent acceptance of black-college basketball as a game on equal status with those rated 'best in basketball.'" He accepted the invitation with one reservation: his team would come only if it could lodge downtown like all the other teams. McLendon had observed Tennessee A&I in its previous NAIA tournament appearances and agreed with Charles "Chuck" Taylor of Converse, who was convinced "that among other pressures, the negative psychological impact on a team housed and boarded separately was too great to overcome in the week-long tournament." Previously, the Tigers had been housed in two different hotels. According to McLendon, "each was of dubious quality, each in a depressed area of the city, or they stayed in the Paseo YMCA or in separate homes provided by local hosts."[9]

Although this was McLendon's first season at Tennessee A&I, and he clearly understood the urgency of garnering national attention for the college's athletic programs, McLendon chose to take this bold stand without consulting either the athletic director or the president. "Because I knew one thing: if they said no, that would have been an impasse," he later explained to Alan Govenar. "If they said yes, then they would have gotten in trouble with the state authorities. So it was better for me to do it and get fired or get chastised or reprimanded or something than for the president to get involved, because he could always say, 'Well, I didn't know anything about it. I didn't have any idea he would do something like that.' And when he heard about it," laughed McLendon, "that's what he said he would have said."[10]

Duer was sympathetic to McLendon's request, having earlier fought successfully to achieve piecemeal integration in some of the downtown hotels, and he asked the coach to wait by the phone until he could poll the executive committee and the Kansas City Junior Chamber of Commerce, the tournament's cosponsoring organization. Duer called back within an hour, saying, "We agree unanimously with your point of view and wish to inform you that your team will be staying at the Hotel Kansas Citian." Due to the persistent efforts of these two men, downtown Kansas City hotels were integrated, and McLendon's Tigers were able to eat at the same restaurants as the other teams. Thus, not only was another significant step made toward having black colleges accepted on an equal basis, but the integration of the tournament continued to have a ripple effect on the community. McLendon proudly noted, "Tennessee State was the first black-college team, or any other black group, to stay in downtown Kansas City." But when his squad checked in at the Hotel Kansas Citian, the team found that all the maids but two had quit in protest. In response, McLendon told his players to help the two remaining women clean their rooms, teaching them another lesson in solving problems with dignity and self-respect. When the Tigers left Kansas City after the tournament, the hotel manager told McLendon they were the best team ever to stay there.[11]

In recounting this incident, McLendon stated that "during those times it was good not to be bitter because you lose focus. You get all wound up in the emotion of the thing instead of the point you are trying to make. Some things you couldn't do anything about, and the fact that you tried to do something was a statement." Indeed, his team did succeed in remaining clearly focused on the task before them, for although the Tigers came into the tournament unseeded, they managed to capture the championship. The black newspaper the *Kansas City Call* ran a banner headline: "Tennessee State Wins NAIA Basketball Tournament." The accompanying story began: "The first Negro team ever invited to compete in the NAIA pre-Christmas 'Tip-Off' tournament, the Tennessee State A&I Tigers, walked off with the championship Saturday night before some 3,500 spectators at Kansas City's Municipal Auditorium. . . . Picked as the team to beat by the press-row experts after their opening game in which they upset the number one seeded Southwest Missouri State Bears of Springfield 77–57, the Tigers rolled over all opposition in the three-day meet and annexed the crown by coasting past Rockhurst College of Kansas City, 94–72 in the finals."[12]

After the Tigers defeated tournament favorite Southwest Missouri State by twenty points in the opening game, the *Kansas City Star* ran an article declaring this "a great homecoming for Johnny McLendon," saying that even he, after all of his success on the basketball court, was surprised by the margin of victory. According to the *Star*, "A championship in this affair would be extra pleasing to McLendon and the Tigers, since this is the first time a Negro school ever has been invited to play in any sort of national collegiate cage tournament." The article went on to point out two curious facts about McLendon: first, that he was "dwarfed by his players since the Tigers average 6 feet, 2 inches, and the coach stands only 5–8"; and second, that "in contrast to other coaches these days, McLendon shows little emotion as he watches the action on the floor."[13]

The Tigers' semifinal game against Arkansas Tech proved to be a much tighter affair, the score tied at 76 with just a few minutes to go. After what the *Kansas City Times* described as a whirlwind attack by the Tigers' Henry Kean, Ben Jackson, and Sam Moore, McLendon's squad hung on to seal the victory. Kean, the son of Tennessee A&I's athletic director, led the Tigers' scoring attack with 23 points, while Vernon McNeal, Jackson, and Marvin Roberts tallied 17, 15, and 14 points, respectively.

In the finals, the Tigers had a comfortable halftime lead of 46–29, but Rockhurst came out smoking and, with less than six minutes left in the contest, had pulled within 6 points of their rivals. But Tennessee A&I's sharpshooting five-eleven All-American guard, Chicago's Vernon McNeal, brought his team a safe lead "with four spectacular goals." With George Altman and Henry Kean adding buckets, the Tigers rolled to an easy victory. McNeal's deadly shooting earned him MVP honors and 24 points in the championship game, while Kean chipped in with 23. According to the *Kansas City Star*, "Tennessee A&I used blinding speed and firepower, plus a rebounding superiority, to flash past Rockhurst College in the finals, 94–72." The *Pittsburgh Courier*'s Wendell Smith wrote, "According to the daily newspapermen who covered the tournament in Kansas City, the Tennessee State team was one of the best coached to ever appear there. They played within a system and performed like athletes who knew exactly what they were doing at all times. What better tribute could be tendered Johnny McLendon?"[14]

McLendon and his fast-breaking team were the talk of the tournament, and he was justifiably proud of having captured the championship in front of his hometown family and friends, bringing the prestigious trophy back to his campus in Nashville. No one was more pleased than the university president, Walter Davis, who took winning so seriously that McLendon joked, "I had to restrain him at times." In McLendon's inaugural year at Tennessee A&I, the Tigers posted a sparkling 29–4 record and eclipsed the century mark in scoring seven times, while McNeal became the first player from the school to be invited to an NBA trial workout by the Boston Celtics.[15]

However, the Tigers' victory was even more significant in terms of racial equality. "For McLendon, winning an integrated tournament championship in his hometown of Kansas City must have been a high point in his long and brilliant coaching career," wrote sports editor John I. Johnson in the *Kansas City Call*. "What a homecoming this triumph must have been for this man who has won 308 games against 74 defeats during his coaching career. It may have proved to him, certainly proved to us, and should have proved to his opponents, that race and color may bar a man but it does not and cannot keep him from attaining high standards."[16]

Tennessee A&I was not the only black-college powerhouse in basketball that year. Texas Southern University, coached by the legendary Ed Adams, who would later become the first black coach inducted into the Helms Athletic Hall of Fame, defeated McLendon's Tigers 103–100 in the District 29 finals in March 1955, thus becoming the second black college to enter the NAIA tournament. Due to the high quality of play in District 29, and the fact that the district now had forty-five member schools, making it three times as large as other average districts and over twice as large as the next in size, McLendon, A. W. Mumford of Southern University, and Talmadge Hill of Morgan State University formed a special committee to petition the NAIA executive committee for increased representation in the national tournament. The NAIA was again receptive, Duer already working on the problem. It divided the district in half, creating a new "District 6" and thus providing space in the thirty-two-team bracket for two black-college teams.[17]

The 1956 national tournament was thus the first in which more than one black college participated. Tennessee A&I and Texas Southern University were the representatives of Districts 29 and 6, and Central State of Ohio entered the thirty-two-team field as the representative from District 22, a fitting tribute to the pioneering efforts of Mack Greene. Although McLendon's Tennessee A&I team lost in the third round to the eventual champion, McNesse State College of Louisiana, 76–68, Texas Southern showed how far black colleges had come by reaching the finals, also losing to McNesse, 60–55. Although tension kept Texas

Southern from pulling off what many would have considered to be one of the biggest surprises in tournament history, theirs was still the best showing by a black-college team. The NASC was quite proud of its accomplishment, looking forward to even greater success to come. Still, this particular tournament was fraught with race-related difficulties and certainly had its share of anxious moments.

Specifically, two days before the start of the tournament, Delta State College of Cleveland, Mississippi, the champion of the Alabama-Mississippi district, withdrew from participation when it failed to get "protection" from playing against blacks, the executive committee unanimously denying the college's request that its players not have to face a black team. A carefully prepared statement to the press made it clear that the executive committee and representatives of the Alabama-Mississippi district agreed that conditions were so tense that they might result in a regrettable incident at the national tournament. Therefore, "at this particular time it would not be wise for a team from that district to enter the tournament."[18]

Yet another team from the Deep South, McNesse State College, also faced pressure to bow out of the tournament but refused and played anyway. The governor of Louisiana, Robert F. Kennon, who accompanied the team to the tournament, never approached the NAIA, but he was obviously looking for a race-related issue that would justify the demand that he pull the team out of Kansas City and bring them home. Ironically, McNesse played all three black teams on its way to the 1956 tournament championship.

Despite the fears of a racial flare-up, however, the tournament came off without incident. John I. Johnson wrote afterward, "Kansas City did itself proud last week when it played host to a large group of fine young athletes from a wide area of the country and treated them all so graciously that I became increasingly in love with my city." He concluded by congratulating the NAIA for not only paving the way for integration in college sports but being responsible for opening other doors in Kansas City, namely those of hotels, restaurants, and movie theaters.[19]

First Black-College National Championship

McLendon looked forward to the 1956–57 season, having recruited two outstanding cagers from the basketball-rich state of Indiana a year earlier—John "Rabbit" Barnhill, from Evansville, and Dick "Skull" Barnett, from Gary. Barnhill had earned the name "Rabbit" because of his speed on the court; Barnett would be called "Skull" because he shaved his head as soon as he enrolled in college. According to McLendon, "Those two players, John Barnhill and Dick Barnett, made Tennessee State the center of attention of all black colleges." Over the years, McLendon had developed pipelines to outstanding talent. He had friends in the right places—coaches, teachers, and administrators at winning high schools in Gary, Evansville, Kansas City, Chicago, and Durham.

A second-team All-State selection, six-one guard Barnhill was not very well-known beyond his hometown, but the principal of his Evansville high school held a summer position at Tennessee State and tipped McLendon off about the young man. "The principal said the coach at Evansville didn't have a running team and that Barnhill always wanted to run," McLendon told Bill Richardson of the *Kansas City Star.* "I went up to Evansville to see him and talk to his mother. She was going to church so I went along and sat prayerfully next to her. I got her aside later and talked about John coming to Tennessee State, and when I left she felt I would take care of him."[20]

Unlike Barnhill, Barnett was well-known, as the six-four forward had led Gary's Roosevelt High School team to the finals of the state championship, where it was defeated by a powerful Crispus Attucks team from Indianapolis, led by All-American Oscar Robertson. Barnett's high school coach, J. D. Smith, convinced his All-State forward that playing for Coach McLendon at Tennessee A&I would be his best choice, not only to further develop his basketball skills but to hone his character. In the twenty-five years McLendon coached at the college level, he had players from Roosevelt for twenty-one. "Barnett was promised to me when he was in the tenth grade," McLendon told Richardson. "By the time Barnett was a senior in high school he was attracting quite a bit of attention. But J.D. said Barnett wouldn't be successful playing for anybody else in college except me. I drove up there, put Dick in my car, and we went right to the campus in Nashville."[21]

Although it was already dark when McLendon arrived in Gary to meet with Barnett and his family, his mother told the coach her son was down the street at the playground and he could speak with him there. As McLendon approached the playground, he heard the basketball bouncing and the sound of it ripping through the net. The coach realized at that moment that Barnett was someone special. Although McLendon was obviously pleased to have Barnett play for the Tigers, this exceptional player was a concern to the coach, for he sensed that the young man lacked the self-discipline necessary to excel in his team-oriented system. According to Barnett and his teammates, he was basically just a street kid from a very poor neighborhood who took longer than most to grow up.[22]

Although they were close, Barnett and McLendon sometimes disagreed, usually over the disciplinary tactics the coach used to keep his star in line. After one particularly egregious trespass during Barnett's freshman year, McLendon not only considered kicking him off the team but also advised his prize recruit to go to the bus station and make his way home. However, the university president interceded. "Dr. Davis asked me to make a deal with him," recalled McLendon. "The deal was that Dr. Davis would go down to the bus station to rescue Barnett and keep him here and would look after him when he got back. I said yes, and in effect was paroling Barnett to Davis." According to McLendon, Davis operated with the underlying philosophy that a coach should never penalize a player if this meant hurting the whole team. "When Dr. Davis stopped Barnett at the station, he told him that it was the first time he had ever heard of a college president asking a coach not to send a player home," McLendon said. "And, because it was so unusual, Dr. Davis told Barnett not to let him down. He didn't. And we didn't have any more trouble."[23]

Recalling the incident years later, McLendon said Barnett's undisciplined behavior—missing curfew and other infractions—forced him to draw the line. "Naismith taught me that if you are going to make some rules, you have to make them apply to your best player or they're not worth anything," he stated. His star player would have to accept the consequences for his actions. When Barnett went even further, defying the school's disciplinary committee, he was on the verge of being permanently expelled from the university. McLendon, however, convinced the committee to allow him to discipline Barnett. According to Russell L. Stockard, "This he did with a regimen that was more instructive than punitory. The results of Skull's pre- and post-practice sessions with Coach McLendon were life changing in attitude and performance."[24]

Barnett learned to accept McLendon's disciplined approach to both basketball and life, and the player and the coach benefited greatly from the arrangement. Many years later, Barnett wrote that his beloved coach "had an easygoing, gentle, understated nature that did not reflect his great inner-spirit for overcoming competition and injustices in sports and more so in other aspects of life. He had an iron fist in a velvet glove. It was both that nature and spirit that enabled him to overcome and to prevail at so much in life. He has been an example that has influenced me to this day in much of what I have attempted and accomplished in my life since I first met him in 1955."[25]

Another lesson McLendon had learned from Dr. Naismith that applied to Barnett was to support individuality as long as it wasn't a detriment to the team. Barnett was famous for his unorthodox trademark jump shots, in which he tucked his legs under his body, looked at the hapless defender, and said with a sneer, "Too late—fall back, baby." Although the coach had never seen anything like it, he "didn't tamper with that," Barnett said. "It was like a lay-back—he would go up and back at a 40 degree angle," McLendon recalled to William Rhoden in the *New York Times*. "It was an undefendable shot. When he'd hit the floor, he was often off balance. Sometimes, he'd exaggerate it. One time, he fell clear up in the second row after the shot." Whatever the method, the shot went in the basket often enough for Barnett to become the highest scorer in Tennessee State University history.[26]

According to author Nelson George, for McLendon, "Barnett's flair was essential to the team's competitive chemistry." "I had to cool him down," McLendon told George about his superstar. "He thought basketball was supposed to be played behind his back. He was kind of a hot dog, let's put it like that. I told him, 'The first time you make a bad pass going behind your back I'm going to pull you out.' He said, 'I don't make bad passes.'" However, one of his teammates recalled that at least once Barnett did commit an unforced error while attempting to be a little too creative. As McLendon had promised, he pulled Barnett from the court. After a brief conversation and cooling-off period, Skull went back into the game, played brilliantly, and brought his Tigers another victory.[27]

To further prepare his team for integrated competition, McLendon organized, directed, and won the first integrated college tournament in the South in 1956. The teams entered in the NAIA Southeastern Tip-Off Tournament in Nashville were Fisk University, Rockhurst College, North

Dakota University, and host Tennessee A&I State University. Speaking of this event years later, McLendon stated that there must have been an understanding between the governor of Tennessee and the university's president, allowing the competition to take place under the condition that white teams would come exclusively from outside the state. Making the most of this pioneering opportunity, McLendon also started scheduling his team to travel to white schools outside Tennessee coached by his NAIA friends. Hungry for integrated competition, McLendon's Tigers traveled throughout the Midwest to take on other NAIA colleges in Chicago, Kansas City, and as far away as North Dakota. Closer to home, Tennessee A&I even played secret scrimmages against all-white David Lipscomb College of Nashville, everyone involved vowing to keep this experiment as silent as possible.[28]

Word spread around the Nashville community that McLendon had assembled a team that was worth watching. White fans started coming to see the fast-breaking, high-scoring Tigers perform, especially sharp-shooting Barnett, who loved to play to the fans. An administrative aide to Walter Davis, Homer Wheaton, told Dwight Lewis of the *Tennessean* that "Barnett and company did more to promote desegregation and integration in Nashville than anything or anybody else." In their history of athletics at Tennessee State, authors Dwight Lewis and Susan Thomas wrote that Davis realized that the basketball team could go a long way toward breaking down barriers of segregation, so he set aside reserved seats for whites in the school's gym. He soon realized, however, that segregated seating created an uncomfortable atmosphere and directed that some of the reserved seats be sold to blacks as well.[29]

With all of this behind him, McLendon was confident in his team's poise and ability going into the 1957 postseason competition. He knew his players were well-conditioned and would be able to withstand the grueling, weeklong tournament if they played well enough to stay in it. "When I came to the NAIA, my goal was to have the best conditioned team in the nation, and I would teach that all during my career," McLendon told Darin David, a staff writer for the NAIA. "Fatigue is only psychological. I never called time-outs to rest anyone; that time was only for strategy. Once you sell it to the guys, you've got something. You have to learn to do skills with speed because anyone can do them with a lot of time."[30]

As required by their coach, all the Tiger players took their training and practice sessions quite seriously, but Dick Barnett took conditioning a step further. "Barnett had a personal training program of his own," McLendon told Lewis and Thomas. "He had a basketball in his hand everyday. They didn't like people to practice in the gym on Sunday mornings, so they locked it up, but Barnett always found ways to get in. Finally, they just had to open it up and keep it open for him." McLendon recalled that Barnett would be in the gym playing by himself, pretending that as many as three people were guarding him. "He had little motions and a little dialogue he would go through. It was interesting," said McLendon. "He learned self-control and discipline that way."[31]

Although his team, affectionately called the "Whiz-Kids," went into the 1957 NAIA national tournament with a 26–4 record, the Tigers were unseeded by the NAIA tournament committee. Having used amazing accuracy and a blistering fast break to defeat Winston-Salem Teachers College (coached by McLendon's friend Clarence "Big House" Gaines) 100–80 for the District 29 championship, the Tigers were confident they could compete with anyone. Exhibiting consistent team skill, courage, and determination, McLendon's cagers climbed to the top rung of the championship ladder, defeating Adrian, Michigan (87–69); Portland University (87–70); Western Illinois (90–88); the number-one seed, previously undefeated Pacific Lutheran (71–70); and, in the final game, Southeastern Oklahoma (92–73).

The eight thousand fans who attended the semifinal games were treated to a thrilling conclusion when the Tigers' Barnett scored to put Coach McLendon's team ahead of Pacific Lutheran with a leaping fifteen-footer with only nine seconds to go. The tense battle had been close all the way, as the Lutes had a 42–40 halftime lead on the strength of two free throws in the last eleven seconds of the period. The pattern for the second half was established early as the Tigers tried to get their fast break going, the Lutes intent on slowing down play when they had possession. Following a 60–all tie, Pacific Lutheran took a 5-point lead with less than two minutes to go. After a twisting jump shot by Tennessee's center, "Diamond" Jim Satterwhite, and a short push shot by guard Henry Carlton, the Tigers got the break they needed. Carlton and Barnhill of the Tigers tied up All-American Roger Iverson, who had the ball in the Lutes' stalling game, desperately trying to protect the lead, which had dwindled to 1 point in the last minutes. With twenty-eight seconds left, Tennessee took the tip, and "Barnett swept

McLendon mapping out strategy for the Tigers' 1957 NAIA championship run with Dick Barnett, Jim Satterwhite, Bill Matthews, Ron Hamilton, and John Barnhill. (Courtesy NAIA)

across the free throw circle, leaped, and fired. It went through cleanly," wrote Ed Garich in the *Kansas City Star*. According to several of his players, McLendon jumped out of his seat when the shot went in, then quickly sank back down again to resume his calm demeanor. Pacific Lutheran came down the floor and tried to get off a shot but failed.[32]

Almost fifty years later, fellow Naismith Hall of Fame coach Marv Harshman, of Pacific Lutheran, remembered the game well, recalling that McLendon's Tigers played with a rare combination of high discipline and the flair of maximum freedom. "You could see his team was very well coached," said Harshman. "They started their fast break with an efficiency of passes, and ended up scoring a lot of layups. We tried to slow them down with a zone defense. It obviously did not work." "Of course, with our fast break offense, we get the ball inside for more layups," McLendon told John Steen of the *Nashville Banner* after the game. "We stress rebounding, so we'll take quick shots from the breaks or screens, relying on tip-ins to score." Remarkably, McLendon's starting five played almost the entire game, with sixth man Joe Buckhalter spelling Satterwhite when necessary. Barnett scored 32 points for the victors, while Satterwhite and the Tigers' captain, guard Ron Hamilton, chipped in with 13 and 10 points, respectively.[33]

The *Kansas City Star* of March 17, 1957, reported that "Tennessee State of Nashville needed only five minutes to achieve a season long ambition last night as the Tigers broke past Southeastern Oklahoma 92–73, to win the championship of the 19th Annual NAIA Basketball Tournament. A crowd of 7,000 sat in the Municipal Auditorium to watch the Tigers turn the floor into a race track for the first five minutes of the second half and score 16 points while the Savages hit only 2. That was the ball game." With "the lightning flurry of Barnett, Barnhill, Joseph Buckhalter, and Ron Hamilton doing the bulk of the scoring, the Tigers expanded a 40–37 half time lead to an insurmountable 56–37 superiority." According to Ed Garich, who covered the game for the *Star,* "it was the blinding speed and daring basketball—combined with an attacking defense—that won it for the Tigers." As befitted the times, Garich thought it appropriate to point out that "Tennessee State is the first Negro College to win the NAIA."[34]

The Associated Press story on the game proved to be noteworthy, as it was picked up by newspapers across the country. Entitled "Red-Hot Tigers Roár to NAIA Cage Title," it read: "The Tennessee State Tigers of Nashville, first all-Negro entry in the National Intercollegiate (NAIA) basketball tournament back in 1953, won the small-college cage trophy with a decisive victory over the favorite Southeastern Oklahoma Savages last night. . . . Tennessee State thus became the first all-Negro team to win a major basketball tournament in history."[35]

"The boys deserve the credit," McLendon told the press following the game. "They never loaf and have a dread fear of losing." Although the Tigers' phenomenal 52 percent scoring clip had made a big difference, the coach specifically credited the job of freshman center Buckhalter, who defended against Oklahoma's All-American center, Jim Spivey, averaging 42 points a game in the tournament, as sealing the victory. "Joe blocked four straight hook shots by Spivey, forcing him to move outside of the key to get clear. They lost their rebounding edge then, and we pulled ahead right after that," said McLendon. Buckhalter, from Tilden Technical School in Chicago, proved to be a fan favorite, often taking two short steps and jumping to touch the backboard halfway up, while scoring 20 points. Whenever

McLendon's first NAIA national champions, 1957. *Standing, left to right:* Marshall Hurst, Remus Nesbitt, Ron Hamilton, Dick Barnett, John Barnhill, Rubin Perry, Coach McLendon. *Kneeling, left to right:* James Satterwhite, Joe Buckhalter, Albert Cook, Henry Carlton, Nurlin Tarrant. (Courtesy Tennessee State University)

he shot inside on driving layups, he flattened the palm of his hand against the backboard to keep his hand from hitting it.[36]

According to Tennessee playmaking guard and Kansas City, Kansas, native Ron Hamilton, who also had a superlative game, netting 20 points for the victors, "the people of Kansas City treated us royally." "We were treated just like the other players," recalled Nurlin Tarrant, although John Barnhill recalled the team being watched closely by tournament officials. "They were scrutinizing everything we did," Barnhill told Ed Miller of the *Virginian-Pilot*. Noticing that nearly every other team in the tournament had a rooting section, a group of more than two hundred Kansas Citians, expertly organized by political and social activist Bruce Watkins, sat together, inspiring McLendon's quintet on to its history-making victory. The fast-breaking Tigers averaged more than 91 points per game, and Barnett, Barnhill, and Satterwhite were chosen as NAIA All-Americans. Tennessee A&I's relentless all-court pressure and fast-break tactics were the result of McLendon's intense conditioning program, which required his athletes to run three miles a day in less than twenty minutes leading up to the tournament.[37]

"The team was not cocky, but confident," Barnhill recalled. "We intimidated the opponents during the warm-ups by dunking the ball at every opportunity and loved doing the shuffle dance to express our joy following another Tiger victory." Buckhalter recalled the tremendous pride his coach instilled in his players, how McLendon frequently reminded them that this was their chance to make history as the first black school to win a national championship. "That was motivation enough," said Buckhalter. "It was all we needed."[38]

Satterwhite and Tarrant both recalled that McLendon was a master at teaching the Xs and Os, the intricacies of the game. The coach's preparation was thorough, and every player understood his role and was committed to executing the strategy as perfectly as possible. And then McLendon left them alone. "I train my boys the best I know how and advise them before every game and during intermissions," he said. "I tell them of mistakes and plan strategy with them for the remainder of the game. Then I leave matters to them. Except to replace a tired boy or send in a play occasionally that they should run, I let them go." During the championship games, however, McLendon kept pulling the strings, changing his strategy, alternating his plays and players. His timeouts were significant, each pause packed with well-orchestrated plans that paid off.[39]

According to Tigers star Barnett, Coach McLendon's philosophy of excellence was the key to the team's success. "Coach was very adamant in terms of his physical and mental applications and training," recalled Barnett. "He had the ability to inspire young men to fit into a system with the belief that they could beat anybody. Because we believed we were champions, we played that way." The results spoke for themselves. The only unfortunate incident of the championship evening came when the announcer, perhaps overwhelmed with the moment's significance, awarded the championship trophy to "Coach McLendon and his team from *East Tennessee State University*."[40]

John Steen pointed out in the *Nashville Banner* that McLendon found the NAIA championship especially satisfying for two reasons.

"The Tigers were awarded the only trophy named after James Naismith, inventor of basketball, under whom the A&I coach studied at the University of Kansas," wrote Steen. "And hundreds of McLendon's boyhood friends from Kansas City, Kansas, saw the title game." During the close tournament games, McLendon's father became so nervous that he walked out into the hall. His mother kept watching the game, his father describing her behavior as "praying the ball into the basket." After McLendon's Tigers captured their national championship, his father made his way down to the court, shook his son's hand, and then bearhugged him. "My mother [who was seventy-six years old] ran all the way to the dressing room to congratulate me after we'd won Saturday night," said McLendon. "She pulled my head down and said, 'I'm so proud of you, Son, but I still have my doubts about anybody who would let their whole life be determined by what five boys do with a ball.'" An educator who did not consider sports a particularly noble career, she then declared, "Son, why didn't you pick another profession?"[41]

Following the first Tennessee A&I championship, Mack Greene marked the historic importance of the victory in the *National Athletic Steering Committee Newsletter:*

> As is generally known, the Tennessee State University won the 1957 NAIA Championship in Basketball. This was a significant milestone in both the history of Tennessee State University and the NASC. And of equal significance to many of us is the singular and proud fact that J. B. McLendon was the deserving coach of the winning team. Most of us will recall that it was he who initiated the preliminary strides which culminated in the organization of the NASC. The precursor to the NASC was the National Basketball Committee of which Mr. McLendon was chairman. The committee was stating nationally eight years and more ago that the basketball teams among our colleges were as well coached and played as brilliant games as any in the nation. It was a thrilling sight to see Mac receive the trophy, which symbolized the truth of his pronouncement made years ago.[42]

The black press also justifiably praised the efforts of the new NAIA champions. Bill Nunn, sports columnist of the *Pittsburgh Courier,* displayed pride when he observed: "At long last the willingness to produce and the ability to teach have paid off in major tournaments for a Negro College five. To those who have been saying all along that Negro teams can compete with the best, if given the opportunity, Tennessee's thrilling victory gives added incentive for believing even better things are yet to come." Cal Jacox, sports editor of the *Norfolk Journal and Guide,* wrote: "In winning the national NAIA basketball championship, Tennessee State University gave colored college athletics its biggest boost. For years, arguments have been raging over whether Negro College teams would be able to compete with white teams in major competition. The success of TSU should put an end to that speculation." Marion Jackson, sports editor of the *Atlanta Daily World,* added: "A&I's spectacular success will provide a weathervane for our colleges in mixed competition. It shows that competent personnel and first-rate coaching can trail blaze frontiers of democracy unknown to us before."[43]

However, the hometown *Kansas City Call* exhibited the greatest pride in Coach McLendon's accomplishment. Under the banner headline, "Tennessee State Tigers Win NAIA Championship," an article entitled "Historic Win for Tan Team" described how the team had "made the jump from its belated 1953 starting opportunity to the top rung of the organization in four shots at the most coveted crown in small-college basketball." In a lengthy editorial entitled "A Great Coach, Period," sports editor John I. Johnson proudly stated: "Search far and wide and you won't find a more likeable or more efficient basketball mentor than Johnny B. McLendon, a transplanted Kansan who three years ago sunk his roots deep into the athletically rich Tennessee University campus soil and blossomed-out last week as the winner of one of the most coveted basketball championships in the U.S.A., and of course, that means the world. Johnny B's boys, the Tennessee State A&I University Tigers, walked off Saturday night with the 1957 NAIA diadem."[44]

According to Johnson, before this championship, McLendon's "victories earned for him the distinction of being a great Negro coach," as "the racial tag was always employed in evaluating his greatness." Johnson argued that some of his skeptics would say, "Oh sure, he was a good Negro coach, who has won a few games in the colored tournaments," wishing him and his team well but granting them little respect for real ability. Such opinions were understandable, said Johnson, as "they have come about because of the rigid restrictions the Negro coaches have been forced to work under. Having very few chances to test his teams and his ability against that of widely recognized and highly touted white coaches," the black coach "has had to spend his life and talents behind the curtain of inopportunity." Acutely aware of this, McLendon had made sure his team understood their opportunity, and "he and his boys seemed intent on making the best of it. They started out as if they meant to go all the way." After the final whistle sounded, signaling their historic victory, and the auditorium had almost emptied of the eight thousand fans, Johnson found "Johnny B. staggering about with the huge, beautiful four-foot championship trophy in his arms." "The transplanted Kansan had come home from Tennessee to achieve his greatest triumph," concluded Johnson. "He had returned to prove to the nation that he is a great coach and this time no tag of Negro was attached to the recognition."[45]

Al Duer also realized the historic significance of these events, writing proudly after the Tennessee A&I victory: "The democratic principles upon which the NAIA was founded and to which it has held unwaveringly through the years, resulted for the first time in an all Negro college annexing a national basketball championship. In doing so, the team's performance has caused the tournament to be rated in the top five in the organization's history. The new champions," stated Duer, "conducted themselves in a manner that upheld the traditions of sportsmanlike conduct of the highest order for which this tournament has become nationally recognized. Their victories were made possible by superb team play that stressed speed and consistent brilliance of individual team members. They are in a class by themselves."[46]

In an interview with Mike Hudson, a reporter for the *Roanoke Times*, McLendon recalled how the team's flight home was delayed by two hours because of a bomb scare. The Eastern Airlines plane carrying his championship Tigers turned back to the Kansas City airport about twenty-five minutes after takeoff. Despite the threat, the Tennessee coaches and players remained calm. After the plane was searched, the pilot stated that it was safe to reboard, and they took off again for Nashville. The next day, a Monday, Coach McLendon walked into the Tennessee gym and stopped short: out on the floor, his players were playing three-on-three, full-court. "We had just won one championship," said McLendon. "But they were ready to go back and win another one."[47]

Two-Time National Champions

The following year, in 1958, Tennessee A&I State University earned its second national tournament berth, easily defeating North Carolina College 115–65 for the District 29 title. Entering the tournament with a sparkling 26–3 record, Tennessee A&I became only the second school in the twenty-year history of the NAIA basketball championship to win two consecutive titles when McLendon's Tigers defeated Western Illinois University 85–73 in the finals at Kansas City's Municipal Auditorium before nine thousand fans. The game ended a twenty-seven-game victory string for Western Illinois, which entered the weeklong tournament as the only undefeated team in the country. It also avenged an earlier Tiger loss to Western at a holiday tournament in Macomb, Illinois, 79–76. Coach McLendon had just been named NAIA Coach of the Year, and his team proved the wisdom of this award with its daring and well-coordinated play. The Tigers had a relatively easy time getting to the final game, taking Northern Michigan by 68 points; Anderson, Indiana, by 21; East Texas State by 19; and Texas Southern by 25. All who witnessed the semifinal game between Tennessee A&I and Texas Southern, with its final score of 110–85, agreed that it was a great exhibition of fast-break basketball. "Of less consequence, although some fears had been expressed in this regard, was the fact that the game marked a first encounter of two black-college teams in NAIA tournament competition," wrote McLendon. "The crowd responded in the usual manner and black teams had not been deliberately bracketed to oppose each other in early rounds as had been predicted."[48]

The well-played 1958 finals were a shooting match from the start, with Western Illinois taking a 1-point halftime lead, 43–42. The lead changed hands nine times through the first twelve minutes of the second half, the teams never more than 3 points apart. With eight minutes left in the game, the score was tied at 69. The Tigers then moved ahead to 71–69 on two free throws by Barnett. Here, McLendon's forces went into their "two-corners" delay game to protect their slim lead with high looping passes, forcing the tired Western Illinois team into committing costly fouls. Henry Carlton recalled that the Western Illinois players had so thoroughly prepared to counter the Tigers' fast break that they seemed "dumbfounded" when he and his teammates executed their delay game. McLendon, who called this approach his team's standard delay procedure in a tight game, had ironically detailed this innovative strategy the previous year for the *Converse Basketball Yearbook*. Of the 16 points scored by the champions in the time remaining, 12 came at the free-throw line, as the Tigers eased the lead into a more comfortable region.[49]

Barnett was deadly from twenty feet out, and his 31-point performance in the finals backed up a 35-point effort in the semifinal game. Also effective on outside shots were John Barnhill and Henry Carlton. The Tigers went the distance playing only five men, with James Satterwhite and Ron Hamilton providing good protection inside. All five players for Tennessee scored in double figures, and Satterwhite finished as the leading rebounder, with 20, as the Tigers won the battle of the boards. Top man in the opinion of press row was Dick Barnett of Tennessee A&I, who earned the Most Valuable Player Award given by Chuck Taylor and was included on everybody's All-Tournament team. The Tigers' lightning-quick guard John Barnhill was chosen for the Second All-Tournament team.

Sitting at the press tables intently watching the NAIA finals was the great All-American Wilt Chamberlain, of the University of Kansas Jayhawks. Asked by *Kansas City Call* sports editor James C. Brown what he thought of Dick Barnett after seeing the likes of Oscar Robertson in the NCAA tournament, Chamberlain replied: "Here is another great basketball player and just about one of the best floor shots I have ever seen. It's just too bad he didn't select one of the major schools, for he would have been ranked with the best of them." What Chamberlain failed to realize, however, is that Barnett chose to play for McLendon at little-known Tennessee State and, by doing so, helped make history for himself and all African Americans.[50]

A wild, delightedly cheering throng greeted the two-time NAIA national champions as they returned to Nashville from their history-making campaign. The press reported that two thousand students dedicated the entire day to a victory celebration that began with steak dinners for the players, coaches, and student representatives. According to the *Call*, "The lauding fans moved to Kean's 'Little Garden' for a victory rally honoring Coach of the Year J. B. McLendon and his Whiz Kids with speech-making and school yells of the 'Tiger Rag' topped with movies from the semi-final and championship games under two red, white, and blue NAIA championship banners." "I think that last year's

Celebrating the Tigers' second NAIA national championship, 1958. (Courtesy Tennessee State University)

victory was our greatest thrill," Captain Ron Hamilton told the adoring fans, but "this year we had more poise and we played our best." Barnett revealed that team members built up their spirits before each game by doing the "Stroll," made famous by R&B vocalist Chuck Willis. As the team joyfully showed off its pregame dance moves, the crowd shouted with glee, knowing that most would return the following year for another championship. As for McLendon, he chose to stay in Kansas City visiting family instead of returning to campus for the celebration. Already plotting strategy for another championship run, he knew that there would be time enough for additional celebrations.[51]

While preparing for another national championship march, McLendon found the necessary time to reflect on his psychology of coaching in an article entitled "Coaching to Win." He argued that "coaches should know more about the factors of psychological impor-tance which determine sustained interest and application of effort in

Chuck Taylor of Converse presenting the MVP trophy to Dick Barnett, 1958.
(Courtesy NAIA)

competitive athletic participation. They are the objectives sought after
by those who want consistent seasonal and year-to-year performance
by athletic teams." McLendon proceeded to outline some of the psychological factors of the utmost importance to all involved in competitive athletics:

> First, the objectives of the coach and the team must harmonize.
> They must be clear to both and represent a return to truly
> educational objectives in athletics rather than the average fan's

objectives. Second, there must be set forth an objective which is greater than winning but which carries winning with it. Winning should be considered not as a goal in itself but rather as something incorporated in the goal. Substitute goals, such as "striving for excellence in performance" or "trying for a credible team effort," are objectives which have a more permanent appeal to the psychological attitude. Winning games in the process of attempting to reach a greater goal is a more worthwhile and meaningful experience than winning as an end in itself.[52]

Dr. James Naismith once said, "Basketball is a game many can play but few can master." "In this statement," McLendon wrote, "lies the challenge in the entire problem of both physical and psychological conditioning for all competitive athletics—mastery of the game." Basic to this approach is the belief that the coach, in response to this challenge, must devise means by which individual players and their teams "can visualize the myriad requirements in fundamentals, techniques, and skills necessary for mastery of the game. Then through his methods, his spirit of determination, and his zeal for achievement [the coach] can imbue his players with the need to apply effort continually and conscientiously. Team members must practice and play with mastery of the game as their objective," he concluded, perhaps thinking about his two-time national champion Tigers. "In their progress toward this goal, interest and effort will be sustained, and there will be many victories along the way."[53]

Making History: Three in a Row

Seeking an unprecedented third consecutive NAIA title, McLendon's cagers came to the tournament in Kansas City with an even more impressive record than the previous year, with twenty-seven wins against only one defeat. McLendon's fast-break style of basketball was at its zenith: the Tigers were the top-scoring team in the nation, with an average just below 100 points per game, and Barnett was the second-leading scorer in the NAIA, with a 29.9-point average. During this remarkable season, Tennessee A&I won three tournaments—in Atlanta; on their home court, in the South Central NAIA Tip-Off Tournament; and in Quincy, Illinois, at the NAIA Holiday Tournament, where they defeated Southern Illinois University, Youngstown University, and Western Illinois

University, scoring an average of 108 points over three games. In January, the Tigers both set a school record by scoring 150 points over Knoxville College and, ironically, won a slow-down game over Rockhurst College, 36–17. Rated the number-one small-college team in the nation by United Press International, McLendon's cagers suffered their only defeat of the season when they lost to UPI's fifth-rated small-college team, Kentucky's Georgetown College, 88–83. "It was a good ballgame, but we made too many mistakes against a good team," McLendon commented after the game. Perhaps the loss made them stronger, for they did not lose another game the rest of the year, ending the regular season with twenty-five victories and only one defeat.[54]

In the final home game for McLendon's brilliant seniors—Barnett, Barnhill, and Satterwhite—the Tigers won a convincing victory over Lincoln University, 96–63, in Kean's Little Garden while five thousand fans looked on appreciatively. Barnett led the scoring, netting 32 points to close his four-year total at 3,022, while Barnhill and Satterwhite contributed 27 and 23 points, respectively. According to the *Tennessean*, "When the fabulous Skull left the floor shortly before the end of the game, he got a thunderous ovation from the crowd that jammed every corner of the gymnasium." The Tigers then traveled to Wilberforce, Ohio, where they captured their third consecutive Mid-Western Conference championship by defeating Central State College, 89–73.[55]

One of the most astute observers of college basketball, Marion E. Jackson, sports editor of the *Atlanta Daily World,* closely followed the Tigers and was convinced that McLendon and his cagers were a team of destiny. "Tennessee A&I State University players are students of the game, but above all they are gentlemen," wrote Jackson. "Watch their finesse in all phases of the game. The NAIA champs deserve their laurels—and the Tigers play to win. No wonder Tennessee A&I State University has become the home of champions."[56]

Its championship-caliber basketball tested and retested in the pressure-packed crucible of Kansas City's Municipal Auditorium, Tennessee A&I State University lived up to advance notice, slamming through to a record-breaking third straight title in the 1959 NAIA basketball tournament. Its masterful performance erased the earlier two-straight record, held jointly by the Tigers and Southwest Missouri State (1952–53). Other records also fell to Coach McLendon's tremendous team. The Tigers set a new single-game scoring mark in the quarterfinals, defeating Illinois Normal, 131–74. They also set a new single-game field-goal mark of 55 percent in that game. Dick Barnett set a new career scoring mark of 451 points in the four tournaments the team participated in and was again named Most Valuable Player by the press. He was also the first black player named to the Converse All-American team and the Associated Press Little All-American team. Later, Barnett was chosen by the Syracuse Nationals in the first round of the NBA draft, going on to enjoy a fourteen-year tenure in professional basketball, scoring more than 15,000 points during his illustrious career. Coach McLendon loved saying that he could sleep well at night knowing that Dick Barnett was on his team.

Barnett, the first member of his family to attend college, never graduated from Tennessee State. After completing his athletic eligibility in 1959, he had earned only enough credits to be classified as an "upper" sophomore. Thirty-two years later, however, at age fifty-four, Barnett earned his doctorate degree in education from Fordham University, becoming a college professor and president of Dick Barnett Enterprises, a sports-marketing company. Barnett has often said that one of the proudest moments of his life came when he told McLendon that he had just been awarded his Ph.D. This was also a great source of pride for Coach McLendon, and he let everyone know about it, just as he did when he learned about the many other achievements of his ex-players.[57]

But it wasn't all records and easy victories for the Tigers in the twenty-first annual NAIA national tournament. At halftime of four of their five games, they were just even or behind. They barely caught Southwest Texas State in the semifinals after lagging by 9 points halfway through the game. During the second half, the Texans pulled out to what appeared to be an insurmountable 53–39 lead, and an upset seemed all but assured. But again the Tigers refused to wilt. McLendon's squad picked up the pace of their full-court pressing attack, narrowing the deficit to 53–50. Barnhill and sophomore center Ben Warley scored 4 points apiece in the final four minutes, and sophomore forward Gene Werts supplied the defensive gem of the evening when he blocked an opponent's chip shot with two minutes to go. With fifteen seconds left in the contest, Barnett's jump shot from the side gave the defending champions a 64–62 edge, and the Tigers could look forward to playing for their third straight championship.

Earlier, in the first round, Nebraska Wesleyan tested the Tigers with a halftime score of 33–all. With nine minutes played in the second half, the defenders had only a 45–44 lead. But with Barnett firing 10 points in the final ten minutes, the Tigers pulled it out to win, 75–57. In the second round, Tennessee A&I was just even at halftime. Youngstown of Ohio pulled ahead slightly early in the second half, then fell back, but was only a point down, 68–69, with ten minutes to go. With just three minutes left in the game, the Tigers held only a 4-point lead before going on to win, 89–80.

This pattern continued in the final game before eight thousand fans, Tennessee A&I behind at the half, with Pacific Lutheran leading, 46–45. But again sheer will, ability, and desire pulled the Tigers to the title. The two teams battled toe to toe throughout the second half. Neither could get more than 5 points ahead, and with five minutes to go, Tennessee A&I held only a 79–76 margin. Once more Barnett, Barnhill, and Warley, along with freshman guard Porter Meriwether, grabbed the opportunity and made the difference, leading to a final score of 97–87. Barnett popped in 26 points to capture scoring honors, but according to Bill Richardson, in the *Kansas City Star*, "the Tigers who threw the lethal punches to the Lutes were sophomores Warley, 6–7 center, and Gene Werts, 6–6 forward. Warley and Wertz made the boards A&I property and led a charge against the Lutes' frontlines that opened the way for the Tiger drivers."[58]

"They were just great; they knew they had to play to win, and they did," the Tigers' elated coach told a reporter for the *Tennessean* after winning his historic third consecutive championship. For their outstanding play, Barnett and Barnhill were chosen for the All-Tournament team. The Tigers ended the season with thirty-two wins and one loss, averaging more than 96 points per game. "They were amazing players with the idea that they were on a mission," said McLendon. "I told them that they could make a great change in basketball in this country if they worked for it. I knew if we kept the team good enough that if we got a chance, we could deliver. They would see that Tennessee State was as good as anybody."[59]

A number of professional scouts seemed to agree with McLendon's assessment, coming to evaluate Barnett and several other Tigers as potential NBA prospects. These included Red Holzman and Vince Boryla of the New York Knicks and Ed Macauley and Marty Blake of the St. Louis Hawks. Phog Allen and A. C. Lonborg, of the University

McLendon's third consecutive NAIA championship team, 1959. *First row:* Robert Clark, John Barnhill, Dick Barnett, Porter Meriwether, Hilary Brown. *Second row:* Richard Mack (assistant coach), John B. McLendon (head coach), Rossie Johnson, Eugene Werts, Ben Warley, James Satterwhite, Melvin Davis, Harold Hunter (assistant coach), Gregory Pharr (manager). (Courtesy Tennessee State University)

of Kansas, were also present in Municipal Auditorium to witness McLendon's historic third consecutive championship, along with George Mikan, the NBA's first superstar, formerly with the Minneapolis Lakers, and Chuck Taylor, Converse's ambassador to the basketball world.[60]

Looking back on these championship years and his Tennessee A&I powerhouse Tigers, McLendon told Bill Richardson that "those were very good teams and great guys. On two of the Mondays after we got home from winning the championships in Kansas City, the players were back in the gym shooting baskets. We went three years without an unexcused absence or tardiness from practice, and we played the entire 1958 championship game against Western Illinois without a substitute. But nobody on the bench complained," declared McLendon. "They knew the five guys out there on the floor were doing an outstanding job."[61]

For his unprecedented accomplishments, McLendon was named Coach of the Year. The championships confirmed what McLendon had long fought to prove. "We were looking for indicators all those years showing that our teams could play," McLendon said. "What we were looking for was a way to tell the public that our teams were just as good." In honor of its third straight national title, Tennessee A&I was named International College Division Champions in 1959 by the UPI. McLendon proudly told Bill Richardson that he "would take his chances against anybody" in the country. In fact, according to the *Kansas City Call*, opinion in some quarters held that that "the mighty basketball power Coach Johnny McLendon has constructed on the campus of Tennessee A&I State University at Nashville, may have outgrown the small-college caliber of the competition it meets in national championship play in Kansas City." Clarence "Big House" Gaines declared that "McLendon's team was on par with the top basketball powers," but proving this would be difficult. "The biggest aim now is to get some big colleges on our schedule," McLendon remarked. "It's not an easy thing to do."[62]

McLendon's Tigers were clearly the best team in small-college basketball for three years running, maybe the best anywhere. Chuck Taylor, considered an authority on basketball, said as much after Kentucky beat Seattle in Louisville for the 1958 major-college championship. "Chuck said he'd probably get in trouble with some of his friends, but he told them a little school down the road—meaning Tennessee State—could beat the major-college finalists in the same afternoon," McLendon said.[63]

Currently president of the Tennessee A&I basketball alumni association, Nurlin Tarrant had no doubt that the championship Tiger teams could compete with major-college teams. An All–New York City guard from Brooklyn, he didn't crack the Tigers' starting lineup. In New York, he had competed against players from North Carolina's 1957 NCAA title team and, in Harlem's Rucker League, against pros like Wilt Chamberlain, so he understood what it was like to face the best. "We had such a unique team and great ballplayers at Tennessee State," he told Ed Miller of the *Virginian-Pilot*. "We had a killer fast break and we also pressed. You've got to conclude we could have played with them."[64]

McLendon became the first college coach to win three consecutive national championship trophies in 1959. (Courtesy Joanna McLendon)

The black press was understandably glowing in its praise of McLendon's unprecedented accomplishment. Under the title "The Amazing Mr. McLendon," Cal Jacox wrote in the *Norfolk Journal and Guide:* "In his five years as Tennessee State mentor, Johnny Mac has solidified his position among basketball's greatest coaches. . . . The record-breaking achievements of McLendon and his players are now part of the game's colorful history. . . . But their biggest accomplishment from here is occurring off the court. . . . Via their brilliant exploits, they've convinced the skeptics that the caliber of play on the colored collegiate sports front is on par with that displayed elsewhere in the nation."[65]

The *Pittsburgh Courier*'s Bill Nunn declared: "Give Negro College teams a chance to participate with the best and we'll beat the best. What is important is that winning the NAIA dribble derby three times running proves, without a doubt, that the Tigers of 1958–59 could have held their own with any team in the country." Referring to McLendon and his team, Nunn continued: "When you have struggled for success and recognition against the toughest kinds of odds, it is hard to measure in terms of pride what a man of high principle must feel under these circumstances. . . . The bows and the cheers belong to each and every one of you!"[66]

Governor Frank G. Clement of Tennessee, who frequently attended Tigers home games, sent McLendon a congratulatory telegram, which read: "We have all become 'bragging Tennesseeans' since your exceptional team has established such a fine sports record both during this event and previous ones in competitive sports. Congratulations to all of you for last night's terrific success in winning 131–74 over Illinois Normal. I am certainly for you as governor and as one who loves good sports. I look forward to further good reports of your team's achievement in the semi-finals and finals."[67]

In his twenty-two years in NAIA competition, McLendon won 495 games while losing only 123, an average of more than 22.5 wins and only 5.6 losses a year. Of equal significance, five of his players from these NAIA championship teams went on to play in the NBA: Barnett, Ben Warley, and Porter Meriwether, who were drafted by the Syracuse Nationals; and Barnhill and Joe Buckhalter, who were drafted by Marty Blake of the St. Louis Hawks.

The only racial incident that occurred during the three Tennessee A&I championships took place in 1959, when the Illinois Normal cheerleaders and band started playing and singing "Bye Bye Blackbird" while the Tigers were warming up on the other side of the floor. While some NAIA tournament officials went over to ask the cheerleaders to stop, McLendon took his team off the floor. He said later that he just wanted to calm his players down and tell them "to show these people from Illinois Normal that they deserved their respect." Apparently, this strategy worked, judging from the Tigers' record-setting trouncing of Illinois Normal, 131–74. An NAIA official said to McLendon afterward: "You may not get 'em to love you. But they sure do respect you." Although some schools from the South continued to raise occasional protests, black colleges had become an accepted part of the NAIA tournament.[68]

Meanwhile, the NCAA, in an apparent move to capitalize on the success of the NAIA tournament, especially in regard to black colleges, decided to conduct a championship for the nation's small colleges, beginning in 1957 in Evansville, Indiana. The historic achievements of McLendon's teams were regarded with particular embarrassment by the NCAA. NAIA executive director Al Duer made a strong pitch at the NCAA gathering to save the NAIA, but the delegates proceeded by unanimous vote to stage their new tournament. Duer wrote to a friend that "everyone here knew for sure that the aim of this move of the NCAA was to put us out of business. . . . My good friend, Mr. [Walter] Byers [NCAA president] has put us Number 1 on his wanted list and makes no secret he is after our scalp." According to historian John R. M. Wilson, "This suspicion seemed borne out when the NCAA set up a black regional tournament, the victor of which would qualify for the Evansville event." Some in the NAIA feared that despite the organization's pioneering efforts, it might be upstaged by the more prestigious NCAA.[69]

The NASC's Mack Greene urged all black colleges to retain dual membership in the NAIA and NCAA so that league winners and tournament champions could remain eligible for the national tournament of their choice. According to Wilson, "Many of the schools followed his advice and held dual membership in the NAIA and NCAA, and since rules and competitive levels varied, they often waited until the last minute to decide which playoffs to favor with their presence." While McLendon welcomed the integration of the NCAA, he continued to remain intensely loyal to the NAIA and spoke out forcefully on its behalf. The national championship coach was quoted in a 1958 newspaper article stating that the NAIA "has done more in the last five years to advance the cause of equal opportunity in team sports on a national basis than any other national organization." Every NAIA committee, he pointed out, including the executive committee, included a black member. According to McLendon, his "Coach of the Year" award signified the depth of the NAIA's intense desire to recognize achievement and merit regardless of race.[70]

McLendon's bond with the NAIA's Al Duer was based upon mutual respect that would strengthen with the years. The coach took special pleasure in referring to Duer as "the Abraham Lincoln of college sports." Many years later, he added that the NAIA's progress toward integration under Duer "was unprecedented in USA sports history" and that "no other athletic organization had the moral leadership to even entertain the idea." Every year, McLendon faithfully returned for the weeklong NAIA tournament in Kansas City, sitting in the stands or at the press table with a look of pride and satisfaction on his face. "This is where it all began for the black basketball player," he said. "I don't want to lose sight of that."[71]

During his tenure at Tennessee A&I, McLendon also tried to persuade the leadership of New York City's highly prestigious National Invitational Tournament (NIT) to invite one of the top teams from the black colleges and universities to participate, but the authorities were not ready to accept his request, believing that the black teams would fail to measure up to the competition. At the same time, A&I's president, Walter Davis, asked McLendon to submit an application to the Missouri Valley Conference, one of the top conferences in the nation, so that the Tigers could face integrated competition throughout the season. Although the commissioner of the conference, Norvall Neve, was interested in the application, the conference schools would not hear of it. McLendon believed they took this position because they were afraid his school would dominate the conference, although there is no evidence to support this assertion.[72]

Twenty-five years later, on October 27, 1984, Dick Barnett and many of the original "Whiz Kids" from the 1957–59 NAIA championship years returned to Tennessee to salute their former coach and mentor John B. McLendon Jr. The salute took the form of an exhibition game in which Barnett and other former Tigers played former college All-American and NBA All-Star Oscar Robertson, leading a team of other non–Tennessee State pro and college stars. According to the event program, "This special exhibition basketball game salutes Coach McLendon's love of the sport, his emphasis on teamwork and his never-ending effort to encourage the philosophy of sportsmanship wherever he goes." McLendon received congratulations from people throughout the nation, including

U.S. senator and former NBA great Bill Bradley, who wrote: "It is fitting that an endowment/scholarship fund be established in your name because of the tradition of greatness you helped to establish, and by the examples you have set. Your achievements and commitment to basketball are greatly admired and respected."[73]

The proceeds from the exhibition game went to benefit the John B. McLendon Jr. Scholarship Fund, which had been initiated at the twenty-fifth reunion of the 1957–59 NAIA champions in Kansas City, the site of their historic achievements. As the former teammates renewed friendships that had endured for more than a quarter of a century, they shared a unanimous feeling of love and respect for their coach, a feeling that he had not received the recognition that his life-long record of excellence demanded. The players, believing that a lasting monument to his greatness and his ability to guide young people was in order, established a scholarship fund at the institution that had witnessed his most glorious basketball triumphs, Tennessee State University. The John B. McLendon Scholarship Fund thus became an endowment to provide young people the opportunity to receive an education and become productive and useful citizens. The fund was administered by the four players who formed the executive committee establishing it: Joe Buckhalter Jr., John Barnhill, Dick Barnett, and Ron Hamilton.

CHAPTER 6

Blazing New Trails
The Cleveland Pipers, 1959–62

After his Tennessee A&I Tigers won their third consecutive national title in 1959, McLendon chose to confront an equally significant challenge. Not satisfied with his historic three straight national college championships, he had his eyes on a bigger prize: coaching teams with both black and white players. Ed Sweeny, owner of a leading plumbing, heating, and air-conditioning company in Cleveland, was sufficiently impressed by what he saw in McLendon to offer him the job of coaching his AAU Cleveland Pipers as the team entered the National Industrial Basketball League (NIBL). The NIBL was a high-level post-college league of nine company-sponsored teams from across the country, comparable to midlevel NBA teams. Sweeny's plan was not only to hire McLendon but also to lure some Tennessee State stars, who he assumed would accompany their coach to play for the Pipers.

"In a national magazine preview of the 1959–1960 season," Sweeny told Jack Clowser of the *Cleveland Press,* "I read that McLendon was the top fundamentalist in basketball today. I didn't even know he was a Negro—not that it would have made any difference to me—and I decided to go after him." Sweeny was also impressed to read in the *Converse Basketball Yearbook* that, in twenty years of coaching, McLendon's winning percentage was over .800, second only to that of legendary coach Adolph Rupp, from the University of Kentucky. "I found out he [McLendon] was an institution at Tennessee State," Sweeny continued. "He had security there and they had a home for him. But he finally concluded ours was a proposition that could open a new field for his talents."[1]

"I was the general manager and there were three daily newspapers [at the time]—the *Press,* the *News,* and the *Plain Dealer,*" recalled Mike Cleary, now executive director of the National Association of College

Directors of Athletics. "We went out with the sports editors, plus the NBC and ABC affiliates, and said, 'We're thinking of hiring a black coach. What do you think?' They said, 'You're nuts. Cleveland's not ready.' That made Ed even more eager to say 'We're hiring him.'" Sweeny, business manager George Dunmore, and Cleary negotiated the selection and hiring of Coach McLendon, who was offered a two-year contract, starting at around twelve thousand dollars—almost twice the salary he was earning at Tennessee State as head coach and associate professor of physical education. Although McLendon initially turned down the offer in April, Sweeny's determination eventually paid dividends. On June 30, Chuck Heaton reported in the *Cleveland Plain Dealer* that the forty-four-year-old McLendon had signed a contract with the Cleveland Pipers. In doing so, he would become the first black coach in the NIBL.[2]

The new Pipers coach and his wife moved to Cleveland later that summer, leaving behind two children enrolled at Tennessee State—John III, a junior, and Querida, a freshman. Querida went on to graduate with a degree in business education. She taught in a public high school in Cleveland for a few years, then earned her master's degree at the University of Kentucky in Lexington while her father was coaching at Kentucky State University in Frankfort. She married and had a daughter, Tracy. John III left college after his junior year and went on to work at General Motors in Cleveland, staying on the job for twenty-nine years. He married and had two daughters. Throughout the years, both he and his sister stayed as close to their father as possible, given his demanding schedule. McLendon's wife Ethel, who had been teaching at Tennessee A&I State University in Nashville, took a position in social work upon moving to Cleveland.

Although reluctant to leave Tennessee State, where he was revered for making history, McLendon accepted the job because, as he told Ron Thomas, he was "one of the people yelling the loudest about the lack of black head professional coaches, and being a member of the NIBL was the accepted step between college and professional ball." It was the highest coaching position that had ever been offered a black man. McLendon also understood that coaching in the AAU could open up other doors. "The NIBL provides most of the talent for the United States Olympic basketball team and I'll have an opportunity to be part of the program," he told George Dunmore in an interview for the *Pittsburgh Courier*. "Moreover, it gives me the opportunity I never

In 1959, McLendon became the first black coach of an integrated team with the Cleveland Pipers of the National Industrial Basketball League. (Courtesy Joanna McLendon)

dreamed would happen to me. I know the challenge is a terrific one, but I think I'm equal to the task." Followers of basketball from both races wondered if white players would respond to a black coach, but McLendon was confident of his ability and looked forward to the Pipers' inaugural season.[3]

"I think the one single thing about this job that made me feel best,"

McLendon told Clowser of the *Cleveland Press,* "was when Mr. Sweeny told me he had called in prospective players individually and asked them if they would have any reservations about being coached by a Negro. All said no. An All-American ballplayer is essentially an All-American boy."[4]

To introduce McLendon to the Cleveland public and test fan interest in high-caliber postcollegiate basketball, Sweeny and his associates invited him to coach a college All-Star team against Johnny Dee's Denver-Chicago Truckers, the amateur basketball champions, to benefit the Cleveland Heart Fund. According to McLendon, two of his Tennessee State seniors, Dick Barnett and John Barnhill, were invited to play for the All-Stars, and five other great players from Southern institutions helped prove the Pipers' point that a college-level integrated team coached by a black man could be successful. "We'll use the style I've always thought was best," McLendon told Chuck Heaton of the *Plain Dealer.* "We'll be using the fast break and doing a lot of shooting. These boys come from various systems but most of them are All-Americans, and I'm figuring they can adjust." McLendon declared he would use a ten-man squad against the National Industrial League champions, employing two teams and substituting them as units to maximize the playing time for as many boys as possible. Going into the game, the talent-laden Denver team had the advantage of having played together all year, whereas McLendon had only had a couple of days to work with part of the squad and even less time with the full unit.[5]

Under the headline "Truckers Thrashed by Pipers," Heaton described the game in the *Plain Dealer:* "Fortified by some of the slickest college basketball players ever to appear in Cleveland, the Sweeny Pipers did a fine selling job for the round ball sport last night. With forward Dick Barnett burning the mesh for 29 points, they upset the D-C Truckers, 123 to 105, at the Arena." This happened on April 5—McLendon's birthday. Joining Barnett for Pipers scoring honors was six-eight John Richter from North Carolina State University, who not only contributed 25 points but also led his club in rebounding. Two five-nine guards, Don Hennon of the University of Pittsburgh and Lou Pucillo of North Carolina State, provided the last-quarter spark for the Pipers, ultimately scoring 18 and 17 points, respectively. "This was a great birthday present for me," McLendon beamed. "The fellows went all-out to win this one, and they did." Following the game, Sweeny praised

McLendon's coaching abilities, stating, "I'm tickled with the way the boys played but naturally a little disappointed at the turnout" (announced as twenty-five hundred). He then spoke with the visiting All-Americans about joining his Pipers team. "Winning this game, in a first-time post-college experience for a black coach," said McLendon, "gave notice that there was a vast reservoir of players and coaches who were available for post-college basketball and sports." As Marion Jackson wrote in the *Atlanta Daily World*, "McLendon had passed his test."[6]

As McLendon often observed, if Sweeny was looking to integrate his team, he certainly accomplished this. The Pipers now had a black coach, six black players (including Tigers John Barnhill, Ben Warley, and Ron Hamilton), and seven white players. "We didn't do John any favors," Cleary recalled. "Of the white players, all of them were from below the Mason-Dixon Line." Yet, Cleary continued, "we did not have one moment of racial conflict on this team. In fairness, if there was any knock on John, it was he was so easy on the white players." In an interview with author Robert W. Matthews, Dan Swartz, a former Morehead (Kentucky) State College star who played under McLendon with the Pipers and later put in a year with the Boston Celtics, said, "John was fair." He recalled that Warley once missed a practice and McLendon quickly let him know that wouldn't be tolerated. "He got on me pretty good," Warley recounted to Matthews. That convinced the white players, said Swartz, that all of them were equal in the coach's eyes.[7]

Two of McLendon's white players recalled that race was never an issue on the Pipers team. One of them, Gene Tormohlen, a former University of Tennessee All-American, didn't know much about McLendon except that he liked to run the ball. During an interview with Ron Thomas for his book on the NBA's black pioneers, Tormohlen remembered McLendon as "a quiet, mild-mannered human being," who easily earned the respect of all the players. "This is something I don't know that I can say for any other coach in America," said Tormohlen. "Everybody liked him—even if you didn't play. He was your friend. Johnny was someone everybody loved. Being in pro basketball for thirty years, I've never heard anyone say anything bad about Johnny McLendon." Jack Adams, a former Eastern Kentucky University star who was chosen as an alternate for the 1960 Olympic team, remembered McLendon as an incredibly patient and knowledgeable coach, a great

McLendon welcomes All-American Johnny Green to the Cleveland Pipers, 1959.
(Courtesy Joanna McLendon)

communicator, and an overall fine person. "He was respected by all his players," said Adams. "And he treated all of us with respect as well."[8]

Although keenly aware of prejudice throughout American society, McLendon always took a positive approach to human behavior. "I've reached a stage of experience where I'm no longer sensitive," he told Cleveland reporter Ben Flieger in 1961. "My approach is to assume that everyone in any situation has intelligence. And that intelligence

McLendon with Cleveland Pipers Ralph Crosthwaite, Corny Freeman, Doyle
Edmiston, Gene Tormohlen, 1959. (Courtesy Spencer Research Library, University
of Kansas Libraries)

brings with it a certain amount of fairness." He stated that his team
had no race problem because he regarded everyone alike. "I'd even
say," he concluded, "that in Cleveland there hasn't been a single time
when my being a Negro has put me at a disadvantage." He later wrote
that "Cleveland was the best city in America for my experiences," as
fans there were fair in their appraisal of new athletes, having already
been initiated into integrated sports by the Cleveland Browns and the
Cleveland Indians.[9]

When McLendon began coaching in the NIBL, only two other teams
had black players. The only racial incident McLendon recalled from his
days coaching the Pipers happened at a hotel in Bartlesville, Oklahoma,
where the team had checked in before a game with the Phillips 66ers.
The hotel refused to put television sets in the rooms of black players,
presumably because the manager felt they would be stolen. After being
apprised of the situation, Pipers captain Jack Adams decided, along with
his coach, to move the team to another hotel, informing the management

of the 66ers of the insulting behavior. The hotel issued an apology to McLendon later that evening. Perhaps the incident motivated the Pipers to play their best, for that evening the Cleveland squad performed superbly, handing the 66ers their first home-court defeat in two years.[10]

McLendon praised his team for being an exceptional group of men who proudly modeled behaviors reflective of their coach's high standards. According to McLendon, "I do believe the conduct of my players and the fact that we were never involved in a technical foul proved that a racial mixture of players who respect themselves, their coach and their opponents, as well as their supporting fans, had a great chance for success regardless of color or regional background."[11]

Sportsmanship was sacred to McLendon, so much so that at the college level he had even benched some of his players "for giving an official a dirty look." "Now with the Pipers, the situation is not the same," McLendon explained to Flieger in the *Cleveland Press,* "because these boys are older and more set in their ways. I simply asked them to cut down on their remarks, to keep them clean—and never give up a defensive position while arguing."[12]

With the Pipers, McLendon applied training methods similar to those that had brought him success in the past. As before, conditioning was the key. "Give me a man who will dig in practice, and I'll give you a ballplayer who will dig in a game," he said. "We worked out three times a day," Tormohlen told Thomas, "and the workouts weren't easy. He had everybody in shape because that was his philosophy: 'We're going to run the ball.'" Another team member, Joe Wise, who had played against McLendon's Tennessee A&I team when he was at Lincoln University in Missouri, recalled how some of the Pipers' three-on-three full-court drills would last for an hour or more of continuous movement. Wise stated that as a result he and the other players got into the best shape of their lives. "McLendon was extremely well organized, an excellent communicator, highly disciplined, and ran a very tight ship," said Wise, "and no one questioned his judgment out of respect for what he had accomplished and the kind of person he was." "I can tell that many of my boys haven't had conditioning work like this before," said McLendon, "but these fellows are giving everything they have to do it my way."[13]

The Pipers opened their first NIBL season on the road with an upset 104–96 victory over the Akron Goodyear Wingfoots, one of the two

Planning strategy for the Pipers' inaugural NIBL season, 1959. *Back row, left to right:* Dick Berghoff, Doyle Edmiston, Corny Freeman, Gene Tormohlen, Ralph Crosthwaite, Chuck Curtis, Delton Heard. *Front row, left to right:* John B. McLendon, Joe Wise, Ron Hamilton, Jim McCoy, Tony Windis. (Courtesy Mike Cleary, NACDA)

remaining charter members of the league. Former University of Kentucky All-American Johnny Cox led the scoring for the Pipers with 25 points, while two of McLendon's cagers from Tennessee State, Ron Hamilton and John Barnhill, chipped in with 20 and 16 points, respectively. Although pleased with the come-from-behind victory, McLendon stated that his team had "played far below their potential." "These boys still haven't had a chance to work together as a team for any time due to Army obligations and injuries," said the coach, following with a bold prediction: "When they get used to each other, watch them go." After the win, Sweeny offered his congratulations to McLendon. Then, to the owner's surprise, the coach inquired: "Can you get me a gym for early tomorrow morning? Right after they win a game and might get to believing they're pretty good, that's when I like to work 'em the hardest. They made some mistakes which can be eliminated."[14]

McLendon's philosophy of basketball worked brilliantly, for

although the Pipers were relatively inexperienced, they finished their first season under his charge in fourth place at 16–16, with the highest-ever finish for a first-year coach. "My boys don't like to lose and for that I'm a pretty lucky coach," declared McLendon. "We have speed, endurance, and determination. We'll have to depend on these three factors. That's all we really got." As they prepared for the national AAU tournament in Denver, McLendon was informed by the Pipers' owner that the team was on its own in regard to expenses, including their airfare back home to Cleveland. In spite of this hardship, McLendon's team won two games in the tournament, against the Philadelphia Wicks (118–78) and the Army All-Stars (90–79). A late-season addition to the Pipers, Ben Warley, from McLendon's Tennessee championship squad, led the team in scoring with 33 points and grabbed 26 rebounds in the victory over the Army All-Stars, which had won the consolation honors a year earlier. Guards John Barnhill and Ron Hamilton each garnered 14 points for the Pipers.[15]

The Pipers were eventually eliminated from the tournament, falling before the Peoria Caterpillars by only two points, 84–82, when former Kansas State All-American Bob Boozer scored in the final seconds to give the Cats the victory. Cleveland had time for a couple of last-second shots, but they failed to connect, and the inaugural NIBL season ended for McLendon's team. After visiting the Peoria locker room to congratulate the victors, McLendon met with his team to tell them, "The next best thing to winning is playing a good game. You did tonight." Cox and Barnhill were chosen for the NIBL All-Star team, and Hamilton earned an honorable mention. The Caterpillars went on to win the tournament.[16]

After the season ended, however, Cox, who became a free agent when the team's ownership changed, signed on to play for the Akron Goodyear Wingfoots. Still, going into their second season, McLendon and general manager Mike Cleary bolstered their team's chances considerably with the addition of NIBL MVP Dan Swartz from Morehead State College; NIBL All-Star Roger Taylor from the University of Illinois; and Jack Adams from Eastern Kentucky University, who had earned an NIBL honorable mention. McLendon was confident that Swartz would provide the ingredient necessary for success. "I think we could have finished first instead of tying for fourth with Swartz last season," he said. "He's fast and rough—the type who is virtually impossible to stop from shooting without fouling. He's tough on defense, he can rebound, and he'll outscore his individual opponent every time." The Pipers would also have Ben Warley for the entire season. Warley had played in the last four games the previous year and was named to the All-AAU Tournament team after averaging 24 points and 18 rebounds over three games. Adding more height, speed, and depth, along with better scoring and improved defense, the Pipers became a solid championship threat. As the team prepared for its second season, veteran Cleveland sportswriter Jack Clowser urged fans to come out to cheer on the Pipers, writing that this was the best basketball team the city had ever seen.[17]

At the end of the 1959–60 season, Sweeny's financial problems caused him to sell the team for twenty-five thousand dollars to sixteen Cleveland-area businessmen, most of whom had been previously active in various civic and business ventures. The Pipers were a low-budget operation because player salaries, which averaged around four thousand dollars, would be paid in part by the team and in part by the owners' local companies. McLendon met briefly with the new owners in late March, but a contract was not immediately forthcoming. "We feel McLendon did an outstanding job with the material he had," said Marsh Samuel, speaking for the ownership group. "We hope to sit down and talk with him when he returns from Denver next week." One of the most outspoken members of the group was thirty-year-old George M. Steinbrenner III, the son of a wealthy Cleveland shipbuilder. He became president of what was now called the Cleveland Basketball Club, Inc., and Samuel was named vice president. This would be Steinbrenner's first venture into professional sports ownership, and his controversial actions would portend his future as owner of the New York Yankees.[18]

On April 6, 1960, McLendon received a letter from Sweeny's lawyer informing him that he was released from any obligations under his two-year contract and was free to look for another job. McLendon, however, left little doubt of his desire to stay on as coach of the Pipers. In an article by Chuck Heaton that ran in the *Cleveland Plain Dealer* on April 8, McLendon declared: "I would like to be able to develop the thing we started here last season. The project can mean a great deal to the city, and I would like to be in on it." He told Heaton of his plans for the upcoming season and related his confidence in the future of the team. "There is no doubt in my mind that we can build a solid club," stated McLendon, "one that will start the season out with a chance of winning the title."[19]

While these negotiations were taking place, McLendon was busy preparing a strategy for his team to take on University of Cincinnati All-

American Oscar Robertson and a group of college All-Stars in a highly publicized two-game set. The first game would be played April 9 in Robertson's hometown of Indianapolis, Indiana, with the second game scheduled to be played at the Cleveland Arena the following afternoon. Playing before 6,000 screaming fans in Butler Fieldhouse, Robertson netted 40 points as his college All-Stars pulled away in the second half to defeat the Pipers, 118–106. Hamilton led the Cleveland scoring with 26 points, while Barnhill and Cox chipped in with 21 and 17, respectively. Back home in Cleveland the following afternoon, the Pipers defeated Robertson and the All-Stars, 120–119, in front of 9,139 fans, by far the largest crowd of the season. Hamilton's basket with four seconds left provided the margin of victory. Robertson finished with 39 points for the Stars, and his final field goal had given the collegians a 1-point lead with eleven seconds left. But Hamilton dribbled half the length of the floor, faked beautifully, and connected with his left-handed hook shot for the victory. Hamilton clicked for 25 points for the winners, Cox contributed 20 points, and Jim McCoy and Gene Tormohlen both made 17-point efforts.

Although there seemed to be some question of whether Steinbrenner and his group of directors would rehire McLendon, Heaton announced in the *Cleveland Plain Dealer* on April 22 that "John McLendon was signed as coach of the Cleveland Pipers basketball team for next season, thus ending several weeks of uncertainty." "On his record, he has to be our choice," said Steinbrenner. "The Pipers won more games than any first-year team in the league's history. And in the National AAU playoffs, we won two before losing by only two points to the eventual champion, the Peoria Cats. Certainly, McLendon deserves most of the credit." According to the press, a heavy factor weighing in the decision to rehire McLendon was a description of the quiet, mild-mannered Kansas native found in a recent publication by Bud Browning, well-respected coach of the internationally known 1960 NIBL champions, the Phillips 66ers. McLendon, Browning said, was "without question, one of the finest sportsmen I've ever met anywhere. He is a talented coach and an outstanding gentleman."[20]

Heaton acknowledged his satisfaction with the decision to retain McLendon: "McLendon proved popular with players, coaches, fans, officials, and sports writers in his first season in the strong coast-to-coast amateur league. His players respected his basketball knowledge and officials were pleased with his quiet, gentlemanly conduct on the bench." In the official Pipers program for 1960–61, the team's directors proudly declared that "the aim of this group is to provide Cleveland with the finest basketball anywhere and, to that end, it has assembled one of the top ten teams in the world. In Johnny McLendon, the Pipers have one the nation's ablest coaches, a man who inspires the best efforts in his players and exemplifies the finest qualities of American sportsmanship."[21]

In the meantime, McLendon was preparing a speech that he would present on April 24 at the annual *Cleveland Call & Post* All-Scholastic Awards Dinner. The Pipers' coach used the occasion to speak about how sports had served as a powerful venue in bringing democracy to American society. "Along with the accepted value of athletics as a factor of tremendous educational and moral influence, we can seriously study athletics as a definitive social force in our lives," McLendon told the young athletes. He continued: "Give Government its reward for laws tempering social justice; respect Education for its program of training. Understand and be thankful for Religion and its precepts. Realize the inter-relationship between all these sociological agents, but still be aware that the greatest strides toward true brotherhood, national, international, and racial understanding have been made through the medium of athletic competition. It is here that action speaks." McLendon concluded his talk with a plea that the young men understand that their talent could have positive social consequences: "Competitive athletics have provided the great arena, the great stage for the objective demonstration of ability, where the judgment of a man strictly on his performance can be the basic reason for respect of the man."[22]

On May 6, the Lake Erie Association of the AAU issued a proclamation congratulating the group of worthy sports-minded Cleveland businessmen for keeping the Pipers in their city. Around the same time, McLendon received a poem entitled "Cheer for a Coach," sent by fan Berea Breezer:

The Cleveland cage fans can depend on

That brilliant mentor, John McLendon,

To keep the Pipers piping-hot

And always round the highest spot.[23]

The Pipers versus the U.S. Olympic Team

On August 6, 1960, in an exhibition game in Canton, Ohio, before a sell-out crowd of forty-seven hundred fans, McLendon's Pipers upset the powerful 1960 Olympic squad in overtime, 101–96. The game marked the only defeat a U.S. Olympic team has ever suffered at the hands of an American amateur club. Perhaps the greatest amateur team ever assembled, the 1960 Olympic team included future NBA stars Jerry West, Oscar Robertson, Jerry Lucas, Walt Bellamy, and Terry Dischinger.

Early on, the Olympians zipped to an easy 11–4 lead, and it appeared that the Pipers were no match for them. But the Pipers came back and trailed only 41–38 at halftime. During the second half, the teams traded baskets, and Adrian Smith of the Olympic team canned a free throw in the final seconds of regulation play to tie the score at 88, sending it into overtime. During the overtime period, the Olympians showed their lack of conditioning, missing their first seven shots; they could not stop Cleveland's Dan Swartz, who scored 8 overtime points to lead to the upset victory. Warley took game scoring honors, with 26 points. Swartz and Barnhill added 19 points each. West Virginia University ace Lloyd Sharrar netted 12 points for the Pipers, and Jack Adams contributed 10. On the Olympic side, Robertson led with 20 points, and West added 17. Making the Pipers' victory even more remarkable was the fact that their tallest player, Gene Tormohlen, was on the bench with a severely injured leg. As the final buzzer sounded, all the Pipers raced onto the floor to celebrate their victory.

McLendon's team had used the fast break to score and to break down their highly praised opponents to the point at which they would be physically unable to cope with the Pipers' style of play. Although the Olympic team included players with superior talent, the Pipers, inspired by their coach and his unique mission, effectively used the one advantage they enjoyed, putting the fast break into high gear and adding another of McLendon's strategic maneuvers, the "four-second rule." This rule required every member of the team to clear the backcourt and be on his way to the goal or his position in the set offense within four seconds, every time the Pipers got possession of the ball. The continued pace was too much for the Olympians, who eventually succumbed, 101–96.

In a press conference following the game, McLendon agreed with

Olympic coach Pete Newell that speed and conditioning had made the difference. "We had much more time to practice for this game. We also are better organized," he graciously told the press. "But I am very happy to win. It sure means a lot to me." The Pipers' Jack Adams was particularly pleased with the victory, since he had been chosen as an alternate player for the U.S. team and felt he deserved to make the squad. After the triumph, McLendon carried film of the game with him because fellow coaches could not believe that his team had won. Newspaper accounts of the game usually appeared in small type on the back page so the public did not lose confidence in their Olympic team.[24]

Four days later, the teams clashed again in Morgantown, West Virginia, the college hometown of Jerry West. Revenge was clearly on the Olympians' minds. "We'll be set to take 'em this time," an Olympic official declared. "We weren't ready for the first game." The Olympians, clearly embarrassed by their earlier defeat, took control of the game after the early minutes, finishing with a solid 91–69 victory over the Pipers before a spirited crowd of more than sixty-five hundred. Robertson led both teams in scoring with 26 points, but it was Walt Bellamy, the six-eleven center from Indiana University, who, according to McLendon, made the difference. He finished with 18 points, while West netted 12 for the victors on his return to his home court, excelling at both defense and ball handling. Swartz led the Pipers' scoring with 14 points, with Adams and Warley contributing 13 and 12 points, respectively.[25]

Marion E. Jackson editorialized about the game in the *Atlanta Daily World:* "The untold 'Big Story of 1960 Sports' was written but went unnoticed in the fusillade of pre-Olympic furore. Now that the controversy, heartbreak and triumph of the XVII Olympiad are gone, the Number 1 success story of a Negro, who is walking pretty near alone in the coaching side of professional sports, should be given an airing." Jackson went on to assert that this slight might reveal the racism still inherent in American society:

> The man in-the-news who deserves loads and loads of accolades —Kansas born John B. McLendon—celebrated coach of the Cleveland Pipers. He is the only coach in history to ever defeat a United States Olympic team. The Cleveland Pipers defeated the U.S. Olympians, 101–96, but in the fanfare, tumult, and shouting prior to the departure of the Stars and Stripes team for Rome,

everyone overlooked the fact. . . . So monumental and towering is the masterpiece which McLendon wrote into the record books that it is a Mt. Everest of the game. It is the most impressive memorial erected by a team since Dr. James Naismith invented the sport. Almost equally remarkable is the fact that despite the unprecedented defeat of the U.S. Olympians, it was buried for the most part in the obscure sections of the nation's sports pages. Was it because J. B. McLendon is a Negro?[26]

NIBL and AAU Champs

Going into his second NIBL season, McLendon could hardly contain his optimism. On November 23, 1960, he told a Cleveland Cage Club audience: "Our team is much better than last year. It has good depth and has more offensive power, plus better defensive ability. I believe we have the team to do the job. We lost more last season than I ever did before. I think I have the team here to get me back on my feet." A few days later, he received the news that the Pipers had sold more than four hundred season tickets. He also received a poem written by several fans, which further bolstered his spirits:

> To the Basketball Coach on this day,
> His day that starts the season on its way.
> A bit of fanfare for his boys
> A great big crowd with lots of noise.
>
> Good luck, Old Boy—
> Good luck, and more—
> We hope that to the heights you soar—
> A Champion Team—the Pipers roar![27]

The Pipers opened the season with a convincing victory over the Phillips 66ers, 124–96, in front of 4,013 enthusiastic fans at the Cleveland Arena. Ben Warley stole the show for the Pipers, collecting 28 rebounds while netting 16 points. Cleary and McLendon's new player acquisitions were already paying off, as Taylor paced the Pipers' scoring with 25 points, while Swartz contributed 21, Barnhill 19, and Adams 18. All five starters ended up scoring in double figures, including Hamilton, with

11 points, while the Pipers shot 50 percent from the field. The Pipers' season continued at a record pace, the team winning eleven out of their first twelve games, surprising even their coach. McLendon offered several explanations for their remarkable showing beyond mere physical talent. "We've a minimum of rookies compared to other squads," he stated. "And the seasoned players are all strong competitors, fellows who don't like to lose. They're mainly players who 'carried' other teams by themselves before coming here. Now they're together, tough-minded and united in team pride on the idea of winning." He added, "They don't crack often in tough games, the games you have to win to be a champ." Jack Clowser of the *Cleveland Press* was so impressed with McLendon's team that he declared that the Pipers were close to professional basketball's best, revealing that both the National Basketball Association and the American Basketball League were wooing them.[28]

McLendon's Pipers compiled the league's best record, 24–10, and captured the league title, defeating the highly favored Denver Truckers, 136–100. McLendon expressed great pride in pointing out that this was a tremendous team effort by the Pipers, as all five starters had scored 20 points or more for the second time that season. Adams led the way with 28 points, while Barnhill scored 24, Taylor 22, Swartz 21, and Warley 20. For the season, McLendon's running game produced four of the league's top scorers, Swartz leading with an average of more than 24 points per game, Adams finishing second with 22.3, and Barnhill setting the record for guards with 21.2. Ben Warley, named Rookie of the Year, was second to Dick Brott in rebounding (with 523) and garnered a scoring average of 20.3. For his stellar play, Swartz was named league MVP for the second straight year, and Warley, Adams, and Taylor joined him on the NIBL's All-League team.

The second-seeded Pipers then went on to win the weeklong AAU national tournament in Denver, where twenty-eight teams competed for the title. On their way to the championship game, the Pipers defeated Los Angeles's Kirby Shoes, 92–81, and Seattle's Kirk's Pharmacy, 120–90, and won a thrilling overtime victory over New York's Tuck Tapers, 97–94. McLendon's Pipers capped their memorable season by beating the hometown Denver Truckers 107–96 in the championship game before 10,500 partisan fans at the Coliseum. Adams scored a game-high 28 points, Barnhill chipped in with 21, and Lloyd Sharrar, filling in for the injured Warley, scored 16 points and picked off 23 rebounds, the best of any player on the court. Adams was voted the AAU tournament's Most Valuable Player. McLendon's cagers were the class of the tournament, and AAU All-American honors were justifiably granted to Warley, Swartz, Adams, and Taylor. McLendon was elated with these victories and lavished praise upon his players. "The fellows were just marvelous in their attitude. They never forgot the objective of winning the championship," McLendon stated in an interview with Chuck Heaton of the *Cleveland Plain Dealer*. "They set a fine example of self-discipline. I can't praise them enough. I certainly am proud of their play and their attitude."[29]

Ironically, the Pipers had had to overcome the shortsightedness of their Cleveland directors before they could compete in the finals. According to Cleary, after McLendon's cagers defeated their first three tournament opponents, the coach received a call from Steinbrenner informing him that his expense account had been cut off and he should bring the team home. Feeling strongly that his team had earned the right to compete for the championship, McLendon struggled to find the resources to keep his players in the competition. Fortunately, a Denver banker came up with the $720 needed to keep the Pipers housed and fed for another few days. Perhaps this made the team even hungrier for victory, as they brought the championship trophy back to Cleveland, McLendon and the Pipers smiling all the way.[30]

The only blight on the Pipers' impressive season came months later when the *AAU Bulletin* came out. The back cover always showed a photo of the previous year's championship team, but mysteriously, the Pipers' photo was nowhere to be found. McLendon later reasoned that some small-minded individual had made the decision not to include his team's photo. "This certainly did not represent the attitude of the AAU," he recalled, "as I was appointed to its executive committee and to serve as its representative on the Olympic Committee from 1968–1976."[31]

Coach of the U.S. All-Stars in Russia

While McLendon and his team were celebrating their 1961 championship, the AAU and the U.S. State Department invited them to play a three-week series of exhibition games in the Soviet Union, including four games against the Russian National, or Olympic, number-one and -two teams. McLendon, loyal to the Pipers, wanted to take the entire squad. However, George Steinbrenner wasn't satisfied with the present players. He wanted a team with stars and therefore composed a squad made up of the Pipers' starting five and seven NIBL, AAU, and college All-Stars. Coach McLendon chose Adams, Barnhill, Swartz, Taylor, and Warley to represent the United States from the Pipers; Johnny Cox and Jim Francis from the Akron Goodyears, Jerry Shipp and Gary Thompson from the Phillips 66ers, Mike Moran from the Denver Truckers, and Paul Neumann from the New York Tapers were also chosen for the U.S. team. Steinbrenner specifically chose Ohio State All-American center Jerry Lucas to be the headliner for the squad.

McLendon began his legendary two-a-day practices on April 9 at Baldwin-Wallace College in Ohio. With more than a hint of nationalistic bravado, Lucas was quoted in the *New York Times* on April 17, declaring: "This is a good team, if not better than our last Olympic team, which won the Gold in Rome. The Russians may have put a man in orbit first, but I think we might be able to show them a thing or two." Coach McLendon echoed the young star's sentiments: "We've studied films of the Russian national team, and I feel we're ready for any type of defense. Jerry has played against the Russians, and that will be a help to us." He noted: "We may play it by ear for a while. We've approached this so that we'll be ready for anything. And we're going to force them to do it our way. Furthermore, we're going to play the running game."[32]

An editorial in the *Cleveland Press* by Jack Clowser reasoned that McLendon was the perfect coach to lead the Russian tour: "The Pipers coach typifies everything we hope to exhibit in international athletics. This fine man has done honor to Cleveland by his mere presence here the last two years. His magnificent sense of sportsmanship will make an indelible impression on the Russian people. Furthermore," he pointed out, "there is an added and important factor that McLendon is a Negro. That gives our side an extra propaganda weapon. The Kremlin has long pointed to America's disgraceful segregation habits as proof of its contention that we hold the color of a man's skin to be more important than his character."[33]

McLendon certainly understood that the formula for picking the coach of the team representing the United States was a sensitive one, and he felt immense satisfaction that the AAU had confidence in his ability to represent his country and the sponsoring organization. "The fact is democracy and my presence is democracy in action," he proudly wrote for the *Atlanta Daily World*. "The goal toward which all decent men struggle is simply to make the phenomenon possible and operative everywhere in America in any area of human relationships."[34]

The challenge of molding a team out of a group of individual All-Stars was considerable. An hour before leaving New York for the Russian tour, McLendon wrote to Marion Jackson of the *Atlanta Daily World*: "Here we are a real team, not too strong, not too weak, just a good solid club with tremendous desire and high morale following my cue of conservative approach to what we know is a formidable opponent." He had watched numerous game films of the Russians, observing that they were tireless, rugged, and much bigger than his own team. Understanding that speed and pressure defense would be the key to success, McLendon planned his game-winning strategy accordingly.[35]

McLendon also understood that representing America abroad, especially in the Soviet Union, carried enormous symbolic as well as real responsibilities. "Our shortcomings notwithstanding," he wrote, "my boys and I will do our best to be honorable in our efforts and proud of our endeavors regardless of winning or losing. My team always gives its best."[36]

Shortly before McLendon and his team were scheduled to leave New York, heightened Cold War tensions between the United States and the Soviet Union delayed their trip for a few days. The ill-fated Bay of Pigs invasion of Cuba had just taken place, and anti-American demonstrations in Moscow were among the most violent in recent years. Feeling the strain of geopolitics, the U.S. team and its coach left on April 20 via Helsinki, Stockholm, and Copenhagen, arriving in Moscow a few days later.

In their first game against the Russian national team, before fifteen thousand zealous fans, McLendon's players were tense and nervous, and their play was erratic. The coach had decided to start Lucas at center, Adams and Warley as forwards, and Taylor and Thompson as guards. The Russians set a fast pace, building a 13–5 lead, but the U.S. team forged to the front, 24–23, at the fifteen-minute mark and never looked back. The offensive play of Swartz, who scored 17 points, Thompson's defense, Taylor's outside shooting, and Lucas's rebounding (with 21) were enough to defeat the Russians, 78–68. In an article rushed back to the United States by C. Stanley Brown of the American Embassy in Moscow, McLendon wrote: "It was another team triumph

Coach McLendon and his U.S. All-Star team, 1961. Ohio State All-American Jerry Lucas is standing in the back row, third from the right. (Courtesy Joanna McLendon)

with the players carrying out their assignments with tremendous spirit. Barnhill, Warley, and Lucas excelled with floorwork, bullet passing and clutch rebounding respectively." Russian cosmonaut Yuri Gagarin, the first human to conquer space just a few weeks earlier, was among the throng that witnessed the first game. When he entered the arena, he received a tumultuous standing ovation and sat in the box reserved for Soviet premier Nikita Khrushchev and other high government officials. After the game, Gagarin congratulated the American team and its coach. Clifford Buck, vice president of the AAU, who watched the game, remarked afterward: "The Russians, both men and women, play as if their life depends on it. Ours go out to win, but for them it's not a matter of life or death."[37]

The second game was a tense overtime match played before sixteen thousand shouting, jeering, whistling spectators. The United States had a 39–32 lead at halftime, but the Soviets came back in the second half to tie the score at 77. A shot by the Pipers' Warley missed the basket seconds before the end of regulation time. Warley came back to put the Americans ahead in overtime with a field goal, but the Russians tied the game again at 79. The Pipers' Swartz converted a free throw, then followed with a field goal. The Russians had crept within a point, with only a minute and a half remaining, when Lucas connected from the floor with the clincher. Lucas was high scorer for the game with 20 points, while Swartz netted 15, Taylor 13, and Warley and Barnhill 11 and 10, respectively.

According to McLendon, "in the USSR our team found the fast break to be our saving possession. The circumstances called for our overcoming a skilled and strongly-conditioned aggregation—a difficult combination to defeat. The challenge to the player is a resounding one; in such a situation physical readiness becomes as important as skill. When you cannot stop a team from scoring, you may allow your defense to become secondary or of slight consideration." The situation against the Russians called for some creative strategy, McLendon abandoning all but a semblance of defense and playing a wide-open game in an effort to outscore his opponents. "Strongly-conditioned, determined players operating under such strategy may still give you a chance to get into the victory column," McLendon declared, looking back on this historic international experience.[38]

McLendon's cagers went on to play in Tbilisi, Georgia, and Kiev, successfully completing their eight-game tour by defeating the Leningrad team, 87–65. The U.S. coach and his team were elated, for they had emerged victorious in each of the eight contests. On the return flight, the Pipers stopped in Stockholm to play the Swedish national team. According to Adams, when McLendon observed the caliber of the opposing team, he decided to give them some of his players so that they would not be embarrassed. "That was typical of McLendon," Adams recalled. "He had a knack for handling situations that pleased everybody." McLendon's experience leading this integrated team had been an unqualified success. It marked the first time an African American coach had ever competed internationally, leading a U.S. All-Star team. "Our State Department was elated over our tour," remembered McLendon. This paved the way for future trips all around the world and for McLendon's later extensive involvement in international and Olympic basketball.[39]

McLendon also believed the trip had been effective as a mission to promote better understanding. "All of us learned things and left with a warm feeling for the hospitality of the Russian people," he declared in an interview with Chuck Heaton of the *Cleveland Plain Dealer.* "I believe those we met feel the same about us." There was no doubt that the Russian people were impressed by the affable American coach, who conducted youth clinics between games. One Soviet sportswriter wrote, "He is the hospitality of good breeding and of a well bred man." The only difficulty McLendon and his team encountered with their Russian hosts was their overabundance of hospitality. "The Russians were so hospitable that you could hardly believe it," McLendon said. "Finally we had to restrict the touring so our players would not be too tired for the games." The banquets held in their honor, where four vodka toasts were the minimum, were a particular problem for McLendon, a teetotaler. He finally got around this by substituting cream soda, with the aid of an understanding Soviet official.[40]

McLendon told the Cleveland press that the Russians had treated him as if he were an expert on the game of basketball, taking full advantage of the almost daily clinics he ran during his three-week stay. "I found they were putting too much emphasis on scoring, giving prizes for the top scorers," said McLendon. "I told them they should put more emphasis on other parts of the game—rebounds, passes, and blocks." They liked his ideas and went to work on them immediately. "If we defeat you in the near future," they told McLendon, "you'll be responsible." Although his team finished the Soviet tour undefeated, McLendon, who from this point on became a highly influential figure in the AAU, had witnessed the strides other countries were making in basketball. He thus urged the sport's U.S. officials to take the foreign challenge more seriously. In an article in the *Cleveland Plain Dealer,* McLendon declared that he saw the Soviet cagers as a real threat to U.S. basketball supremacy in the 1964 Olympics.[41]

Upon the team's return to the United States, Cleveland mayor Anthony J. Celebrezze presented a "proclamation" to Coach McLendon designating May 12, 1961, "Cleveland Pipers Day." In 1962, McLendon received an even greater accolade as he was enshrined in the Helms Foundation Hall of Fame, later referred to as the NAIA Hall of Fame. He was the second African American coach to receive this honor, the first being Edward Adams from Texas Southern University, who was inducted in 1959.

The First African American Professional Basketball Coach: The ABL

In 1961, with the NIBL slipping in interest and attendance, Pipers president George Steinbrenner immediately had the team join the new American Basketball League (ABL), which had been founded by Harlem Globetrotters owner Abe Sapperstein. Franchises were granted to eight cities: Chicago, Washington, Pittsburgh, Cleveland, Kansas City, Los Angeles, San Francisco, and Honolulu. Sapperstein himself assumed ownership of the Chicago ABL team, and the other club owners prevailed upon him to also serve, without salary, as commissioner of the fledgling circuit.

To make the league attractive to fans, Sapperstein inaugurated a few innovations. He invented the 3-point field goal, enlarged the free-throw "key" to Olympic size, and promised the ever-popular Globetrotters as prelims from Washington, D.C., to Honolulu. With the utmost bravado, Steinbrenner promised the Cleveland fans "the most exciting basketball team you have ever seen. We are the smallest team in the league, but also the fastest . . . and the brand of basketball played by the Pipers is thrilling and spectacular." Revealing his intensely competitive character, Steinbrenner declared "perfection" the "paramount goal" of the Pipers organization, in the hopes of bringing Cleveland a professional championship. "If we should fail," he wrote, "we shall all feel that, in a sense, we have failed our loyal fans." Although Steinbrenner would have preferred a big-name coach, McLendon enjoyed the loyal support of his team and the Cleveland fans. When the Pipers' board of directors voted on who should coach the team, the vote was sixteen to one in favor of McLendon. According to several board members, Steinbrenner cast the only vote against the popular forty-five-year-old African American coach.[42]

McLendon was not yet hired for the position, for Steinbrenner maintained that he needed the coach to live in Cleveland, near the players, year-round, and he felt that McLendon spent too much time traveling during the summer, conducting clinics all over the country. Even before this stipulation became public, however, McLendon had accepted a job with Cleveland Parks and Recreation, agreeing to conduct clinics teaching basketball fundamentals for youth all over the city. Delighted with the response of the youngsters, he even got some of the Pipers to help him in the evening clinics for older youths. As a result, Steinbrenner reluctantly continued with McLendon as the Pipers' coach, and the team's directors presented him with a new Buick and a "substantial raise." His salary as a professional coach would be over fifteen thousand dollars, and to his surprise, the contract Steinbrenner offered him was for two years. "I feel good about the confidence placed in me," he said. "Actually, I didn't ask for a two-year contract. I feel that my only security is in doing a good job. There would be no question of staying once I ceased to be useful. That's why I have no concern for long term contracts." McLendon eagerly signed on to coach the Pipers in the ABL, and thus, on May 15, 1961, he broke through yet another social barrier, becoming the first black coach of an integrated professional team. Five years would pass before the NBA hired its first black coach, Bill Russell, to replace the legendary Red Auerbach of the Boston Celtics.[43]

Attempting to soften criticism from fans and the press, Steinbrenner said that the delay in signing McLendon had been caused by his trip to Russia as coach of the U.S. team. "There was no lack of confidence in John at any time," Steinbrenner told Chuck Heaton of the *Cleveland Plain Dealer*. "We simply had to wait until he returned in fear that he might be deprived of making the trip if he signed to coach a pro team. I am convinced that no other coach could take the team to Russia and win all eight games. It was a remarkable job," said Steinbrenner. The following day, he was quoted in the paper praising McLendon: "I would rather have John with us than any other coach I can think of. We had a great many applicants but never considered anyone else. To me, his ability to win friends with his gentlemanly manner as well as to win titles on the court makes John unique in his field."[44]

ABL commissioner and former coach Abe Sapperstein was noticeably pleased to have McLendon in the fold, understanding the historic sociological implications. "Cleveland fans are sure to have an outstanding team with McLendon coaching their entry," he wrote. "His appointment also proves that there are no limitations in our league with respect to how far he can go if he has the ability. There is a great future for everyone in the ABL, and McLendon's appointment proves it. He is the first Negro to coach a major league sports group, and we are delighted to have him with us."[45]

McLendon's team had a different look entering the ABL. General

McLendon coaching children in the Cleveland Parks and Recreation Program, 1961. (Courtesy Joanna McLendon)

manager Mike Cleary had pulled off a major coup, luring McLendon's former college star Dick Barnett from the NBA's Syracuse Nationals. Cleary had promised the high-profile shooting guard that if he came to Cleveland, McLendon would design an offense around him. His promise became a reality when Barnett ended the season second in the league, with a 26.2 average, behind league MVP Connie Hawkins.[46]

Unfortunately, the announcement of Barnett's signing cost Cleary his job and would become a source of bitterness between Steinbrenner and the *Cleveland Press*. Luring Barnett from the NBA to play for the Pipers would, Steinbrenner knew, be a national story, and he wanted desperately to capitalize on it. In an interview with well-known sports author Peter Golenbock, Cleary recalled that the Pipers' owner thus made a deal with the *Cleveland Press*: he would give it an exclusive if the paper agreed to run the story on its front page. Steinbrenner struck this deal without telling Cleary, who sent out a press announcement, along with a warning that the information was not to be revealed until

6 A.M. the next morning. A radio sportscaster, however, got hold of the story and aired it on his late-night news show. The news spread quickly, and the *Cleveland Plain Dealer* picked it up early enough that it ran the story at the same time as the *Press*. Without an exclusive, the *Press* removed the story from its front page. When Steinbrenner saw the papers that morning, he was livid. He fired Cleary, who became general manager of the Kansas City Steers and, with former Pipers center Gene Tormohlen playing a key role, later defeated the Pipers to win the first-half league championship. Steinbrenner also told his players, coaches, and business partners that he wanted each of them to cancel his own subscription to the *Press* and to call fifteen friends and ask that they do the same.[47]

Although Barnett's signing had unforeseen repercussions, it did prove to be a very astute strategic move, just as McLendon and Cleary had predicted. With Barnett, John Barnhill, Ben Warley, Jack Adams, Roger Taylor, and Johnny Cox, who had returned to the Pipers from the Akron Goodyears, leading the way, the Pipers were one of the ABL's best teams in the first half of the 1961–62 season. McLendon's squad captured the Eastern Division championship with a 24–18 record before losing the midseason playoffs by only one game to Western Division champions the Kansas City Steers, led by Bill Bridges.

Steinbrenner, however, was not satisfied with McLendon's coaching decisions and constantly interfered with the team's roster. Indeed, he undercut McLendon's authority from the day the season commenced. After the Pipers lost their inaugural professional game in the ABL to the Pittsburgh Rens, 87–82, the new Pipers general manager, Ben Flieger, approached McLendon while they were checking into a hotel. "Word has come from upstairs for the players to be in bed by midnight," McLendon was told. "Well, you go right back upstairs and say I'll tell these players when I want them to report in," McLendon shot back. The coach then turned to his players. "I told you what time I want you in the hotel," he said. "You are to follow my orders. What I say goes."[48]

In an interview with Ira Berkow in the *New York Times*, McLendon stated that he and Steinbrenner were never bitter toward one another: "Steinbrenner was a fierce competitor, extremely ambitious about winning, though he might have been a little out of control. He didn't have losing on his mind at any time." According to McLendon, however, Steinbrenner's uncontrolled, erratic behavior on and off the court, and his attack on McLendon and his team in the papers, did hurt the performance of several players.[49]

Jack Clowser wrote in the *Cleveland Press* that the "Boss" did not appreciate McLendon's quiet, controlled personality or his philosophy about not criticizing game officials. Steinbrenner became so frustrated with an official's call against the Pipers one night that he yelled at his coach, "You've GOT to get off that bench!" Steinbrenner was also so obsessed with the low attendance at Pipers games that he went out and signed "name" players, unfortunately upsetting McLendon's carefully crafted system. Two of the players Steinbrenner signed were Bill Spivey, the former Kentucky All-American, and Bevo Francis, a one-time college basketball superstar who had once scored 113 points for Rio Grande College. Unfortunately, neither player was in good enough shape to run McLendon's legendary fast break, so the coach kept them mainly on the bench, causing Steinbrenner to bristle. Steinbrenner also took offense that McLendon was not playing Ohio State All-American guard Larry Siegfried as much as the owner wanted. Siegfried was the only college player of note to sign with the ABL, and Steinbrenner wanted McLendon to showcase him in the hopes of bringing more college stars to the league, especially his Cleveland franchise. The coach, however, was concerned about Siegfried's ability to run his patented fast-break offense. According to McLendon, Siegfried thought he was in great shape when he arrived in Cleveland but discovered there might be an ability gap between the Big Ten Conference and the ABL.[50]

Loyalty to his players was also a matter of contention between the owner and the coach. "One time he took one of my players and sold him at halftime to the team we were playing," McLendon told Thomas. That player, Grady McCollum from Western Illinois University, was coveted by Red Rocha, who coached the Honolulu team. "Red wanted Grady on his team and Steinbrenner decided it was time to make a little cash," McLendon said. The Pipers' owner told McCollum that he needed to suit up for the opposition immediately so he could play the second half for Hawaii. According to McLendon, this action left all the players hurt and embarrassed. Upon hearing the news from Steinbrenner, McCollum returned in tears. "I told him he didn't have to play against his teammates," recalled McLendon. As for Steinbrenner, McLendon declared, "We'll take him to court," but, realizing that the owner could do what he wanted, never did.[51]

A column by Jack Clowser in the *Cleveland Press*, entitled "Trouble at Top Endangering Pipers," praised McLendon and the players for their hustle, desire, and drive and at the same time launched a scathing indictment of Steinbrenner's actions. Clowser described how Steinbrenner had charged into the Pipers' dressing room after they blew a 10-point lead to the Chicago Majors and lost the game by a point. "John," he reportedly said, "I don't want to tell you how to run your team, but . . ." Clowser then described how Steinbrenner had railed about the lack of team effort, blasting some of the players by name, even charging that some of them were more interested in going out on dates than in playing basketball. Accusing Steinbrenner of undermining Coach McLendon and hurting team morale, Clowser praised the coach for keeping the team together despite a rash of injuries—to Ben Warley, who was leading the league in rebounds and pacing the Pipers in scoring; to hot-shooting guard John Barnhill; and to Larry Siegfried, who was just coming into his own as a pro standout. The *Press* reporter also praised the healthy players for working hard to take up the slack. "For this," declared Clowser, "they should be receiving front-office plaudits instead of criticism." He concluded by warning that "the current Pipers, now beginning to enjoy an upsurge in attendance their brand of basketball merits, will continue as championship contenders ONLY IF their morale isn't dampened by the misguided actions of the club's president." The players stood by McLendon steadfastly while Steinbrenner tried to undercut the coach and induce him to quit.[52]

One time, McLendon told Golenbock, the Pipers drove from Cleveland to Pittsburgh in two station wagons. On the way, McLendon's vehicle had a blowout. The coach instructed his captain, Jack Adams, to take the starters in the other car and go ahead, saying that he would be there as soon as he could. McLendon and the remaining players fixed the tire and arrived at the game about ten minutes before halftime. The Pipers were leading by 14 points when Adams called timeout. McLendon, obviously pleased with his players' performance, simply told them: "I don't have anything to say. Whatever you're doing, keep on doing it." A few minutes before halftime, the Pipers again called timeout, and again McLendon allowed his captain to take the lead, observing as Adams diagrammed one of their patented plays. In the locker room, with the Pipers still way ahead, McLendon was talking to his players when Steinbrenner suddenly opened the door and entered. He began shouting at McLendon, "Who am I paying to coach this team, you or Adams?" McLendon, ordinarily a mild-mannered gentleman, admitted to both Ira Berkow and Peter Golenbock that this was one time he had great difficulty controlling his anger. He told Steinbrenner: "I don't allow anybody on my bench and in my dressing room. You'll have to leave. And I don't allow anyone to talk to me like that in front of my players. Besides that," he continued, "what do you care who's coaching the team as long as we come out of here with a victory?"[53]

On January 10, 1962, the 24–18 Pipers won the ABL's Eastern Division first-half title by defeating the Kansas City Steers, 115–110, in overtime. The game took place as part of a doubleheader in famed Chicago Stadium, where McLendon had longed to play for years without an opportunity. The score was tied at 106 at the end of regulation play. After the Steers' George Pruitt scored a field goal, giving his team the lead, the Pipers connected for three straight baskets by Cox, Warley, and Barnett, sealing the hard-fought victory. Taylor led the Pipers' scoring with 30 points, while Cox and Barnett contributed 20 and 19 points, respectively.

The Pipers' victory set them against Jack McMahon's Western Division champion Steers in a best-of-three play-off the following weekend. As McLendon prepared his team for the play-off games, the pressure the Pipers felt to win from the emotional team owner became even more intense. Cleveland, with its 4–2 edge over the Steers in regular-season play and the home-court advantage for two games, was rated the favorite. Fritz Kreisler, writing in the *Kansas City Star,* remarked: "Of all the basketball qualities, the raw scoring ability of Cleveland is unquestionable. Because of their speed and depth, the Pipers are capable of merely blasting an opponent into submission." Barnett, unable to join the team until mid-December due to a temporary injunction issued in favor of the NBA's Syracuse Nationals, had the best scoring average (22.3) going into the play-offs, but five other Pipers (Adams with 17.8, Taylor with 16.9, Cox with 16.8, Warley with 15.2, and Barnhill with 14.0) were also averaging in double figures. Yet another (Siegfried with 9.6) was just below.[54]

The play-off commenced on January 12 with a stirring Kansas City victory over Cleveland, 106–93, before a Municipal Auditorium crowd of 5,286. According to Kreisler, "It was a ball game of sharp offensive maneuvers and fierce, rugged play under the boards." It became so fierce that a fight between Maurice King of the Steers and the Pipers' Johnny Cox erupted midway through the third quarter, resulting in both players being ejected from the game. The Pipers had a difficult time stopping Larry Staverman of the Steers, who led the scoring with 25 points. Adams led McLendon's Pipers with 23 points, followed by Siegfried with 18. It was the Steers' King, however, who, according to the *Star,* "applied the handcuffs to Dick Barnett, the Pipers' lead pony in their fast-break." "That as much as anything else hurt us," McLendon commented later as he stood outside his dressing room. "We made other mistakes, like going to the outside instead of getting the good shot, but he [King] hurt us the most. In this league you're supposed to match baskets. We didn't [45–32] so we lose."[55]

Back home in Cleveland the following evening, before 4,276 fans at Public Arena, the tables were turned when McLendon's Pipers used a balanced scoring attack to defeat the Steers, 98–87, evening out the series at one game apiece. Using their patented shock treatment, the Pipers outplayed the Steers in virtually every phase of the game. McLendon employed a creative defensive strategy, inserting Archie Dees and Nick Romanoff into the starting lineup to contain the Steers' two big men, Bridges and Staverman. Entering the game after intermission, late in the third period, with only a 59–53 Pipers advantage, the two McLendon mainstays from Tennessee A&I, Barnett and Barnhill, sparked a surge that carried the Pipers to a 69–53 lead, then, early in the fourth quarter, reeled off 16 consecutive points to seal the victory. The Steers' Bridges was the game's high scorer, with 22, while Taylor, Warley, Adams, Barnett, and Barnhill all scored in double figures for the Pipers. McLendon's squad hit on thirty-six of seventy-nine tries from the floor and was equally effective from the foul line, missing on only three out of twenty-five shots. Of concern to McLendon, however, was the Steers' rebounding advantage, as Kansas City had collared 56 rebounds to Cleveland's 35. The coach knew that his team would have to improve in this category if they were to defeat their opponents in the rubber game the following day.[56]

On Sunday afternoon, January 14, in front of a disappointing crowd of 2,313 at Cleveland's Public Hall, a torrid 53 percent shooting performance by Kansas City proved decisive as the Steers defeated the Pipers to win the first-half ABL championship, 120–104. The Pipers' horrible 26 percent shooting average in the first half resulted in a 56–45 deficit.

McLendon's squad picked up the pace in the second half, and their scoring percentage improved dramatically, but their opponents were equal to the occasion. The action became so furious that at one point the teams traded baskets (or free throws) twenty-four consecutive times, spilling over into the fourth period, when the Pipers started their move. Trailing 96–78, Adams, Siegfried, and Barnett scored 13 points within three minutes, while the Steers countered with just 2. After quick baskets by Siegfried and Taylor for the Pipers, the Steers' Bridges responded with 4 tallies to put the decision out of reach. The Pipers' Adams took game high-scoring honors with 30 points, while Siegfried tallied 26 and Barnett 16. Nick Mantis, playing the best game of his career, led the Steers with 25 points, while Staverman and Bridges netted 24 and 22, respectively.

The new champions outshot the Pipers by sixteen baskets. Cleveland was able to keep the game close until the final minutes only by hitting on thirty-eight out of forty-one free throws. "We were off our shooting and made some defensive mistakes," said McLendon. "Kansas City has a good team and they were hot today. We've beaten them six times in ten games, but they were the better team this afternoon." The Pipers' coach was upset with the loss, but he was confident his team would rebound in the league's second half season.[57]

After this final game in front of the sparse Cleveland faithful, Steinbrenner stormed into the Pipers' locker room and angrily announced that "heads would roll." Embarrassed by the disappointing loss, Steinbrenner refused to pay his players—not only their share of the playoff money but their regular salary. When the players went to the Pipers' office to get their paychecks, they were turned away without any explanation. "Guys played their hearts out, and when we got home they didn't get paid," McLendon told Golenbock. "Here was a bad sports attitude. The guys couldn't take it. And here we had another half-season to go. And when he wouldn't pay the players, I resigned to bring it to the attention of the public, 'cause all these guys had families, kids, they were up against it, and they needed the money. I figured they'd get paid if I told everybody."[58]

The players complained to the Cleveland papers, and a story by Bob Sudyk appeared in the *Cleveland Press* on January 16, stating that the Pipers were resentful over not having been paid on time the previous day. Furthermore, certain players were quoted as saying that the team would not play in Pittsburgh the following night unless they were paid. "They talk, talk, talk about wanting a winning team and then pull a stunt like this," said one of the players, indicating the low level of morale. "We were to get a bonus and a suit of clothes for winning our division title. Now we're wondering if we'll get anything," he added. Angered by the players' charges, Steinbrenner told Sudyk: "The boys will be paid tomorrow. Their deposit slips were not put into the bank yesterday and if they don't like it, well that's just too bad. I'm getting sick of all this turmoil. We have the highest paid players in the league, they have no gripes coming. The way I feel now, I'd just as soon pay off the whole bunch and call it quits." The story also indicated that Coach McLendon was solidly on the side of the players and was considering resigning. After Steinbrenner read the story, he called a meeting of the players and demanded they sign a retraction. Otherwise, he would fold the team and not pay anyone.[59]

According to a 1995 article by Wayne Coffey in the *New York Daily News,* an enraged Steinbrenner, after reading the article, said to Sudyk: "That's a pack of lies. I'll have your job for this. You won't be able to get a job anywhere in the country after I'm done." According to Sudyk, Steinbrenner met with his editor and demanded that the reporter be fired. Instead, wrote Sudyk, he got a raise. "As for McLendon, he was faced with a serious moral dilemma," wrote Golenbock. "On the one hand, he couldn't ask his players to sign a statement he knew was untrue. On the other hand, he knew if he didn't, there was little doubt that Steinbrenner would make his players suffer financially and emotionally."[60]

Convinced it was in the team's best interest, McLendon reluctantly requested that his players sign the retraction. The players complied, and Pipers captain Jack Adams sent the signed statement to Bob August, *Cleveland Press* sports editor. Published on the front page of the sports section on January 29, it declared that "absolutely no ultimatum of no-pay no-play was ever issued," and that "there is no seething resentment toward Mr. Steinbrenner by any of us." Furthermore, the carefully prepared statement read: "We would like it clearly understood that Mr. Steinbrenner has our unquestioned support. . . . We admire his drive and determination to win this championship for him and Cleveland." The statement concluded that "somewhere your reporters got some unreliable information and we hope that all this can be set straight so we can get down to the business of trying for that championship." When contacted by the press, McLendon said that the players' statement had appeared in the paper without his knowledge and that he had intercepted and destroyed an earlier statement meant to satisfy Steinbrenner because he "felt on my own personal principle standard I could not allow such an act to be culminated." McLendon accused Steinbrenner of pressuring the players into signing the statement, saying that he had deliberated a long time before making this charge.[61]

McLendon announced his resignation, declaring: "I am and have been able to withstand personal attacks but I cannot stand by and see a good group of athletes intimidated into a position which has seriously affected their personal attitudes and performance. Furthermore, I cannot be party to any act which tends to put a player of mine in an untenable position. This position on my part as coach destroys all their respect for me and confidence in me."[62]

McLendon went on to describe the players' seething resentment toward the owner and stated that he felt bitter about Steinbrenner's underhanded treatment of them. In resigning, McLendon declared, "As much as I sincerely love my team and Cleveland fans and friends and wanted so much to make my home here, I cannot see any course open to me other than the one I am following at this time." In response to McLendon's charges, Steinbrenner denied having coerced the players into making their statement and publicly stated: "The players don't hate me as he [McLendon] would have everyone believe. McLendon can't resign. He must give me sixty days' notice, according to his contract." Because of the public outcry, Steinbrenner and McLendon got together at a hastily arranged meeting and attempted to come to a mutually satisfying result. "I don't like to hurt basketball," declared the coach. "If today's talks are satisfactory in terms of the future then there is a possibility I'll be staying." McLendon and Steinbrenner met privately for several hours, and Steinbrenner was quoted as saying, "I'm hoping that John decides to stay."[63]

Steinbrenner then met with the players, advising them to "go to work with new vigor," saying, "It was a very enlightening afternoon." "We had a good meeting and everything is OK now," new cocaptain John Barnhill explained to Chuck Heaton of the *Cleveland Plain Dealer*. "Everyone is happy and all we want to do is go on and win." However, McLendon did not share these good feelings. After consulting with Ed

Sweeny, the man who had brought him to Cleveland, McLendon resigned, feeling that the present situation was untenable in terms of player morale and the owner-coach relationship. Informed of McLendon's decision on January 30, Steinbrenner told the press: "I'm sorry he chose to leave. I was convinced that he was staying with the team. . . . There always will be a place in the organization if he wishes to return. I'm genuinely sorry this happened."[64]

When the Pipers landed at the Cleveland airport later that day, returning from games in Hawaii, team captain Adams received a call from Steinbrenner. According to Adams, the Pipers' owner informed him that McLendon was going to be replaced as coach and given another position in the organization. Steinbrenner asked him to become the player-coach of the Pipers, but Adams refused out of loyalty to McLendon. He was traded immediately to the New York Tapers for Connie Dierking, former University of Cincinnati center.[65]

During this controversy, the Cleveland press was solidly behind McLendon. Clowser declared that "Steinbrenner maneuvered McLendon into a corner on a matter of principle, and McLendon felt he could not be true to his players and his own conscience unless he resigned his coaching post and told why. This he did in a published statement accusing Steinbrenner of threatening to fold up the club unless the players signed a document denying their previous remarks about a tardy payday." Frank Gibbons was equally sympathetic to McLendon: "It strikes me that Coach McLendon acted honorably and with the proper loyalty when he made several efforts to persuade his employer that the best interest of this team would not be served with a statement he (McLendon) did not believe fitted the facts. Coach McLendon continually distinguished himself in a trying situation. He felt unwanted as coach of the Pipers, but he wanted to do a good job right to the finish." In regards to Steinbrenner's actions, Gibbons added, "All that George has succeeded in doing is to get rid of a coach who is one of the most respected in basketball." Steinbrenner also traded away the three players who had earlier complained about not getting paid during the Russian trip: Adams, Swartz, and Taylor.[66]

After McLendon resigned, Steinbrenner decided to try to minimize the animosity by paying the players and to win over the public by signing the "name" coach he was seeking. Bill Sharman, the former Boston Celtics great who had recently been serving as rookie coach for the Los Angeles Jets, a team that had folded earlier in the month, was immediately named to coach the Pipers. A few days later, in a bizarre move, McLendon was named vice president of the Pipers, in charge of player personnel. Golenbock later observed that "the outcry against Steinbrenner's treatment of McLendon had been so shrill that the owner felt he had to do something to ease the backlash. McLendon, who always sought to protect his players, took the job to help them through the transition to a new coach." In his press release announcing the hiring of McLendon, Steinbrenner wrote: "Needless to say, we are delighted and proud that Mac is back with us. In his new position he will be better afforded the opportunity to accomplish what he does best and enjoys most—this is meeting the public and telling them about his greatest love—basketball and the Pipers."[67]

The irony of this statement was not lost on the Cleveland press, for what McLendon loved most was coaching, and his record over twenty-two years was among the most successful in the nation. On February 2, 1962, Clowser expressed the view of many when he wrote, "As an ardent basketball fan, my primary feeling was that the split between President George Steinbrenner and Coach John McLendon should be smoothed over, for the best interests of the game here." However, Steinbrenner was not about to change his mind, and McLendon, as usual, refused to compromise his principles. The Pipers went 19–11 under Sharman and won the league championship over the Kansas City Steers. Ben Flieger, the new Pipers' general manager, accepted the trophy for the team. After the ceremony, in an act that spoke volumes about loyalty and justice, Flieger gave the trophy not to Coach Sharman but to John McLendon.[68]

Cleary later said that Steinbrenner really irritated McLendon: "He was tough on John, and John wasn't used to handling a Steinbrenner-like personality." However, McLendon, always the stoic, remembered the situation differently: "I never let him [Steinbrenner] get to me. He was quite annoying, but in the back of his mind he wanted his team to win. But he just had ways to upset the team. He wanted to make friends with the players but that [McCollum] incident gave them the distance [from Steinbrenner], and I don't think they overcame it." Years later, a reporter asked McLendon if Steinbrenner disliked him because he was black. McLendon laughed at the question. "I have been asked that forty times," he said. "I could never say George's attitude was racial, because he treats everybody the same. He isn't anti-black. He's anti-human."

"John used to have a great quote when people asked him how George [Steinbrenner] treated him," recalled Cleary, the first man fired by Steinbrenner. "He said, 'He treats us all the same. Like dogs.' It's the most violent thing I've ever heard John say."[69]

In a later interview with veteran sports journalist Dick Schaap, Steinbrenner admitted that he might have made some mistakes as president of the Pipers. "I was too vociferous in exhorting my coaches and players from the stands," he recalled. "I'd get on their backs when I didn't think they were trying hard enough. I guess over-exuberance, enthusiasm and youth made me the kind of owner that, perhaps, I shouldn't have been." The obituary section of the *New York Times* on October 9, 1999, ran a lengthy section on the passing of John McLendon. It included a quote from George Steinbrenner: "He was an outstanding basketball technician. He had the respect of all his players and produced nothing but winners."[70]

The Cleveland Pipers disbanded following their initial season, after Steinbrenner signed Jerry Lucas to an exorbitant contract in a failed attempt to land his Cleveland team an NBA franchise. Due to financial difficulties, the ABL itself folded in December 1962. ABL players scattered throughout the NBA soon afterward, with former Tennessee A&I stars Barnett and Warley returning to the Syracuse Nationals and Barnhill going on to play for the St. Louis Hawks. As general manager, Mike Cleary had obviously been an astute judge of talent: ten out of the eleven players he signed for the Pipers and later the Kansas City Steers went on to the NBA. Aside from hiring McLendon as the first professional African American coach, the American Basketball League's only lasting impression rested in two innovative rule changes: the addition of a 3-point field goal, which would later be adopted by the American Basketball Association and the NBA, and a widened free-throw lane, which the NBA soon copied.

CHAPTER 7

Back to the College Game

Kentucky State College and Cleveland State University, 1963–69

At the conclusion of the 1961–62 season, McLendon was asked by the U.S. State Department to go to Southeast Asia as part of a cultural exchange program to teach basketball at two universities. He traveled to Malaya (now Malaysia) and Indonesia for six months, continuing to spread goodwill and help coaches prepare for the Asia games. Afterward, he returned to Tennessee State University for a year as supervisor of undergraduate and graduate physical education and as an assistant basketball coach, helping his successors and former players—head coach, Harold Hunter, and his assistant, Richard Miller. McLendon took great delight in seeing that Hunter and Miller hardly needed his expertise, as the 1962–63 Tigers had a 25–6 record that season, earning an invitation to the small-college NCAA tournament. In 1964, due largely to McLendon's efforts, Tennessee State became the first black university to host the Olympic track and field trials. By this time, the Tigerbells women's track club had become one of the most accomplished athletic teams in the nation, and McLendon felt the state of Tennessee and the university needed to reward their efforts. The team had won its first gold medal in the 1952 Olympics, but it was not until the 1960 Olympics in Rome, when the Tigerbells' Wilma Rudolph captured three gold medals, that the team and the university Athletic Department got the recognition they deserved.

On February 14, 1962, McLendon received a letter from his long-time friend NAIA executive director Al Duer. "It is with real personal pleasure and great pride," Duer wrote, "that I tell you of your election to the NAIA Hall of Fame as a 'Coach' of basketball. You know my personal high regard for you as a gentleman, as well as your great skill and handling of athletes. . . . My sincere congratulations." Induction into the Hall of Fame became even sweeter for McLendon when he learned

Coach McLendon with the Malaya (now Malaysia) National Team, 1962. Years later, he would travel to fifty-eight countries as an international ambassador of basketball for Converse. (Courtesy Joanna McLendon)

that he would be going in alongside Boston Celtic great Sam Jones, who had played for him at North Carolina College ten years earlier.[1]

Later that fall, NAIA executive director Duer was proud to announce that an All-Star basketball team from the association's colleges and universities had been invited to compete in a two-game series against a Russian national team touring the United States. The games were to be staged in cooperation with the Amateur Athletic Union and the U.S. State Department. Duer and his executive committee named John McLendon as head coach of the NAIA All-Stars, to be assisted by Coach Jim Nelson, from William Jewell College, in Missouri. However, problems over player eligibility soon developed. Historian John R. M. Wilson states that "the NCAA petulantly denied five athletes from dual-affiliation colleges the right to play, threatening them with ineligibility." Thanks to a last-minute agreement with the NCAA, however, three players who had recently graduated from NAIA institutions and were now playing AAU basketball were allowed to join the U.S. team.[2]

McLendon began his two-a-day practices in Kansas City on November 8 with only one week to prepare for the competition. The

Back to the College Game

McLendon's induction into the Helms Athletic Foundation's NAIA Hall of Fame, with Francis Hoover presenting, 1962. (Courtesy NAIA)

Russians won the first game, 75–71, in front of a field house packed with ninety-three hundred spectators in Sioux Falls, South Dakota, home of the NAIA Track and Field Meet. Jimmy Allen, from Arkansas A&M, wound up as high scorer for McLendon's All-Stars, with 18 points; Jerry Shipp, from Southeastern Oklahoma and the Phillips 66ers, and Roger Strickland, from Jacksonville, Florida, garnered 10 points each. Alexandr Petrov took top honors for the Russians with 18.

In the second game, in Mount Pleasant, Iowa, the American team displayed much more confidence and, under the leadership of Georgetown College's Cecil Tuttle, fought the Russians furiously in a torrid first half. The USSR led the All-Stars 50–49 at halftime. The Russian team jumped to a 5-point bulge early in the second half, but McLendon's cagers bounced back to gain a 64–58 lead that held until the last two minutes. With ten seconds remaining, the NAIA team had a 1-point advantage, but a last-second desperation shot by Russian star Genadiy Volnov swished through the net as the buzzer went off, and McLendon's All-Stars lost their second heartbreaker, 83–82. Tuttle was the game's high scorer, with 18 points, backed by Lucious Jackson, from Pan

McLendon with the NAIA All-Star team, 1962. *Front row, left to right:* Jim Boutin, Lucious Jackson, Bill Pickins, Ken Saylors, Jim McGurk, Jim Emmerich (trainer). *Back row, left to right:* John B. McLendon, James Mack Allen, Roger Strickland, Cecil Tuttle, Phil Shirk, Jim Nelson (assistant coach). (Courtesy NAIA)

American College, in Texas, and Dennis Price, from the University of Oklahoma and the Phillips 66ers, who had 16 points each.

Itching to get back into full-time coaching, McLendon accepted a three-year position at Kentucky State College (now University) at the request of his friend Carl M. Hill, who had assumed the duties of college president in 1962. While there, McLendon recruited the school's first in-state white athlete. "I always thought I was at a disadvantage as a coach because I couldn't recruit white athletes," he said.[3]

McLendon employed the same strategies at Kentucky State that had brought him success at Tennessee A&I. "Coach was not a hard-nosed person and did not yell at his players. Yet everyone responded to him and to what he wanted us to do—probably out of respect for the way he treated and respected us as persons," recalled Kentucky center David Barnes. "His practice always lasted ninety minutes—no less and no more—and we always accomplished much at them. There was no dogging it or messing around, but he did make them fun, even the much, much running we had to do to play his style of ball."[4]

In 1964, his team captured the championship of the Mid-Western Athletic Association, its first since 1951, and McLendon earned a berth for another of his teams at the NAIA national tournament in Kansas City. His eleventh-seeded Kentucky State Thorobreds won their first game over a determined Redlands College of California squad, 71–65, giving McLendon a record sixteen straight victories in a national tournament. Thorobreds center David Barnes led the way with 17 points, while teammates James Robertson and Samuel Adams contributed 13 points each. The following evening, before a standing-room-only crowd of 9,682, McLendon's team fell behind early to sixth-seeded Emporia State College of Kansas and trailed at halftime, 45–36. According to Fritz Kreisler, writing in the *Kansas City Times,* McLendon's halftime speech apparently inspired a furious comeback. The Thorobred rally was "led by Barnes and Henry Davis, a couple of spring-legged front-liners who took command under both baskets, and a couple of lightning-quick reserves—Floyd Theard and Harold Batiste. Barnes was especially adept at tip-ins, while Batiste and Theard hawked E-State with a full-court press." Although Kentucky tied the score at 60, clutch shooting by the boys from Kansas proved to make the difference, as McLendon's team went down in defeat, 85–80. Barnes led the Thorobred team again, with 13 points and 14 rebounds, while Davis, Batiste, and Theard tallied 12 points each. Although he did not know it at the time, this would be the final game that McLendon would coach in the NAIA national tournament.[5]

In 1965, McLendon coached and won the first integrated game between state schools in Kentucky, with Kentucky State facing Morehead State. He also authored *Fast Break Basketball: Fine Points and Fundamentals,* the first book on basketball written by a black coach, and was elected to serve on both the NAIA and AAU executive committees. Then, in 1966, the People-to-People program invited Coach McLendon and his nationally ranked Kentucky State College team to tour Iceland and Europe in a six-game tour. For McLendon, this would be another career milestone, marking the first time a historically black college team (and coach) played in Europe. As coach of Kentucky State, McLendon also invited three national teams—from Mexico, Poland, and Puerto Rico—to compete against his Thorobreds, defeating each of

The 1963–64 Kentucky State College Thorobreds, MWAA champions. *Front row, left to right:* Samuel Adams (captain), Floyd Theard, James Barlow, Harold Batiste, James Banks. *Second row, left to right:* James Lewis, O. B. McCane, James Robertson. *Back row, left to right:* James Campbell, David Barnes, Henry Davis, John B. McLendon. (Courtesy Joanna McLendon)

them. This was the first time a historically black college had invited teams from foreign countries to participate in athletic events on its campus. Although McLendon won fifty games and lost twenty-nine in his three-year tenure at Kentucky Sate, he also experienced the first losing season of his coaching career. According to one of his star players, David Barnes, the poor performance of the 1964–65 squad was due in large part to an early-season tragedy, when player James Barlow, who was at the heart of McLendon's team, was killed in an automobile accident. The team never recovered from this psychological trauma, and its performance on the court suffered accordingly.[6]

McLendon also helped integrate teams from other schools. According to Fred Whitted, a leading authority on black-college athletics, although Coach McLendon had recruited Charlie Scott out of

Back to the College Game

Laurinburg Institute to play for him at Kentucky State, he understood the larger historic implications of the drive for racial equality taking place in the 1960s. At the time, the University of North Carolina was trying to find a black player who would help integrate their team as the Tar Heels competed for basketball supremacy in the Atlantic Coast Conference (ACC). McLendon convinced UNC assistant coach John Lotz that Scott would fit the bill; he was not only an exceptional player but also the top student in his high school class. Scott's high school coach, a friend of McLendon's, had helped him recruit one of his earlier players. Following both coaches' advice, in 1966 Scott became the first black man to receive an athletic scholarship at UNC and play for legendary coach Dean Smith. McLendon obviously had a nose for talent, for during his three-year career at UNC, Scott became a two-time All-American and earned a three-time All-ACC selection.[7]

Scott was united with McLendon again in 1968, when the UNC star played a key role on the gold-medal-winning U.S. Olympic basketball team, with McLendon serving as an assistant coach. Scott remembered McLendon not only as an exceptional strategist and tactician but also as a personal and much-beloved mentor to him, Spencer Haywood, and several other players. Scott was only eighteen years old, with one year of college ball behind him, and McLendon helped the young man discipline his schoolyard game to fit into a team-oriented system; later, he helped him understand and appreciate both the historical evolution and the underlying philosophy of the game of basketball. Years later, Scott took great pride in supporting McLendon in receiving the Naismith Lifetime Achievement Award for basketball.[8]

In 1964, McLendon became the first black coach to serve on the U.S. Olympic Committee; for twelve years, he was responsible for scouting and player-performance evaluation. He also became the first black coach to serve on the Olympic coaching staff, under Hall of Fame coach Henry Iba of Oklahoma State University, in Mexico City in 1968 and again in Munich in 1972. Ironically, the possibility McLendon had warned about years earlier—that the United States was taking its foreign competitors too lightly—was realized on his watch in 1972, when the U.S. basketball team went down in defeat because of a last-second shot made by the Soviet Union, in one of the most controversial games in Olympic history.

It was also in 1964 that McLendon was selected to coach the U.S.

All-Stars, a team composed of seven AAU players and five collegians, on tour in France, Poland, Czechoslovakia, and Russia. The Americans drew standing-room-only crowds of twelve thousand in Brno and sixteen thousand in Moscow. They won eight of their fourteen games, with the Soviet Union, represented by its 1964 Olympic team, trimming the Americans in three straight meetings.

That same year, McLendon was chosen to coach the NAIA All-Star team in the Olympic trials at St. John's Arena in New York. Joe Brehmer of Rockhust College and Gus Fish from Emporia State College were named as his assistants. For the upcoming trials, the U.S. Olympic Committee awarded the NCAA three teams, the AAU two, the armed forces two, and the NAIA one. According to Wilson's history of the NAIA, representation in the Olympics continued to be a focal point of the NAIA's struggle with the NCAA, which in fact was merely a subset of the all-out war between the NCAA and the AAU to dominate American amateur athletics. "In 1960," according to Wilson, "NCAA President Byers walked out of a USOC meeting to protest the NAIA being allowed to participate in the Olympic trials. The NAIA's upset of NCAA champion Ohio State that year poured salt on the wound and appeared to earn the undying enmity of the NCAA chief." McLendon, who found himself unwittingly embroiled in this conflict between the athletic organizations, prepared his NAIA team to handle the pressure and measure up to the competition accordingly.[9]

Led by NAIA All-Americans and later NBA stars Lucious Jackson from Pan American College and Willis Reed from Grambling College, McLendon's cagers were the surprise of the trials, finishing at third place in the eight-team competition. In their final game, with only twenty seconds remaining, Ralph Telken of Rockhurst College supplied the key basket, while Lou Skurcenski of Westminster College tallied 22 points, McLendon's NAIA All-Stars toppling the NCAA Whites in the third-place game, 77–74. Until then, the NAIA had struggled through eight ties and as many lead changes before Lucious Jackson put his team ahead to stay at 69–68. Moments later, Jackson tucked in another field goal, then added a free throw for a 72–68 NAIA advantage. In addition to Skurcenski's 22 points and 10 rebounds, Wilbert Frazier from Grambling tallied 10 points, and Willis Reed pulled down 12 rebounds and finished with 9 points. Joe Caldwell of Arizona State University led the Whites, with 18 points and 12 rebounds.

This was the highest finish ever for the NAIA in the Olympic trials, and everyone in the association agreed that McLendon had done a magnificent job coaching the team. Jackson, selected for the 1964 Olympic team, played a key role in America's gold-medal performance. However, according to Wilson, "the NCAA members succeeded in keeping Reed from joining Jackson as the second NAIA athlete on the squad." Unfortunately, Wilson wrote, "the tension between the NAIA and the NCAA would not ease for another three decades"; indeed, this tension might have contributed to the delay in electing Coach McLendon to the Naismith Memorial Hall of Fame, which was finally accomplished in 1978.[10]

In 1965, McLendon served under John Kundla from the University of Minnesota as associate coach for the World Student Games in Budapest, the team also playing games in Finland, Sweden, and Czechoslovakia. An evaluation sent by Nicholas Bodis, special assistant for athletic programs in the U.S. State Department, to Carl M. Hill, president of Kentucky State University, through the U.S. Embassy in Helsinki, clearly indicated the standards Coach McLendon set as manager of this tour: "The College All-Star Basketball Team performed in a superior manner in every respect. In spite of the fact that they soundly trounced all the Finnish teams in competition, the sports enthusiasts and the press were unanimous in their praise. This included the communist press. They were most cooperative, personable, and press coverage was more than twice that received by the Cleveland Orchestra. The group, in every respect, was outstanding."[11]

Due to his international basketball experience, McLendon, while at Kentucky State, was chosen to serve on the first Advisory Panel on International Athletics, assisting the State Department in planning exchange programs involving athletes and coaches. In 1967, he coached the U.S. team to its first Intercontinental Championship at a tournament held in Lisbon, becoming the first black coach to win an international competition. With Michigan State's John Benington, he cocoached the U.S. championship team in the World Student Games in Tokyo, winning six games and losing none. McLendon also coached the U.S. team in the 1967 World Under 6-Feet Championship in Barcelona, capturing the first-place trophy by defeating the host team, 76–68. "We wanted to prove to the world that the little guys still can play basketball," he said. That same year, he was appointed chief basketball consultant to the

Virgin Islands Basketball Federation. The following year, McLendon served in the same capacity for the Bahamas Basketball Federation. In 1968, as noted earlier, the U.S. Olympic Committee asked him to serve as assistant basketball coach under head coach Henry Iba of Oklahoma State University, his chief responsibility scouting. With all these successful experiences, in 1969 McLendon was appointed to the International Basketball Board. Along with all his other accomplishments, as a board member, he devised a scouting book for international competition and started a library of films showcasing the brand of basketball played in thirty-five different countries.

After attending the 1967 World Basketball Tournament in Montevideo, where Brazil defeated the United States, McLendon wrote a lengthy article in the *Cleveland Plain Dealer* declaring that "the U.S. will become second class in basketball. . . . Unless we arrive at an understanding which will have all our amateur athletic groups contribute willingly toward the construction of our international competitive units, we will soon be regulated to the sidelines." McLendon argued that the United States must take international tournaments much more seriously, as the competition did. "Our athletes in international competition are dazed by the competitive atmosphere," he wrote, "and need to prepare themselves not only physically, but also psychologically for the experience." As an advocate of international basketball for more than twenty years, McLendon believed that the spirit of the games went beyond what happened on the court. "This year's World tournament was an illustration of the international good will and understanding which can exist and become operative when athletes of many countries meet in competition," he said.[12]

Return to Cleveland

In June 1966, McLendon became the first black coach to be hired by a predominately white university, Cleveland State, which was trying to establish a new identity after changing its name from Fenn College just one year earlier. Cleveland State president Harold Enarson had been made aware that there were no black head basketball coaches at predominately white colleges, and he wanted his newly established university to be out in front on this issue. Enarson therefore aggressively pursued McLendon to serve as head basketball coach and professor of physical education, with Ohio governor James Rhodes and the school's board of trustees providing enthusiastic support. It was agreed that Jim Rodriquez, who had stepped down voluntarily after seven years as head basketball coach at Fenn College and one at Cleveland State, would assist the new coach. Robert Busbey, newly named athletic director, expressed his pleasure in adding McLendon to the staff: "His record speaks for itself. Cleveland State is getting a man with broad experience and exceptional character who will add to that high degree of personal excellence and integrity which we desire of our university family. His addition represents a solid building block in the development of a dynamic program, even before our new facilities are available." Busbey added, "We are pleased that he will have a real part in the program as it unfolds."[13]

For his part, McLendon expressed pleasure in returning to Cleveland: "I have always felt that Cleveland was a great town for basketball, and I would like to see Cleveland State's team earn a share in that public enthusiasm." When McLendon was being recruited for the position, he had been told of Governor Rhodes's plans for a new $15 million, 16,000-seat sports arena, a major part of a $110 million six-year capital campaign. This arena would provide a much-needed home court for Cleveland State's basketball team and its greatly enhanced physical education facilities. One of the most successful coaches in college basketball history, with a winning percentage of .800, McLendon liked the idea of building a program at an institution that seemed ideally positioned for an expanding future. "I like the fact that this institution is going to be one of the major developments in the Cleveland area, and I want to be a part of it," said McLendon. "Whatever basketball can do to help it along, I want to be a part of. If the basketball program moves simultaneously with the way other things about the university grow, it'll be something I'll be very proud of."[14]

At Cleveland State, however, McLendon inherited an extremely poor program, the team having won only four of eighteen games the year before. He realized the challenge before him but declared that he firmly believed that "through hard work and concentration we'll come up with a good and representative team." "It will take some doing and time," he stated. But he was confident in the caliber of high school basketball in the greater Cleveland area and in his ability to recruit some local talent. When asked by sports information director Merle Levin how he planned to be successful at Cleveland State, which was making the transition from a private college, with a strong academic emphasis on engineering and accounting, to a public university, McLendon replied, "The woods are full of good basketball players; it's coaching that makes the difference." He also understood and appreciated the high academic standards the university took pride in upholding. "The material here is above the average, and we will certainly try to divert their attention to a fine college at home," declared McLendon. "Education for the youngster has always been my first concern, and I know he will get a sound education at CSU." Other people associated with the athletic program were also confident in McLendon's ability to recruit high-caliber athletes. "The name of John McLendon is worth a lot in recruiting," said Busbey. "But we weren't interested in John just for his record. There are plenty of guys around with good records. John is a gentleman, as well, and he teaches more than just good basketball."[15]

From the first practice, McLendon's team understood their coach's commitment to expert conditioning and his trademark fast-break basketball. To qualify for his squad, all candidates were required to run two miles in twelve minutes, and he was pleased to see that several of his players recorded times nearly three minutes faster. "I stress teamwork in the running style, and I think we'll have a lot of fun this winter playing this type of game," said McLendon. When Cleveland State won its first game of the year over Ohio's Hiram College, 86–70, the students gave the coach and team a standing ovation. Although McLendon's team lacked height and experience—nine of his fourteen players were freshman—it was off to a positive start. Don Ross, an All-State freshman guard from Virginia who had come to Cleveland because his father competed against McLendon during his playing days at Virginia Union and greatly admired him, scored 36 points for the Cleveland State Vikings. Everybody, including the administration, was so happy with the initial victory, McLendon recalled, that "the students wanted them to close down the school."[16]

The Vikings followed their initial victory with wins over Muskingum College, 94–77, and Slippery Rock College, 91–79, and enjoyed a thrilling defeat of host school Indiana University of Pennsylvania in the Christmas Tree Basketball Tournament, 85–83. Although the team then suffered two successive defeats, to Kenyon College and Eastern Illinois University, the Vikings seemed to be adapting well to McLendon's style of play. Going into the new year, Ross led the team with an average of 24.2 points per game, while another freshman, Tom Blackman from Alabama, was second in scoring, with 15.3 points per game. Senior Denny Lenk, despite the wealth of talent from the underclassmen, was still the most complete ballplayer on the squad.

McLendon's fifth victory of the season was perhaps his most memorable and ironic. On January 11, 1967, Coach McLendon earned his five hundredth career collegiate victory against Ohio's Walsh College. He later frequently recalled this milestone game with amusement: "Before the game I chatted with their coach, Ken Gold, who said, 'You're going after your 500th tonight? Tell you one thing, Coach, you won't get it here.'" Gold's team didn't take a shot for thirteen minutes, and then it was a forty-footer that went in. The Vikings tried their fast break, but their opponents stalled. Cleveland State led 12–11 at halftime. "We finally won 24 to 22 but we held onto the ball the last three minutes," said McLendon. "I'll remember my 500th victory forever," he declared after the game. "I teach fast-break basketball and our team scored just 24 points—it was unbelievable." "I won my first college game back in 1940 at North Carolina College," McLendon told Bill Nichols of the *Cleveland Press*. "It was my first game as head coach and we beat Hampton Institute, 59–40. We scored more points in that game twenty-seven years ago, than both teams did Wednesday."[17]

After losing a few key players because of low grades during the winter quarter, McLendon's team finished the season with an 8–13 record. Entering his second season without his three top scorers and a proven big man, McLendon relied heavily on the scoring of three sophomores: six-two guards Mike Campbell and Sam Thomas, both from Cleveland, and six-six forward Harvey Smith, an All–State rebounding star from New Jersey. Hailed as one of the top prospects ever to enroll at Cleveland State, Thomas lived up to his advance billing, leading the team in almost all areas, only to be placed on academic probation after the fall quarter. Unfortunately, he wasn't the only player lost to grades and disciplinary problems that second season. Left with only eight players after the Christmas break, McLendon's Vikings finished a frustrating season with seven wins and fifteen defeats.

In his third and final year at Cleveland State, McLendon led the Vikings to their best record in history, recording twelve wins in a twenty-six-game season. Led by junior captain Campbell and sophomore sensations Thomas and Smith, both of whom were now eligible to rejoin the team in January, McLendon's cagers recorded a major upset over nationally ranked Central State University of Ohio, the previous year's NAIA national champions, 41–40. Calling it Cleveland State's "biggest victory in its history," the *Cleveland Plain Dealer* stated that "Harvey Smith's 15-foot jumper with 2:22 left to play gave the Vikings their first ever victory over the defending champion Marauders." Smith was the only player on either team to score in double figures, cashing in 17 points. The taller Marauders led in rebounds, 49–39. However, the Vikings' Sam Thomas took individual game honors with 12 rebounds, and Smith blocked 10 shots to figure prominently in the victory.[18]

Finally at full strength, the young Vikings under Coach McLendon won five out of their last six games, creating an optimistic outlook for the future. Looking back on that season, Thomas remembered how hard everyone on the team worked in order to remain competitive and the feeling the players and their coach had that their efforts were finally paying off. However, McLendon did more than bring respectability to the Cleveland State program. According to Jim Rodriquez, McLendon's assistant coach, "John brought in our first scholarship players," and "along with Bob Busbey, he was instrumental in making physical education a major, which academically was a big help to many of those kids."[19]

McLendon enjoyed his tenure at Cleveland State, but he needed a few more athletic players with greater experience. He also desperately needed the new arena that had been promised by Governor James Rhodes, but it was not forthcoming. Only twenty-five years later would the 13,500-seat Convocation Center be dedicated on the Cleveland State University campus. According to Rodriquez, it was difficult to recruit players to a school that did not have a physical education major, that had makeshift practice facilities at Gray's Armory several blocks from campus, and that had to play many of its games in high school gymnasiums all over the city. To make matters worse, the best player on the team, Don Ross, stayed only one year due to academic difficulties.[20]

Basketball coaches around the country knew and respected McLendon for the trailblazing path he was forging at an integrated university, and they kept channeling many of their star players his way. In the spring of 1968, a skinny six-three forward, recently named the outstanding Long Island high school player, arrived with several other talented players to meet with the legendary Coach McLendon on a

Cleveland State University Vikings, 1968–69. *Standing, left to right:* Jim Rodriquez (assistant coach), John DeStefanis, Dan Palumbo, Bruce Hagins, Matt Taylor, Henry Jordan, Alex Dadas, Kevin Lineberger, Kevin McManamon, John B. McLendon. *Front row, left to right:* Tom McCombe, Ewald Heise, Mike Guilfoyle, Mike Campbell (captain), Jerry Pavlas, Charles Hill, Mike Misja. (Courtesy Jim Rodriquez, Cleveland State University)

recruiting trip to the Cleveland State University campus. His name was Julius Erving. The coach expressed a mild interest in having him play on the Vikings. McLendon operated under the philosophy that it was best to bring in a group of prospects at the same time in the hopes that they would bond and end up playing together. Erving arrived with other promising players, such as Jim McDaniels, who later starred at Western Kentucky University and in the ABA, and ex–Marquette University player Ulric Cobb. "He was offered a partial scholarship as an afterthought as part of a package," said Cleveland State sports information director Merle Levin, remembering Erving's visit. "As I remember it, John was the most interested in Cobb, Marquette's 'Elevator Man,' and the least interested in Erving of the five players he brought in."[21]

Years later, Erving also recalled the visit: "Cleveland State was just one of the places I evaluated. I decided not to go to the Midwest. I wanted to be out of New York, on a college campus, but at a place I would be able to get home easily." Years later, Erving recalled how during the recruiting trip in Cleveland he was taken around by a student who displayed Coach McLendon's business card wherever they went. Erving quickly understood that McLendon knew everyone and that everyone had the greatest respect for him. From that day on, Erving stated, he realized that he was dealing "with someone special, who represented class," and he never forgot it. He ended up enrolling at the University of Massachusetts, staying there for three years, and later brought his superlative talents first to the ABA's Virginia Squires and, in 1976, to the NBA's Philadelphia 76ers. "Sure I wanted him," McLendon told Dennis Lustig of the *Cleveland Plain Dealer* in 1976. "If he would have come to Cleveland State, I would have stayed there." Although McLendon appreciated the opportunity to recruit high school All-Americans like Erving, he knew his program wasn't up to the competition for Erving or other players of his caliber. "The main stumbling block was not having a gym on campus," he recalled. "We tried to sell them on the Cleveland Arena but it didn't work."[22]

Speaking of his three-year tenure at Cleveland State, McLendon did not try to hide his sarcasm: "It's the best place to work I know. It's got everything, except what I need. It's the only state school with no gymnasium, no physical education department, no fieldhouse. Ohio State spent more time taking care of the stadium grass than we spend on our basketball program." As Bob August observed in the *Cleveland Press,* "With no facilities to show off, McLendon had trouble getting players for Cleveland State and more trouble keeping them in school." It was an uphill struggle for a school that had no basketball tradition, leaving the coach with too many obstacles to overcome. McLendon still worked tirelessly, as he always had, to turn things around. "I don't think I've ever done more coaching in my life than I did at Cleveland State," recalled McLendon. Although his 27–42 record over three years at Cleveland State isn't very impressive on the surface, McLendon did bring respectability to the Vikings program. More important, according to the authoritative 1969 *Converse Basketball Yearbook,* McLendon's record over twenty-five years of coaching, of 522 wins and 165 losses, made him the fourth-winningest coach in collegiate basketball history, behind only Adolph Rupp, Henry Iba, and Butler University's Paul Hinkle.

Furthermore, McLendon was ranked third best in winning percentage, his .760 falling behind only Rupp and John Wooden of UCLA.[23]

While coaching at Cleveland State in the late 1960s, the considerate, mild-mannered McLendon became embroiled in the heated rhetoric and actions of the struggle for civil rights, taking place in a country torn apart by racial animosity and the war in Vietnam. As David Zang argues persuasively in *SportsWars: Athletes in the Age of Aquarius,* sports underwent an almost cataclysmic change in the late 1960s and early 1970s, the Vietnam era. The result was a massive culture clash between the old view of sports as a noble, society-supporting, character-building endeavor and the 1960s emphasis on personal freedom and social revolution.[24]

In the fall of 1967, amateur black athletes formed the Olympic Project for Human Rights (OPHR) to organize a boycott of the 1968 Olympics in Mexico City. Its lead organizer, Harry Edwards, a professor of sociology at San Jose State University and a friend of track star Tommie Smith, offered the following explanation: "It was inevitable that this revolt of the black athlete should develop. With struggles being waged by black people in the areas of education, housing, employment and many others, it was only a matter of time before African-American athletes shed their fantasies and delusions and asserted their manhood and faced the facts of their existence."[25]

Of course, McLendon had been asserting his manhood and fighting for equal rights for more than thirty years. Therefore, by the summer of 1968, he felt compelled to speak out on this highly controversial issue. When a group calling itself the Black Youth Conference followed the lead of the OPHR, issuing a call for all black athletes to boycott the upcoming summer Olympics, McLendon responded. Bill Nichols, of the *Cleveland Plain Dealer,* quoted him on August 28, 1968, as stating that he "cannot understand the logic of Negro athletes who qualify for the Olympics and then do not compete." Upon completing a comprehensive report on the group's reasons for boycotting the Olympics, McLendon concluded: "A rebel without a cause can be under suspicion of being stupid. The Black Youth Conference is not stupid. It has a cause, but it is without a cause in Mexico." McLendon pointed out that the U.S. Olympic Committee had recently appointed five African Americans to its roster; that African Americans served on the Olympic coaching staff;

and that the International Olympic Committee had already withdrawn its invitation to South Africa, which, with its apartheid regime, would not be represented in Mexico City by any individual or team. As for the Black Youth Conference's demands that the New York Athletic Club immediately cease its segregation practices and that Muhammad Ali be reinstated as heavyweight boxing champion of the world, McLendon wrote that, although he was in agreement with them on these two issues, there was no relationship between them and the Olympic games.[26]

Although the proposed boycott failed, on October 17, two black American athletes did make history at the Mexico Olympics, staging a silent protest against racial discrimination. Tommie Smith and John Carlos, gold and bronze medalists in the two-hundred-meter race, stood with their heads bowed, each raising a black-gloved fist in the black power salute as the U.S. national anthem played during the victory ceremony. They also chose not to wear shoes, to protest black poverty, and wore beads to protest the lynching of black people in the South. At a press conference afterward, Smith stated emphatically, "Black America will understand what we did tonight." McLendon was one black American who certainly understood the athletes' motivations but strongly disagreed with their actions. Throughout his life, he had always worked within the system to bring about democratic institutional change, and he believed that America could reform itself systemically if pushed to do so. Furthermore, he felt strongly that the actions of these two black athletes had embarrassed the United States around the world and would be counterproductive in the achievement of American racial harmony and equality. To McLendon, negotiation was always preferable to confrontation. In the highly volatile atmosphere of 1968, with the horrific assassinations of Reverend Martin Luther King Jr. and Massachusetts senator Robert Kennedy, he believed that one must work to bring the races together, not tear them further apart.

Inspired by the 1968 Olympic protest, McLendon's black basketball players at Cleveland State wanted to wear black armbands during a game as a form of protest against ubiquitous American racism. McLendon, in an action typical of his measured, thoughtful approach, told the black players he would permit this only if they discussed the matter with their white teammates and the whole team agreed to wear the armbands. Instead, the idea was dropped. McLendon stated that he was not opposed to the protest, but he refused to compromise the team's unity by allowing rifts to develop between friends who could help one another do the right thing. "I think they would have made a bigger point," he said, "if they had gone ahead with the protest and included the white players. I think if they were here today . . . they would realize that they had missed a good shot."[27]

It was in Cleveland that McLendon, divorced for the second time, met Joanna Owens Bryant, a beautiful, engaging, highly educated, and refined woman who served as an elementary school principal in the Cleveland area. Joanna had grown up in the small town of Greensboro, Alabama, and at the age of fourteen enrolled at prestigious historically black Spelman College for women in Atlanta, where she completed her degree in four years with a major in music and a minor in English. Meanwhile, her family had moved to Cleveland, and she joined them there to begin graduate school in music education at Case Western Reserve University. After her first marriage and the birth of two children, Nanette in 1949 and H. David in 1950, she began teaching in the Cleveland school system.

In 1967, Joanna and John McLendon were introduced through mutual friends, Faye and Bill Chavers, on a Sunday afternoon, while McLendon and a number of other coaches were watching and analyzing a basketball game. Joanna remembers the first words McLendon said to her: "Are there any more at home like you?" Their relationship was quite casual in the beginning, as both of them were recently separated from their spouses and extremely busy, Joanna completing her master's degree in educational administration at Case Western Reserve while raising two children, and McLendon in his new challenging position at Cleveland State University. Their relationship grew more serious after their respective divorces, and they were married on March 1, 1969, at the City Hall in Shaker Heights, Ohio, the Cleveland suburb where her children were enrolled in school.[28]

Joanna remembered her new husband vowing to complete his coaching career at Cleveland State, promising to stop traveling all the time and stay in Cleveland forever. Instead of a honeymoon, after their wedding they drove to Chicago, where Joanna visited a close cousin who was ill and her husband attended a meeting of the Olympic Committee at O'Hare Airport. Wanting to share in her husband's passion, Joanna began studying the game of basketball and became an avid fan. "I get awfully excited at a game," Joanna said, "but you should watch John.

He shows no emotion at all. He sits very calmly on the bench, observing." Although Joanna understood that basketball was, in her words, her "husband's mistress," and that he would continue to coach and teach all over the world, she loved their life together. She traveled with him whenever she could, both within the United States and abroad, and whenever he was away from home, he would never forget to call and bring her presents upon his return. The respect that she had for her husband grew even stronger as she observed him fighting for causes in which he believed in his quietly dignified and determined way.[29]

In April 1969, McLendon, still at Cleveland State, received a telephone call from Denver. It was from old friend and former Denver coach Larry Varnell, who had first met McLendon in the 1950s, when McLendon was coaching championship teams at Tennessee A&I. Varnell had followed McLendon's career for fifteen years, and the two would occasionally talk basketball for hours. Now a Denver businessman and a member of the Rockets' board of directors, Varnell had a proposition for Coach McLendon.

CHAPTER 8

The First Black Coach in the American Basketball Association

The Denver Rockets, 1969

The proposition Varnell had for the fifty-four-year-old Cleveland State coach was simple and direct. The ABA's Denver Rockets wanted John McLendon to be their next head coach. McLendon had won the AAU and NIBL titles in Denver back in 1961, and he was well respected in the Mile High City. McLendon was interested in the offer, but he wanted to consider his obligation to amateur sports. He had been an AAU and Olympic official and valued these associations tremendously. When each of these associations assured him that when he left the pro ranks the amateurs would welcome him back, he was relieved, but another important factor involved his wife, Joanna. She was an assistant principal at the second-largest elementary school in Cleveland, and it would be important for her to find comparable work in Denver. After she was hired as principal of an elementary school in Denver's Cherry Creek school system, McLendon committed to coach the Rockets.

Clearly, Cleveland State's lack of facilities, and the broken promises to improve them, was a major factor in McLendon's decision to leave. He was quoted in the *Cleveland Press* as saying that he would miss working with young people, which he found to be one of the greatest rewards of college coaching, but he would not miss the intensely competitive and sometimes unethical side of recruiting. "It's the least attractive part of college coaching, and I think that any coach will tell you the same thing," declared McLendon. "It can actually be humiliating. The boys play a game with you, and they are always the winner."[1]

With the memory of only one difficult season in professional basketball, eight years earlier, with the ABL's Cleveland Pipers, McLendon felt the challenge to prove his skills in the two-year-old ABA. The negotiations were relatively simple and quickly accomplished. "Salary was more or less unimportant for me," said McLendon. "Young coaches look for money, the older ones—like me—look for solid organization and good players. The Rockets have both." There was also the excitement of the ABA and the wide-open kind of basketball the league was known for. "It has a status and structure," he said of the new league. "It offers a kind of basketball you don't see in the National Basketball Association and, frankly, it's more appealing to the public. The superstars will come . . . they'll be there."[2]

McLendon's words proved to be prophetic, for only a few months after his signing, the Denver papers were filled with stories about Spencer Haywood, the six-nine, twenty-year-old superstar of the 1968 Olympic team, announcing that he was giving up two years of eligibility at the University of Detroit to play for the Rockets. During the 1968 Olympics, Haywood had followed little Coach McLendon around, asking about the other teams and how good their centers were, their weaknesses and their strong points. The two had spent considerable time together in Mexico and, according to McLendon, "became fast friends." McLendon recalled: "I was impressed with him, and he knew it, I guess. I also became aware of his personal hardships." Haywood had been born into a family of ten children in tiny Silver City, Mississippi, with no father to support them. Taking the opportunity to escape the rural poverty of his childhood, Haywood went to Chicago and then Detroit to live with his brother. He led his Pershing High School to the 1967 Michigan Class-A championship; spent a year at Trinidad State Junior College in Colorado; and moved on to the University of Detroit for the 1968–69 season, where he scored an average of 32.1 points per game and led the nation in rebounding with an average of 21.5 per game. Will Robinson, Haywood's high school basketball coach and legal guardian, was a longtime friend of McLendon's. Thus, feeling that he had accomplished all he needed to at the college level, Haywood contacted the Rockets' owner and told him he wanted to play for Coach McLendon of the ABA's Denver Rockets. When McLendon heard the news about Haywood joining his team, he was "flattered" but stunned "that out of twenty-six professional teams he decided he'd play with the Rockets."[3]

The Rockets' owners, Don Ringsby and his father, Bill, purposely did not tell Coach McLendon anything until the negotiations had been completed, "because knowing his involvement in amateur basketball and his highly ethical background, we didn't want him to be involved in the negotiations." The story of how McLendon found out about

The First Black Coach in the ABA

In 1969, McLendon became the first black coach in the American Basketball Association. (Courtesy Joanna McLendon)

Haywood's signing is an amusing one. As McLendon told Carl Skiff of the *Denver Post*, the Ringsbys went to his room at New York's Lombardy Hotel at 3:30 A.M. and woke him up. "They started talking about the weather while I sat on the sofa-bed, in my pajamas, wondering what they were driving at," recalled McLendon. "Then they lunged at me and pinned me down on the bed. Don sitting on one arm, his father on the other. They said I'd better lie down while they told me the news—Spencer Haywood would be playing for me this season. I was delighted."[4]

The ABA bylaws permitted a player to be signed before his college class graduated in cases of extreme hardship. As for Haywood, he had a simple explanation for turning pro: "I was faced with the responsibility of supporting my mother and nine brothers and sisters and felt I had to play pro basketball. I looked over all the pro teams and decided I wanted to play with the Rockets because Coach McLendon was there. I admire and respect him and felt he was the man that could bring the most out of me." Ringsby felt that Haywood had the potential to become the most dominant force in basketball at the time, since Bill Russell, the Boston Celtics' player-coach, had recently announced his retirement. Haywood himself certainly wasn't shy about his talent, proclaiming his desire to become the "greatest player to ever play the game."[5]

In the Rockets' press release of August 23, Haywood spoke of his admiration for his new coach: "I like coach McLendon's system. He really likes to run and so do I. We have a great deal of mutual respect for each other, and other than my high school coach, Will Robinson at Pershing High School in Detroit, there is no one I'd rather play for." McLendon felt equally positive about his new star player. "I am extremely happy to have the opportunity to coach Spencer again," declared the coach. "He fits the fast-break style of play perfectly, and he is a proven winner and a fine young man in every way."[6]

Irv Moss quoted McLendon in the *Denver Post* the following day as stating that "Spencer is without a doubt the top player on the collegiate scene today." More than that, the new Rockets coach was impressed with Haywood's work ethic. "He's a player right out of the old school," said McLendon. "He really works hard and with dedication and seriousness." McLendon said the addition of Haywood to the Rockets fit right in with his strategy of using a high-low post offense. The Denver coach declared that he expected terrific results from having players like Haywood and veteran center Byron Beck in the lineup at the same time. "And the more experience they have at playing both center and forward the better it will be," McLendon noted. Haywood's signing also had a positive effect on Rockets season-ticket sales. In the past, Ringsby said, "we had to go out and sell tickets. But now, for the first time since we've been in business, they (the fans) are starting to call us."[7]

Before the season began, a *Denver Post* reporter asked McLendon whether he expected any discipline problems with the Rockets. "Not really," he answered. "The pros are different than college players, even though there're still some pros you have to baby-sit. Nevertheless,

The First Black Coach in the ABA

McLendon welcoming 1968 Olympic star Spencer Haywood to the Denver Rockets. (Courtesy Joanna McLendon)

they're supposed to be more mature. In college, I permitted no smoking, no drinking and no exceptions, except one. He was Norbert (Slim) Downing at North Carolina College. He had smoked a clay pipe since he was twelve and it was part of him. With the Rockets I'll ask them to consider smoking and drinking only in private, never in public." After a moment's reflection, he added: "And I know how to discipline a pro, if I have to. It's back here," McLendon patted his hip pocket. "And it looks like this," he said, pulling out his wallet.[8]

Although he was excited about the challenge before him, obstacles to success plagued the new coach from the very beginning. Upon meeting his team, he immediately implemented his usual fast-paced offense and grueling preseason conditioning drills. Because of the thin air in Denver, this style of ball would be problematic, but McLendon figured that after he got his players in shape, their opponents would be gasping for air. Although a few members of the Rockets supported McLendon's methods, which included running the two miles around Green Lake in twelve minutes or less, the team largely objected to his training regimen. Spencer Haywood believed it was difficult for some players—both white and black—to take direction from a black coach, and McLendon's conditioning drills irritated them. "The style was a running style and pressing defense," Haywood told Ron Thomas. "You have to be in tremendous shape and have to put your body through rigorous training to do that, and most people don't know how to do that. That's when you separate the men from the boys, and a lot of boys stepped up, both white and black."[9]

Byron Beck told Robert Matthews of the *Rocky Mountain News* that "there were a couple of players that were what I would call mental problems. They couldn't get around the track, but get that person on the floor and he could run all day." Lonnie Wright, a popular player who had spent two seasons playing football with the Denver Broncos before joining the Rockets, admitted to Matthews that he had problems with McLendon not only for his training methods but also for the way the coach related to his players. "He would practice us three times a day sometimes," he said. "We didn't make adjustments to his discipline, but I just thought as professionals we did not have enough flexibility. It was just about treating us as adults."[10]

McLendon stated in an interview with Thomas that two major problems in Denver prevented him from getting the players he wanted to make the team successful. First, he had been told that none of the players had no-cut contracts, but when he tried to cut two players, Lonnie Wright and Larry Jones, who said "running was for horses and automobiles," he found out otherwise. Each had a no-cut contract. The second restriction was that the team's owners had apparently decided to keep the roster exactly racially balanced, with six black players and six white ones. McLendon said that the team's chairman of the board, Bill Ringsby, never directly told him about the six-six policy. While the coach wanted to pick his roster based on merit, he felt that the team owner had other considerations. Specifically, McLendon brought in Floyd Theard, who had played for him at Kentucky State, and Ben Warley, a star player at Tennessee A&I and the Cleveland Pipers, to help run his fast-break offense. He also wanted to sign John Barnhill, one of his favorite former players, who had been cut loose by the NBA's Baltimore Bullets, but said Ringsby insisted on keeping roster spots open for white players. Don Ringsby, the club's general manager, later denied that his father had restricted McLendon's player choices. "I can tell you that any time John wanted a player, we let him get him," Ringsby told Matthews. "He had full freedom to coach the team. For him to say we had racial quotas, I find that insulting."[11]

Whatever the case, McLendon's biggest hurdle was perhaps the Rockets' schedule. Opening the season with a brutal run that had them on the road for twenty-one of their first twenty-eight games, Denver suffered a seven-game losing streak. After an eighteen-day road trip that saw the Rockets lose six out of ten games, the end came for McLendon. Of note, however, is the fact that only one of the losses on this trip was by more than 6 points. One came in overtime, another in double overtime, and a third on a last-second shot in regulation time by Indiana's Roger Brown. Dealing with all these problems, McLendon managed only a 9–19 record. Years later, he joked that if Haywood, who was enjoying one of the most amazing individual performances in professional basketball history that season, averaging 30 points per game and 19.5 rebounds, and being named Rookie of the Year and league MVP, hadn't been playing for him, "I would have been 0–28."[12]

In a surprise move, the Rockets fired McLendon on December 9, 1969, the day after his team lost their nineteenth game to the ABA's Western Division leaders, the New Orleans Buccaneers, in overtime, 105–99. Replaced as coach, he was instead offered a position as director of player personnel for the Rockets. Within hours, Theard and Lonnie Lynn, two black players who were close to the coach, were also dropped from the team. Warley still bristled when he spoke to Matthews years after the firing: "What hurt Coach McLendon was that he was the same on the court and off, always a gentleman. The management felt he wasn't rowdy enough. He wasn't jumping up and down and throwing his coat. I guess they wanted him to do like a clown."[13]

"McLendon knew his Xs and 0s better than anybody," said Joe Belmont, the former referee and member of the Rockets front-office staff who succeeded him as coach, "but he needed time for the players to buy into his system." Nevertheless, Ringsby was apparently convinced that McLendon's time was up. "It is with great regret," Ringsby said to the press, "that we must make the change, but we have been greatly disappointed with the club's poor showing through the first third of the 1969–1970 season. We had high hopes at the beginning of the year. With the addition of Olympic superstar Spencer Haywood, the Rockets were picked as one of the strongest team in the league. To date, they have failed to live up to this reputation." "I have the greatest respect for John McLendon," Ringsby concluded. "My biggest regret is that I induced him to leave a successful and happy situation at Cleveland State University this past spring." Years later, Don Ringsby told Matthews that this was merely a business decision. "Quite frankly, I'm sorry I hired John," he said. "I think I did him a disservice. It just became obvious to me he wasn't ready for the pro game."[14]

The following day, McLendon was quoted in the *Denver Post,* stating that he had been unaware of any timetable for success, nor did he have any warning that he was about to be fired. "It might have been different for me if, I suppose," McLendon said, "they had said, 'if you aren't in a certain position in the league by such and such a date,' but no, it came as a complete surprise." McLendon said that he felt that Ringsby "was in a vulnerable position and susceptible to pressure, but his timetable must have been private. He didn't share it with me." McLendon thought the owner understood that it would take a little time for the players to adjust to his fast-break style of play. "I fought for my job, yes," declared McLendon. "We were doing as much as we could do, and I don't know if the pressure on me or the team would have been different if there had been a timetable. There must be a better way to do this."[15]

According to the press, two criticisms commonly launched against McLendon concerned his system of substitutions and his failure to take advantage of the ABA's team-foul rule, the latter allowing intentional fouling near the end of each period, depending upon the number of fouls a team had acquired. Regarding substitutions, McLendon said, "No one knew better than Don [Ringsby] our internal problems, such as the injuries to (Byron) Beck and (Julie) Hammond." McLendon touched on other injuries as the reason his club was not up to par, explaining his varied combinations. "I only had what I called my best unit together for three games," he said, "and we won two and lost another in overtime." As for team fouls, McLendon stated that this was just "a theory that doesn't always work. But when you decide you want a new car you find a lot of things wrong with the old one."[16]

In an article in the *Rocky Mountain News,* Rockets players indicated that McLendon's firing came as no great surprise to them. Although they had felt a change was imminent, most were saddened to see McLendon go. "It's a cold business," Beck explained, "and the coach is usually the first to go." "As for McLendon," said Jeff Congdon, a Rockets veteran who did not appreciate McLendon's system, "I think everyone knew it was coming. When you have as much talent as we have, there has to be a change somewhere. But no one was glad to see this happen to him because we all like him and he was a warm man. Perhaps if we would have gotten a few breaks, things might have been different." With fourteen of the next nineteen games at home and everybody healthy, the breaks began to fall the Rockets' way. Under Belmont, the team completed the season in first place, compiling a 51–33 record, with Spencer Haywood leading the way, averaging over 30 points per game and becoming the league's leading scorer and rebounder. Belmont exhibited uncommon decency when he chose not to take the bulk of the credit for the turnabout. "John would have been successful had he had time here," Belmont told Matthews. "He knows basketball, and he knows the situation. He had them in shape, and I believe John had an overall plan." Even Lonnie Wright admitted that McLendon was probably on the right track. "We didn't reap the benefits of John McLendon until the second part of the season," he told Matthews. "That was probably all due to the fundamental development."[17]

Curiously, Spencer Haywood, the Rockets' ace rookie who had sought a job with the Denver team because of McLendon, had no official comment on his firing. When questioned about this years later, Haywood stated that he should have backed McLendon more forcefully, perhaps even quitting the team after his coach was let go. Haywood said that McLendon was a father figure to him, "the genuine article," and he felt terrible that McLendon was treated so unfairly by the owners, who even used him to entice Haywood into signing with the Rockets. Another player who strongly supported McLendon, Lonnie Lynn, doubted that McLendon was used in this manner but did strongly believe that Don Ringsby, a man who admittedly knew little about basketball, was heavily influenced by a few disgruntled players and never appreciated the complex strategy that McLendon was trying to incorporate. According to Lynn, "McLendon knew basketball better than anybody" and "taught me about every inch of the floor." Both Haywood and Lynn believed this to be a sad situation, for McLendon never got a chance to realize the fruits of his labor.[18]

Chet Nelson, sports editor of the *Rocky Mountain News,* offered an explanation for the firing in an editorial entitled "Too Nice a Guy." Nelson wrote that "the schedule of twenty-one of the first twenty-nine games on the road, plus reported player dissatisfaction, caught up with quiet and friendly John McLendon. This kindly Negro gentleman is simply too nice a person to be wrapped up in the stormy segments of professional athletics. McLendon is a knowledgeable basketball man, a shrewd judge of talent," concluded Nelson, "but he belongs in the AAU game where he became prominent."[19]

When McLendon came home the night of his controversial firing, he was met at the door by his wife, Joanna, who was crying. As usual, he had a calm look on his face, telling her things would work out for the best. Although Joanna, angry at the Rockets' owner for not giving her husband time to succeed, sent an impassioned telegram to Ringsby protesting the firing, McLendon took the situation in stride, stating: "That's professional sports. . . . The team is going to start winning because it is at home for fourteen of our next nineteen games and the new coach is going to look good when they do." Years later, McLendon, typically, harbored no malice over his firing, even when some observers suggested that the Rockets had prospered because of his dismissal. In an interview with Matthews, McLendon said, "I was glad he [Belmont] was succeeding, and especially glad that the players were succeeding." After observing his wife one night become so upset over the injustice dealt her husband that she began sticking pins in a voodoo doll, he counseled Joanna not to worry, that a better opportunity would soon come along. "All I've ever said about the experience," McLendon declared, laughing, "is that it didn't stop me from getting elected to the Hall of Fame."[20]

Looking back on his professional coaching experience, McLendon reminisced: "I was spoiled by the Industrial League experience. That was the best; college is next. I'm really not cut out for professional coaching. You don't have enough control over your team and I depend on the player-coach relationship, and this type of relationship is practically destroyed. They might be sold, and now with the free-agent system, you don't have enough control over who you have." However, in February 1970, when it was announced that his former hometown of Cleveland had been awarded an NBA franchise, the *Press* ran an article stating that McLendon had applied for a position with the new team. Reached at his home in Denver, McLendon freely admitted his desire to bring his expertise to the NBA. "I am very interested in joining the Cleveland group in some capacity . . . either as coach, general manager, or working in personnel," he said. The opportunity to coach in the NBA never came. "I do think I should have been given a chance to coach in the NBA, but they weren't ready for it," McLendon told Thomas. "When I started applying for it, I got some of the best letters of refusal you ever saw."[21]

Years later, McLendon spoke with deep sincerity about the special relationship he enjoyed with his young players and the important role coaching played in his life. "Today, it is the last frontier to capture the attention of youth and do different things to help them. Most institutions of society have relinquished that role," he maintained. "I always liked the idea of what you can do with five players out there with unusual skills. I liked to see individual skills develop and merge into a team. I like to see more discipline in high level sports," concluded McLendon. "When you do that with great individuals, you get a great team."[22]

CHAPTER 9

National and International Ambassador of Basketball for Converse, Inc., 1969–89

A few days after McLendon was fired by the Rockets, Grady Lewis, vice president of Converse Rubber Company and fellow Naismith Basketball Hall of Famer, offered him a position as the company's national and international promotional representative, telling him, "Whatever is good for basketball, and good for Converse, you do—and do it anywhere around the world."[1]

McLendon knew Chuck Taylor, whose signature brand of Converse canvas basketball shoes had a strong hold on the market across America in the 1960s. The friendship between the two led Converse to hire McLendon, and he soon emerged as a most worthy successor to the legendary Taylor, whose basketball knowledge and promotional zeal had helped to make Converse the dominant name in athletic footwear for many decades throughout the world. In order to continue the Taylor legacy, Converse wanted McLendon to be more centrally located and asked him to move to Chicago. He and Joanna purchased the home where Grady Lewis used to live, on Clyde Drive in Downers Grove, a pleasant middle-class suburb nineteen miles west of Chicago.

Joanna took a position as principal of an elementary school in the LaGrange school district, while McLendon enjoyably spent the next twenty years teaching basketball clinics and promoting Converse shoes around the world. In this capacity, he traveled to fifty-eight countries in Europe, Asia, Africa, South America, and the Middle East, teaching the fundamentals of basketball and the value of sportsmanship in life. In 1971, he was appointed as the only U.S. representative to the World Basketball Rules Committee; the following year, he was reappointed to the U.S. Olympic Committee, serving again as chief scout for the U.S. Olympic basketball team for the games in Munich. Many believe that

McLendon contributed more to the worldwide proliferation of basketball than any other individual. Indeed, videos outlining his basketball precepts can be found in the homes of coaches throughout the world. McLendon held private clinics, ran summer leagues, became a motivational speaker, and taught his strategies to high school and college teams. According to Lewis, McLendon was outstanding at his job, always thorough, enthusiastic, and professional. "Everybody loved and admired him," stated Lewis, "and Converse was proud to have him on its team."[2]

With Lewis at the helm, McLendon joined others in initiating direct communication between Converse and high school and college coaches in the Chicago area and beyond. Hired by Converse upon his graduation from the University of Kansas in 1976, Roger Morningstar, who roomed with McLendon at a sales and promotions convention in Denver, was immediately impressed by the famed coach's demeanor and personality. "Coach McLendon had a tremendous ability to put himself in other people's shoes," recalled Morningstar, "and consequently everybody loved and admired him. His contribution to making Converse and basketball one was substantial in the United States and throughout the world." In the 1970s, Converse found new ways to advertise its sneakers, placing them on the feet of the NBA's top players, who in turn would promote the shoes. Ironically, Julius Erving, whom McLendon had attempted to recruit for Cleveland State almost a decade before, became the first pro pitchman for Converse in 1975. The corporation added college and NBA superstars Ervin "Magic" Johnson and Larry Bird as spokesmen six years later. Further, "it was through McLendon's quiet urgings that the company [Converse] began hiring Blacks in their factories and on their sales and promotional teams," Howie Evans wrote in the *Cleveland Call & Post*. Indeed, Evans was one of the first African Americans to join the Converse staff in the early 1970s, and he joined because of McLendon.[3]

"Converse had a problem with extra shoes that were shopworn," McLendon told Matthews, "and I created a thing called 'Operation Bigfoot.' And one year I gave away 8,000 pairs of shoes to all the colleges and universities I could think of in this country—mostly the little schools, the smaller NAIA schools. They were going to destroy those shoes because they were shopworn anyway." McLendon took great delight in delivering shoes to the poor kids at the Martin Luther King

National and International Ambassador of Basketball

McLendon as an assistant to Coach Henry Iba with the 1972 U.S. Olympic basketball team. (Courtesy Joanna McLendon)

Boys Club on the West Side of Chicago. "They would just pick up those shoes as fast as they could," he recalled. "They didn't care what size or anything. They just wanted a pair of new Converse basketball shoes." While McLendon was working for Converse, other coaching opportunities came his way, but he declined. "Thinking about the problems associated with the highly competitive nature of college recruiting gave me second thoughts of returning to the coaching ranks," said McLendon. "Besides, I got to do a lot more for people in the Converse position, and that brought me immense satisfaction."[4]

Among the many contributions he made to young American athletes while working for Converse was telling them that athletics should be considered a stepping stone to greater achievement, not viewed as all encompassing. "Athletics is a vehicle to assist in scholastic objectives and education," he told a group of high school and college athletes on January 28, 1980, at the 100% Wrong Club's award dinner, sponsored

McLendon awarding the Converse MVP trophy to Joe Pace, Coppin State College, NAIA Tournament, Kansas City, 1976. (Courtesy NAIA)

by the *Atlanta Daily World*. "A man should want to go to school and participate in athletics, not just be an athlete." McLendon, charging the media with being partially responsible for developing the theory that sports is everything in life, advised the athletes that this is not the case. "The media will mislead you to think that the end of life is athletic achievement, but this isn't so," said the recently inducted Hall of Fame coach. "The end of life is making yourself respected, a worthwhile citizen." McLendon also instructed the young athletes about the true meaning of the word *champion*. "Champions are people who are not afraid to condition themselves to the *n*th degree and who are not afraid to be the best," he said. "A champion is one who has mental toughness and psychic, inner power. One who uses adversity as a motivating factor and not as an excuse for mediocrity and defeat."[5]

On average, McLendon conducted ten to fifteen clinics per month, traveling the world for Converse. "It's not really work for me," he quipped. "It's one of the most pleasurable things I do." In the summer of 1980, at the request of Mao Tayo-Yun, people's commissioner of basketball, McLendon took his lifetime of experience to the ancient city of Nanking, on China's mainland, where he and 1980 NAIA championship coach Lonnie Nichols of Cameron University conducted a two-day, eleven-and-a-half-hour basketball clinic for more than two hundred coaches, representing all sixteen provinces of the largest nation on earth. "We had 206 coaches in attendance and I've never seen anything like it," said McLendon. "When we would come into this huge fieldhouse in Nanking, the whole audience would stand up at attention and applaud, and they'd do the same thing when we left each day." The coach was impressed with the Chinese love for and commitment to basketball, predicting the country would become an international power in the near future.[6]

This first trip to China was so successful that the following spring the U.S. State Department requested that McLendon return, along with the University of Washington's Marv Harshman, a fellow Hall of Famer, to conduct clinics over a five-week period in Suen Yang for 256 men and women coaches, instructing them in how to teach basketball to Chinese youth. The two American coaches met with the women's national team in the morning and the men's in the afternoon. They each lectured for an hour, then demonstrated the skills and strategies they had discussed for the remainder of the period. The people's commissioner of basketball had each of the clinics videotaped, resulting in a large coaching manual that would be used throughout the country. According to Harshman, both he and McLendon were treated as celebrities and told by the commissioner that "basketball will flower in China because of what you are doing." Indeed, looking back at the great strides the Chinese have made in the sport, these two American coaches were certainly right to take pride in their efforts.[7]

In April 1979, Coach McLendon and Tony Banks, a Midwestern

business executive who had lived in Africa for five years, joined with the *Black College Basketball Yearbook* in creating an opportunity for two historically black colleges to participate in the Pan African Classic in Dakar, Senegal. McLendon was proud to report that highly rated North Carolina A&T won the international tournament, defeating Senegal, 76–73; Virginia Union edged out Ivory Coast for third place. The tournament was a huge success: euphoric crowds jammed the Dakar Sports Arena, overflowing the five-thousand-seat capacity. All the games were televised and received extensive newspaper and magazine coverage. Visiting coaches and players were besieged with requests for autographs and bombarded with questions about life in the United States.

Impressed with the Africans' caliber of play, McLendon later noted that the Americans and the Africans, specifically the Senegales and the Ivoriens, not only played good basketball against each other but also exchanged ideas on how their game might be improved. On returning to the United States, the Hall of Fame coach insisted that it wouldn't be long before NBA scouts took up permanent residence in Abidjan, Dakar, Bangul, Libreville, Lagos, Kinshasa, Brazzabille, Thies, and other African basketball hotbeds. McLendon took special note of the Africans' quick reactions, composure under pressure, precision, and technical efficiency around the basket. Several players for Senegal and the Ivory Coast had rendered sensational performances. "They could play for anybody," McLendon avowed. "On a broader plane," noted U.S. ambassador Herman J. Cohen, "this experience, the first of its kind, also enabled the black American teams to increase their understanding of their African heritage. Likewise, it provided an opportunity for Africans to know black Americans on a first-hand basis."[8]

In 1972, McLendon became an advisor to the Chicago Public League Basketball Coaches Association and began organizing and supporting annual Public League basketball clinics and an All-Star game. In 1980, he organized a visit to the Chicago Martin Luther King Boys Club by the Ivory Coast's men's national team, which would participate in the summer league over one month and eighteen games and help the Chicago team improve its game. This was a first-time international experience for Chicago youth, and McLendon would organize a similar program for Cleveland youth in 1990. In 1988, McLendon led Chicago boys' and girls' team entrants in the International Youth Tournament in the Netherlands, a new opportunity for Illinois public school student athletes. His longtime friend Ken Denzel traveled to Champaign, Illinois, where the High School Athletic Commission was meeting, to obtain special permission for the students to travel abroad during their spring break, representing the United States. Dorothy Gaters, coach of the girls' team from John Marshall High School, recalled that over nine days her team lost only one game, and the boys' team from Simeon High School was also successful. Gaters said that Coach McLendon gave all the young students an inspirational talk on how to conduct themselves abroad to function as excellent goodwill ambassadors for the United States. They all lived up to his expectations, since neither she nor her players wanted to let Coach McLendon down.[9]

Norm Sonju, retired founding president and general manager of the Dallas Mavericks, and presently the chairman and CEO of the Christian Family Camp-in-the-Woods in upstate New York, had first met McLendon in the early 1970s, when they were neighbors in Downers Grove. Sonju was so impressed by McLendon's generous spirit, and all the social and psychological barriers he had overcome in his life, that when the dean at George Williams College asked him to take over the basketball team for a couple of years, he consented with one stipulation—that John McLendon be his full-time assistant. The dean agreed, and McLendon was there to lend his expertise whenever Sonju needed him or had to leave town. The two men established a lifelong friendship. For one week every summer over twenty-five years, Sonju brought McLendon to his New York camp to serve as the main instructor at the basketball clinic that he held for 132 boys, ages twelve to fifteen. Sonju recalled that more than forty professional athletes served on his staff over the years, but none was as purely loved or respected, by the professional athletes on down to the campers, than the man everyone called "Coach Mac." Sonju, recalling the laudatory role McLendon played in integrating collegiate and professional athletics, said, "There was no finer person in the world to move that along than John McLendon."[10]

While working for Converse in 1977, McLendon received the prestigious Metropolitan Award from the New York Basketball Writers Association. Two years later, he received the Push for Excellence Award for the Outstanding Man in Athletics; the NAACP Recognition Award; and the Outstanding Achievement Award from the National Health, Physical Education, and Sports Association. In April 1979, McLendon received perhaps his highest honor, becoming the first black coach inducted into the Naismith Memorial Basketball Hall of Fame in Springfield, Massachusetts. He often said that this was one of the proudest moments of his life. College athletic directors, basketball coaches, the National Athletic Steering Committee, former players, and journalists like Howie Evans, sports editor of the *New York Amsterdam News,* had been calling for the Hall of Fame's recognition of black coaches, especially McLendon and Clarence Gaines, for a number of years. Under the headline "Basketball Hall of Fame Ignoring Black Coaches," Evans had persuasively argued the case for McLendon's and Gaines's enshrinement, contending that the only explanation for the neglect of these two deserving coaches must be their racial makeup. Some also contend that the various NCAA representatives who wielded power in the Hall of Fame selection process kept McLendon out long enough to kill his eligibility for induction in the coaches' category. When he did finally make it in, McLendon was chosen in the contributors' category.[11]

Nevertheless, after years of waiting, and after having been nominated five different times since 1970 by a host of former players, friends, and colleagues, on January 26, 1979, McLendon was immensely pleased to receive the congratulatory letter from the Hall of Fame's executive director, Lee Williams. The letter began with Williams extending his official and personal congratulations upon McLendon's "selection to Basketball's greatest single honor. Our distinguished Honors Committee has recognized your greatness in the game and we now welcome you to a permanent place in Basketball History." In his letter, Williams informed McLendon that he would be inducted the following spring and then added a handwritten note: "Time has a wonderful way! How pleased I am for you." The official announcement became even more gratifying when McLendon learned that he would be inducted alongside another University of Kansas Jayhawk, Wilt Chamberlain, and a Chicago friend, DePaul University coach Ray Meyer.[12]

In an article by Gerry Finn that ran in the *Springfield Union* on May 1, 1979, just before the enshrinement, the journalist noted that McLendon "was feeling melancholy." "It's sort of like being back in the classroom," said the new Hall of Fame inductee, his eyes growing moist. "I had no idea we'd [he and Dr. Naismith] wind up together in a place like this. Especially me. When he was teaching me there in Kansas, I couldn't even get into the school swimming pool. Oh, I take that back.

McLendon with presenter Bob Davies, Naismith Memorial Basketball Hall of Fame induction ceremony, 1979. (Courtesy Naismith Memorial Basketball Hall of Fame)

I did get in once. And they drained the pool the next day." McLendon insisted to everyone present that he owed most of his success, as an outstanding basketball coach and as a champion of his race's fight for recognition in the sport, to Dr. Naismith. "It took time and patience, but things did change," McLendon told Finn. "When the doors were still closed, I only prayed the black schools would sustain their record of excellence in the sport. They did, and the contributions to basketball

McLendon with Wilt Chamberlain and other University of Kansas notables—Don Baker, A. C. "Dutch" Lonborg, Bill Johnson, and Ted Owens—at the 1979 Naismith Hall of Fame induction ceremony. (Courtesy Spencer Research Library, University of Kansas Libraries)

by blacks in all phases of the game are obvious." He then declared with a big smile, "You bet I feel good about it."[13]

"It's been tough on me at times," he admitted to Finn. "But I always had my association with Dr. Naismith to fall back on in time of trouble. So, this day is very special for me . . . perhaps more so because it puts me back in touch with what has been the greatest influence on my life. I'm here. Dr. Naismith's here. I can't believe it."[14]

In the Hall of Fame citation, McLendon was honored not only for his remarkable coaching career but also, appropriately, as "the acknowledged leader of the emergence of the black colleges of the U.S. into the varied National Championship programs." He was introduced by his close friend Bob Davies, four-time NBA All-Star guard from the Rochester Royals, who had been enshrined in the Hall of Fame ten years earlier. During the ceremony, McLendon spoke of the obstacles he had overcome in order to get there. "The biggest problem I had in life," said McLendon, "was trying to get through those years when prejudice and segregation were too much a part of some areas' lives. It was a struggle to make people recognize that black people were great athletes. We couldn't make the newspapers then. We weren't discovered by the media until the 50s, or by the pros until Jackie Robinson in '47 in baseball." He went on to explain that his "whole program was to try to get my players and other coaches and their players to sustain the kind of excellence that would qualify those schools and those athletes—and black athletes elsewhere—as contenders for athletic national championships and positions."[15]

Friends, family, former players, and Converse coworkers jammed the Hall and the Honors Court where McLendon was enshrined. When the ceremonies were concluded, McLendon posed for television cameras, newspaper reporters, and admirers, as some one hundred people fought their way through the crowd to have their picture taken with him. According to Howie Evans, McLendon signed autographs for well over an hour, obviously enjoying every moment. Having returned from conducting basketball clinics in Africa just a day before, he must have been tired, but he certainly did not show it. "I'll wake up later today or tomorrow," he said when someone asked how he felt. A few days after the Hall of Fame weekend, Lee Williams wrote another letter to McLendon: "Please know how proud we are that you have been inducted. Throughout your basketball life you have enhanced the game in so many ways. You have and are giving of your time and talents so that basketball is much the better and constantly growing because of your participation."[16]

Above the entrance to the Naismith Memorial Basketball Hall of Fame are meaningful quotes by outstanding Hall of Famers throughout the years. Unlike the others, one quote speaks directly to significant social change in modern American history. Understandably, this quote is from John B. McLendon Jr.: "Basketball has been a powerful force for understanding and improved race relations in our society."

That he was successful in the struggle for racial equality, there is no doubt. According to Howie Evans, McLendon "was a civil rights activist long before Martin Luther King and others became involved in the civil rights movement." "Over a career that dated back to the 1930s," Evans noted, "Coach Mac set a standard of excellence that became as much a part of his profession as did the many innovative systems, drills, and fundamental foundations he created. He was one of the greatest teachers of basketball in history." Reflecting on the 2006 inspirational film

Glory Road, chronicling the 1966 upset victory of Texas Western over an all-white University of Kentucky quintet, Evans declared that "there wouldn't be any *Glory Road* or black players in the NBA if it wasn't for the tireless efforts of John McLendon."[17]

There is an ironic postscript to the story of McLendon's election to the Hall of Fame. Eighteen years afterward, McLendon received a Hall of Fame card displaying his likeness on a medallion. It read that he was "elected coach in 1979." Upon receiving the medallion, McLendon immediately wrote a highly assertive, passionate letter to Joe O'Brien, president of the Naismith Memorial Hall of Fame, urging him to recall this item, to *"cease and desist its production and reproduction at once!"* In this letter, which revealed his strength of character, McLendon pointed out that he had been nominated five times as a coach but had not been elected in that category. Since there was a five-year limit on any one nomination at the time (a rule that was later rescinded), he had had to wait three more years before he entered the Hall of Fame as a contributor. "It took nine years for me to finally make it," declared McLendon, "and I do not intend to give this new more meaningful position away to be listed as a 'coach' *unofficially,* a real subterfuge here *and* in the Hall's guidebook since 1990. Do not have my life in Basketball misrepresented now and into the next century. I have been continually complimented and honored greatly for the past eighteen years just to be in the Hall of Fame. I am *not* proud to be honored for a place accorded me *unofficially* to replace me in the position I 'earned' *officially.*" Apparently, McLendon's letter received a favorable response, as the error was ultimately rectified, and he was officially listed as a "contributor" once again.[18]

For his efforts both on and off the court, McLendon was subsequently inducted into fifteen other halls of fame, including the CIAA's (1978), the National Sports Hall of Fame (1979), the NAIA's (1983), North Carolina Central University's (1984), Tennessee State University's (1984), the Mid-Eastern Athletic Conference's (1986), the Pigskin Hall of Fame (1993), the North Carolina Sports Hall of Fame (1996), the Illinois Basketball Coaches Hall of Fame (1996), the Cleveland Sports Hall of Fame (1998), the State of Kansas Sports Hall of Fame (2004), and the Cleveland State University Athletic Hall of Fame (2007). In 1992, the Atlanta Tip-off Club honored McLendon with the Naismith Outstanding Contribution to Basketball Award, and he thus joined a select list of legendary coaches—John Wooden, Ray Meyer, Hank Iba, Adolph Rupp, Pete Newell, Red Auerbach, Nat Holman, Frank McGuire, and Clarence Gaines—who helped develop basketball to the point of its modern popularity. In 1995, the Black Coaches Association presented him with its Lifetime Achievement Award at its annual banquet in Kansas City, and three years later the University of Iowa honored him with its Distinguished Alumni Achievement Award.

McLendon was chosen as one of the NAIA's top five coaches when the organization celebrated its fiftieth anniversary in 1987 and as one of the top ten coaches of the century by CBS basketball analyst Billy Packer during the game's one hundredth anniversary in 1991. The following year, *Sports View* magazine designated John McLendon Jr. as "Coach of the Century," and in 1995 he was recognized by *Basketball America* as one of the six coaches with the greatest influence on the evolution of basketball in the United States. At a function of the 1997 NBA All-Star Game in Cleveland, all-time NBA and Boston Celtics great Bill Russell referred to Coach McLendon as "the best and greatest coach of all time." Sam Jones, who had played for McLendon and overheard Russell's comment, quickly agreed. Yet none of these numerous honors or awards changed this humble man. "The thing about Mac," said Leroy T. Walker, an assistant under McLendon at North Carolina College and later president of the U.S. Olympic Committee, "is that he is unaffected by his greatness."[19]

Known as "Mr. Clutch," Sam Jones was one of the linchpins of the fabulous Boston Celtics juggernauts of the 1950s and 1960s. His uncanny, accurate bank shots, lightning quickness, and cool demeanor helped the Celtics win ten NBA championships in the twelve years he played for the team. A member of the NBA Hall of Fame, he was chosen as one of the fifty greatest players in NBA history. Although Jones played for Coach McLendon at North Carolina College for only one year, during the Eagles' 1951–52 championship season, he was very close to him. After McLendon left North Carolina College to coach at Hampton Institute, Jones found himself playing against McLendon's new team. A prolific scorer, Jones stopped by the opponents' bench and said to McLendon, "Coach, I hate to do this to you." Although it had taken Jones about eight games to make the starting lineup his first year at North Carolina under Coach McLendon, he went on to become one of the most outstanding players in CIAA history. Elected to the NAIA Hall

McLendon smiling with justifiable pride over a few of his championship trophies earned in collegiate, NIBL, AAU, and international basketball. (Courtesy Joanna McLendon)

of Fame in 1962, he credits McLendon with helping him make an easy transition to the famed Celtic fast-break championship style of basketball. In a 2005 interview, Jones fondly remembered McLendon as an outstanding individual, a strict disciplinarian, and a man whose knowledge of basketball and sterling character earned the respect of all around him.[20]

Basketball great Julius Erving also understood Coach McLendon's exceptional nature, for when he went up against Kareem Abdul Jabbar in the 1992 "Clash of the Legends," he chose McLendon as his coach. Before the highly publicized game, according to Erving, he and Coach McLendon strategized for two hours. In an interview several years later, Erving shared his deep respect for McLendon, stating, "I wanted him on my side."[21]

Isiah Thomas, a Chicago native who starred in the NBA and hired McLendon as a consultant for the Toronto Raptors when Thomas joined the team as an executive in 1995, remembered McLendon fondly as "the father of fast-break, up-tempo basketball and other things that made the game the exciting sport it is today." "I first met Coach Mac when I was an eleven-year-old kid trying to learn how to play basketball at the Martin Luther King Boys Club in Chicago, where McLendon was chairman of the board," Thomas said. "Coach Mac would be wearing that wide perpetual smile of his, and he'd enjoy giving those shoes away and seeing us all excited. He became my friend and mentor for life. We'd spend hours talking about how the game is played, and the things he taught me about basketball and about life contributed heavily to every success I've enjoyed in every area of my basketball career."[22]

McLendon was also a role model and mentor to many Chicago-area coaches. Horace Howard, who coached at several area schools, met McLendon in the early 1940s and was a member of his NAIA championship teams at Tennessee State. "In the almost fifty years that I knew him, Coach always was there for me and others," Howard said. "He came to my schools to conduct clinics and to observe and give advice to me about coaching. If he noticed that a youngster didn't have decent gym shoes, he would give him a free pair of new ones."[23]

Legendary Chicago Marshall High School girls' basketball coach Dorothy Gaters, with a winning percentage of nearly 90 percent and more than eight hundred victories, was tutored by McLendon for many years, beginning in 1980, and she and her team traveled with him in 1988 to participate in the International Youth Tournament in the Netherlands. A *USA Today* newspaper article concluded in the early 1990s that Coach Gaters had developed the best high school program in the country, of boys or girls, and that no others compared. "What I have been fortunate to accomplish in basketball has been in large part because of Coach McLendon's great influence on me and what he has taught me, both on and off the court," recalled Gaters. "Each of my teams and players have been a reflection of him, as much as of me." She recalled that not only did people admire McLendon's intellect, but they also adored him for his great character and kindness. "But he wasn't just rich in the wisdom and knowledge of basketball," stated Gaters. "Coach Mac knew something about everything. He didn't curse, he didn't smoke, and he didn't drink, and never hollered when he coached. He was a library of information. Never once did I go to him for advice that he didn't have the answer. It was rare for him to criticize anyone. He had a way of getting his message across." Gaters and Marshall High School's men's basketball coach Luther Bedford, who together organized the Chicago Public League Basketball Coaches Association, give the John B. McLendon Award every year to the coach who best exemplifies some of McLendon's virtues of sportsmanship and integrity.[24]

As president of this association, Bedford wrote a tribute to Coach McLendon in 1991, thanking him for his continued interest in student athletes and coaching staff and for actively inspiring others with his untiring energy. "You have always been a sterling character, a genius for organization, and you display a rare wisdom that places you among the outstanding leaders of our country and the world," wrote Bedford. "Your human qualities and your love for your fellow man endears you to thousands of athletes and coaches. Your genuine interest in Chicago's athletes is demonstrated with a generous kindly presence. Your magnetic personality, your rare gifts of human expressions and a wisdom you have acquired through wide experiences, stands out among the masses." After praising McLendon for the numerous basketball clinics and tournaments he had conducted and arranged for Chicago-area athletes, Bedford declared, "Coach McLendon, you are sincere, unfailing in your kindness; you have strength of character, high ideals and expectations—these qualities have had a positive effect in the development of our athletes."[25]

Ken Denzel, who met McLendon in 1969, when he was launching his not-for-profit International Center for Athletic and Educational Opportunities for inner-city youth, remembered him as a man before his time who, though he took great pride in his title as "father of black basketball," expressed mild disappointment that he never got the chance to coach at a big-time college. Denzel recalled that his friend once applied to coach at Northwestern University but was informed that the Big Ten wasn't ready for a black coach or his style of basketball. Yet McLendon understood the role he was destined to play and always expressed an inner satisfaction with his life. "He had a personal peace and joy about him that were rare," Isiah Thomas recalled to Lacy J. Banks

National and International Ambassador of Basketball

in the *Chicago Sun-Times*. "He perhaps impressed me most with his simplicity of life and the way he lived. He made the difficult seem so easy. And his wisdom and knowledge in dealing with people was second to none."[26]

Indeed, Coach McLendon is consistently spoken of as a man of deep integrity and honor. His longtime friend and fellow Hall of Famer Clarence "Big House" Gaines once quipped that McLendon "was almost too clean to be a coach." "Keep it simple, let them play, don't overcoach, give them guidelines, then make sure you adhere to them and enforce them," McLendon loved saying, explaining his philosophy of coaching and life. His daughter, Querida Banks, proudly recalled that her father wasn't a man of situational ethics. During his initial season at Tennessee State, two star players broke curfew before the team was to play a white team for the first time in school history. Though this was probably the most important game of his career at that point, McLendon wouldn't let the two players even travel with the team. The other players, the athletic director, and even Querida tried to change his mind, but he wouldn't budge. "He stood for what he believed in," Querida said. The players learned that their coach would not compromise his values no matter what the cost, a lesson McLendon taught to all who cared to listen.[27]

Always aware of his responsibility as teacher, McLendon wrote down a "Code of Conduct for Coaches before the Players and Fans," practicing it diligently throughout his career. He understood that respect was the key to the player-coach relationship, essential for teaching, motivating, disciplining, inspiring, and coaching. McLendon wrote that the coach must educate his players (and many times his fans, students, and the public) to respect authority, which in the game is represented by the officials. Furthermore, he believed that "education of the cheerleaders, and band, may prove an assistive force in implementing sportsmanship and improved control of crowd behavior. Coaches are exceptional people," he declared. "They *must* act differently and at no time forget they are under observation at all times, that they are still 'Father Figures,' 'Heroes,' and 'Role Models.' They are 'guidance counselors' during school days and often long afterward. They are responsible for their charges learning life's lessons through competition, for changing boys into men. The coach's leadership is a requirement for the survival of *Athletics as it is supposed to be*." At basketball clinics and conferences throughout the world, McLendon preached that coaches must "insist on the very best in game and bench decorum. Do not allow less. The coach takes the leadership role through his own actions and practices."[28]

In 1987, McLendon authored a small book entitled *McBasket: A Three on Three Full Court Basketball Game,* explaining and diagramming this approach as a "developmental game which guarantees improvement in the offensive and defensive skills of the participants. Inasmuch as it is a full-court game involving three players versus three players under semi to heavy pressure," he continued, "the offensive and defensive competition reveals the depth of player ability more clearly than in a regular basketball game." The following year, he coauthored, with Milton S. Katz, a richly detailed booklet, complete with extensive photographs, about how Al Duer and the NAIA had paved the way for democracy in sports, providing upward mobility and athletic opportunities for black college athletes in post–World War II America. Called "one of the greatest sports stories of the century," this social history rendered long-overdue respect to the pioneering individuals and institutions that forced democratic principles into civil rights action.[29]

CHAPTER 10

Return to Cleveland State: Professor, Advisor, Historian, and "Just a Man"

After living in the Chicago region for twenty years, McLendon returned to the Cleveland area and Cleveland State University in 1989. He and Joanna purchased a split-level home on tree-lined Runnymede Boulevard in the diverse, progressive suburb of Cleveland Heights. Joanna first worked with the Cleveland Board of Education on a two-year project funded by Research Triangle in North Carolina. Following the completion of this assignment, she accepted a position as practicum supervisor of teacher education at Cleveland State University. Now in his midseventies, McLendon served the university as an advisor to the Athletic Department. According to Joanna, her husband also enjoyed listening to his impressive jazz collection, reading the Bible and other books of historical significance, playing chess, and even playing the harmonica on occasion. However, his greatest enjoyment came from interacting with people, and he was always looking forward to new challenges to enhance his life.

A few months after McLendon rejoined the Cleveland State staff, an African American communications major from a small town in Pennsylvania came to his office to interview him for a story to run in the campus newspaper. "I've heard people call you the Jackie Robinson of basketball," the student said. "Well, that's very flattering," McLendon replied. "But let me ask you something. Do you know who Jackie Robinson is?" "No," she replied. The next day, McLendon offered to teach a course on the role of minorities in sports, joining the faculty as a history professor teaching a popular class entitled "The History of Sports and the Role of Minorities in Its Development." Howard Mims, director of the Black Studies Program, worked to make this course a reality.[1]

The course syllabus states: "This course examines the history of the

African-American athlete in the United States of America within the context of the social and political circumstances and conditions that existed during the various time periods of his life and achievements. We will study African-American athletes in various sports while observing social and political phenomena that affected their role and development." The course covered eleven different sports and had a research list of one hundred books, from which the student would choose ten to investigate on his or her own. The one text the coach listed as required reading was Molefi K. Asante and Mark Mattson's *Historical and Cultural Atlas of African Americans,* which provided a context for Coach McLendon's focus on the sports achiever and the sporting event. Although the professor chose to concentrate on other black athletes and coaches in his class, his own life would have provided a compelling case study for the students. For McLendon, what was important was passing on the stories of black athletes and coaches—and the whites who supported them—and detailing how their struggles and triumphs helped change America.[2]

In a press release announcing the hiring of McLendon as special assistant to John Konstantinos, athletic director at Cleveland State, Konstantinos noted: "John McLendon probably knows as much about the game of basketball, its history, the people who made it the great game it is and the ways in which the game has developed as any person alive. . . . McLendon is one of the greatest natural resources Cleveland State could ever hope to draw upon in moving its basketball program forward another notch. We intend to fully utilize that resource and consider ourselves very fortunate that John is available to us."[3]

"We are proud to have John McLendon included in the history and present status of Cleveland State University," said university president Claire Van Ummersen. "John is a true pioneer, not only in the sport of basketball, but also for student-athletes from all sports and the black community at large. It was through John's tireless efforts for equality that black athletes were integrated into all sports and those black citizens were not segregated during their participation. We are proud of the role CSU played in this integration, and we are even more proud to count John McLendon as a continuing member of our university."[4]

Alice Khol, associate athletic director at Cleveland State, worked closely with Coach McLendon on a number of different projects, and they became such close friends that Khol later said she thought of him as a second father. She remembered him as an individual who was unique for his intellect and passion, for his even temperament, calling him "the most gentle man" she had ever known. "McLendon had a calming effect upon everyone," she recalled, "and his passion for social justice wasn't ever about only race; it had to do with an abiding belief in equality, for women, for minorities, for everybody."[5]

Cleveland State University awarded McLendon an honorary doctorate in humane letters in 1992. Earlier he had been granted this honor by two other institutions of higher education—North Carolina Central University in 1977 and Jarvis Christian College in Hawkins, Texas, in 1979. To honor the beloved coach, athletic advisor, and professor, Cleveland State University established the "John McLendon Outstanding Student Award," which is presented annually to the student-athlete who best represents the ideals and personal philosophy of Coach McLendon: "Foremost among these are integrity, honor, and leadership accompanied by a demonstrated commitment to civility, service to others and the concept of team first, last, and foremost." The CIAA named its Hall of Fame after Coach McLendon, and a chair placed at the end of the press table for each CIAA tournament is draped in black and bears his name. The CIAA also paid special tribute to McLendon during its tournament's sixtieth anniversary in Raleigh, North Carolina, in March 2005. Applauding McLendon as "the Father of Black Basketball," the tournament program read, "For his coaching genius, his quiet but strategically planned fight for social change, and for his leadership and organizational skills, 'Coach Mac' has emerged as one who was short in stature, but was a gentle giant in so many ways."[6]

In 1992, the Tennessee Secondary School Athletic Association paid tribute to McLendon as "a great coach, an outstanding individual, and a true gentleman." In "A Special Tribute to a Living Legend—John B. McLendon," Gene Beck wrote: "Many times we overlook the sacrifices made by those who have gone before us. We take for granted life as we know it to be today. There are many leaders who by their ideals and high standards of living have set examples for all to follow. One of these special people is Coach John McLendon."[7]

There is little doubt that McLendon changed the game of basketball forever. According to University of Maryland professor Neil Isaacs, author of *All the Moves: The History of College Basketball*: "To

McLendon and his wife Joanna being honored at the rededication of the McLendon- McDougald Gymnasium, North Carolina Central University, 1991. (Courtesy Joanna McLendon)

talk about the fast break without talking about John McLendon is like talking about the interpretation of dreams without talking about Freud. . . . Under his rigorous training, all of his teams have run, whatever their size, and under his vigorous teaching they have run the classic patterns, filling the lanes, finding the trailers, and converting to offense from any possible situation." William C. Rhoden remarked, in a 1993 *New York Times* article, "McLendon's influence, if not his spirit, will be felt in arenas across the nation, every time a fast break is executed, every time a team presses for forty minutes. McLendon didn't invent the fast break. But as a head coach of Tennessee State between 1954–1959, he helped popularize it and widen the concept of what a fast break could be with well-conditioned athletic players with speed and quickness."[8]

During Black History Month in 1999, host Ernie Johnson Jr. and

Tennessee State University president James A. Hefner—along with Richard Miller, Howard Gentry, Frankie Allen, Harold Hunter, and Bill Thomas—salutes John McLendon by naming the Tigers' court in his honor, 1995. (Courtesy Tennessee State University)

analyst Kenny Smith, of TNT's Emmy Award–winning show *Inside the NBA*, paid special tribute to eighty-three-year-old John McLendon. Smith opened by remarking, "It is not often that you're in the presence of someone you're in awe of not only for what they accomplished for themselves but also for society," going on to describe McLendon as an innovator, a builder of character, and a social pioneer. Acutely aware that McLendon was the last remaining link to Dr. James Naismith, and conscious of McLendon's impact on the game of basketball, Smith pointed out that "every single NBA player is connected to this man in some way." At the conclusion of the show, Johnson and Smith agreed that "Coach McLendon is the root from which great players have evolved." Mike Cleary, executive director of the National Association for College Directors of Athletics (NACDA), stated in 1995 that

McLendon's contributions to the game of basketball are the stuff of legends: "He was the benchmark by which other people are measured."[9]

Marty Blake, the NBA's director of scouting for more than twenty-eight years, certainly would agree with Cleary's assessment, as his relationship with McLendon stretched over more than fifty years. Regarded as one of the leading authorities on college and professional basketball in the United States and, increasingly, throughout the world, Blake has spent more than five decades evaluating basketball talent both on the court and in the coaching profession. As general manager of the St. Louis Hawks in the late 1950s, Blake saw McLendon's Tennessee State teams capture three straight NAIA championships in Kansas City and was so impressed that he drafted two of McLendon's star players, John Barnhill and Joe Buckhalter. "Their fast-break style of basketball used to terrorize teams," said Blake. He and Hawks coach Ed Macauley, an NBA Hall of Famer, took great delight in sitting in the stands at Municipal Auditorium, watching the Tigers play. "McLendon was one of the great minds of basketball and a great international ambassador for the game while he worked at Converse," said Blake. "But even more important, he was a generous man with his time and a great human being. No man had more to do with changing the face of collegiate (or perhaps pro) basketball than the soft-spoken McLendon. Eventually he earned the respect of America's coaching fraternity, and in later years his fame circled the globe."[10]

McLendon was the author of two books on basketball fundamentals and numerous articles on the history of black basketball in America, and coauthor of a work on the NAIA and the integration of intercollegiate athletics in post–World War II America; his contributions to sports and equality in American society are legendary. Through courage, hard work, persistence, gentleness, dignity, and respect for all men and women, he demonstrated that ability, not skin color, should be the measure of an athlete's work. After observing the heartbreak that Olympic athletes felt when they failed to win a gold medal in Rome in 1960, he wrote a poem, "Ode to the Vanquished," which he dedicated to those "winners" who do not always finish in first place but always give their "best." The last stanza of his poem reads:

> Total the sum of life's great test
>
> Find honor is given for only your best.

McLendon with NACDA director and president Mike Cleary, presenting the John McLendon MVP Award to Richard Crumble, Cleveland State University, 1998. (Courtesy Mike Cleary, NACDA)

> Regardless of finish, your place in the sun
>
> Is decided by the race you've run.
>
> From birth, as from the starter's blast,
>
> Not whether you win, but whether you last,
>
> Nor whether you're beaten by others my friend,
>
> But whether you've run your race to the end.[11]

A spiritual man, on May 6, 1960, McLendon became a dedicated member of Bethany Christian Church in Cleveland. He liked to say that he had a strong religious belief in the Almighty, as God had been in his corner at all times. When a revised edition of his earlier book was published as *The Fast Break Game* in 1974, he acknowledged his mother, who prayed for him; his father, who was his favorite fan; his wife and "super fan," Joanna; and "the one who makes all things possible." Appointed to the Deacon Board in Cleveland by Elder R. W. Dickerson in 1993, McLendon continued to serve in this capacity until the onset of his illness and enjoyed speaking regularly during the "God Bless the Children" segment of the Sunday-morning worship service. A member of the men's Sunday-school class, McLendon also prepared each session's lesson plan. Senior pastor Robin Hedgeman recalled McLendon as "a blessing, a man whose message to both children and adults combined biblical principles and life lessons, who was respected by everyone in the community and the church." Indeed, people often remarked that McLendon lived his faith every day. According to former Cleveland State player Sam Thomas, he served as a model for others to follow in both their spiritual and their professional development. McLendon was a lifetime member of the Boys and Girls Clubs of America and a member of the National Association of Christian Athletes; he also served as a Tennessee Volunteer and a Kentucky Colonel. He took great pride in receiving the Boys Club's first Man of the Year Award, authorized by Coretta Scott King.[12]

According to columnist Leslie Scanlon of the *Louisville Courier-Journal*, McLendon will be remembered not only for his many accomplishments, on and off the basketball court, but also "for the quiet and steady way he lived his faith." McLendon's leadership was deeply rooted in his faith, declared Scanlon: "He looked for the good in people and was routinely courteous. He took aside students who shouted insults at the other team and asked them to tone it down. When he traveled, he read his Bible and called his wife before going to bed at night. When he coached, he tried to get his players home in time to attend church." Everyone who knew him said that McLendon was an example of the influence that can be wielded by a person of integrity, a person who gave thanks to God for each new day, who cared more about the character of the young men who played for him than about how many points they scored on the basketball court.[13]

As a social historian, McLendon was acutely aware of the historic role he and others had played in employing sports to help integrate American society. "Sports has been one of the most important agents for breaking down barriers in this country, for it is so visible," he often commented. To accentuate this point, McLendon once wrote an article for a black paper that proved to be so controversial that it refused to print it. The controversy stemmed from McLendon's declaration that legendary football coach Paul "Bear" Bryant had done as much for inte-

McLendon with his daughter, Querida, and his son, John, North Carolina Central University. (Courtesy Joanna McLendon)

gration in the South as any person except Martin Luther King. "Because when he started having blacks on his football team in the middle of Alabama when he was number 1, people could not sit up in the stands, 100,000 strong, and yell for white Alabama. They couldn't say, 'Go white Alabama, stay back black Alabama.' You need someone of importance and power to step out and make a statement," McLendon declared. It didn't make any difference to him whether that person was black or white, or what their motives were, for in the end only the results mattered: "He [Bryant] did it because he wanted to win. Whatever he did it for, he did it. Other people had the chance and didn't."[14]

Looking back on his career, McLendon took great pride in the game that had brought so much joy and meaning to his life. "Basketball has been a powerful force for understanding and improved race relations in our society," he stated. "Many places in this country never would have gotten through the integration process without basketball bringing together crowds of people for a common goal." A man of deep humility and moral courage, with a keen sense of social responsibility, McLendon judged his life to be one of meaningful accomplishment. Of course, he would have liked to coach at a big-time university like Kansas or Iowa, where he had earned his degrees, and he believed that he should have been given a chance in the NBA, but he never allowed disappointment to hinder his progress or slow him down. "I guess I've done it all in the time frame I was in," he was fond of saying. "The thing I'm really proud of is the integrating of basketball on a national level."[15]

Most of McLendon's life was spent in a society that separated people according to color. "In all facets of life," McLendon said, "from growing up in 'free' Kansas to coaching in five southern states, the specter of bias or prejudice was a perpetual shadow over all our ambitions and aspirations. You learned to avoid as many reminders of who you are supposed to be as possible." When he could not avoid racially tense situations, he always found a way to model self-respect and respect for others. McLendon's approach to social change was always to look for allies and work within the system. "During those times it was good not to be bitter because you lose your focus," he told Mary Schmitt of the *Kansas City Star* in 1995, sounding much like his father had sixty years earlier. "You get all wound up in the emotion of the thing instead of the point you are trying to make. Some things you couldn't do anything about, and the fact that you tried to do something was a statement. But that's in the past," he continued. "You should forget it. You can't hold people responsible for what happened then. . . . It's who you are now that counts." Looking back on McLendon's life, Mike Hudson wrote in the *Roanoke Times:* "Petty insults and outright racism weren't right, but they were part of the game. They made him, and his teams, stronger." "You have to play through those things and defeat them," said McLendon. "The game itself is made for people who want to play fair."[16]

A visionary, McLendon could see the social revolution of the 1960s coming, and he used sports as a way to take maximum advantage of it, the game of basketball becoming his medium for bringing forth profound social change. "And in his quiet way," Mike Hudson wrote, "McLendon used this American creation to help dismantle the Jim Crow system that held back the game and divided the nation." McLendon believed that racism and racial barriers usually aren't the will of most of the people but of the few who are noisiest. "If you're in the right, there are always more people on your side than you can imagine," he told Hudson. "There's no racial boundary between people who support

208

Return to Cleveland State University

right." From high school through college and the professional ranks, those who played for Coach McLendon performed with the greatest respect for their coach and teammates and even their opponents. Indeed, this attitude of respect and generosity is arguably his greatest legacy, ultimately more important than all his victories and championships.[17]

At the time of the 1997 NBA All-Star Game in Cleveland, Ken Denzel, a friend of McLendon's from Chicago, who was staying with Coach McLendon and Joanna, mentioned that he had written to the NBA, complaining about its failure to honor McLendon at that game or at any of the weeklong festivities. McLendon, however, was characteristically more concerned about the organization's failure to select at least one of the two great players from his NAIA championship teams, Dick Barnett and John Barnhill, as one of the fifty greatest players of the NBA's first fifty years.[18]

Throughout his life, John McLendon never forgot the man who had made all his success possible. "On a brilliant summer day in 1995," wrote Roy MacGregor in "The Birth of Basketball," "a nattily-dressed black man from the United States headed out in a stiff wind to make his way across a rolling field outside Almonte, Ontario. John B. Mclendon Jr., then eighty years of age, did not even notice the wind as it tried to push him back toward the vehicle that had carried him from the airport to this spot in the Ottawa Valley. He had, after all, just traveled 1,700 kilometers to keep a promise he had made to himself fifty-six years earlier and never expected to break." McLendon had come to Ontario to see the massive granite boulder that had inspired the game that had shaped his career. He had come, as well, to visit the birthplace of the man who had shaped his life, James Naismith. McLendon became active in the Dr. James Naismith Foundation, holding a number of basketball clinics for Canadian children at the Almonte Community Center, just as he had for so many American children in the past. "McLendon respected everything Naismith stood for," said John Gosset, the foundation's operations manager. Because he never forgot where his inspiration and success had come from, McLendon received the James Naismith Basketball Foundation Honor Roll Award in 1998 at a ceremony held in Almonte, the place the inventor of basketball had called home.[19]

Also in 1998, the University of Kansas saluted its basketball legends at Allen Fieldhouse, one of the most famous basketball shrines in America. Basketball's greats were all there—from Dean Smith and Larry

McLendon standing in front of a photograph of his beloved mentor at Naismith's boyhood home, Almonte, Ontario, 1995. It is believed that the ball McLendon is holding is the same one held by his former teacher in the photo on the wall. (Courtesy Joanna McLendon)

Brown, to Wilt Chamberlain and Danny Manning. John McLendon was also there, smiling as he signed autographs for the Jayhawk faithful. Rick Dean, of the *Topeka Capital-Journal,* calling him "the overlooked basketball pioneer," wrote, "The welcome he received upon his return to campus as part of the KU Legends weekend was befitting not only his stature as one of the oldest honorees, but also one of the most accomplished." The "Little Coach" had come home to Kansas, the place where his dream of making a difference through basketball had commenced seven decades before. This homecoming gave him great satisfaction, as he was proud to credit his experience at Kansas as the springboard for his coaching career. This would be one of the last such events McLendon would attend, for he became ill shortly afterward.[20]

John B. McLendon Jr., at the age of eighty-four, passed away from cancer on October 8, 1999, at his home in Cleveland Heights. He was

McLendon signing an autograph for a Jayhawk fan after the University of Kansas Legends game in Allen Fieldhouse, 1998. (Courtesy of the *Topeka Capital-Journal*)

survived by his wife, Joanna; daughter Querida; two stepchildren, Nanette Adams and H. David Bryant; two sisters, Anita Williams and Elsie Bevenue; brother, Arthur McLendon; five grandchildren; and five great-grandchildren. His son John had died of a heart attack two years earlier. The first floral arrangements to reach his home came from North Carolina coach Dean Smith, who expressed gratitude to McLendon for teaching him the four-corners offense. An overflow assembly of some five hundred people attended the funeral at Bethany Church, including former players, coaches, athletic directors, journalists, family and friends, and Cleveland mayor Michael White.

Although he suffered great indignities as an African American in a racist society, McLendon carried no bitterness. He chose, rather, to say that he considered himself lucky to be associated with "some of the finest people God ever created." A true pioneer, whose calmness in the face of adversity was universally admired, McLendon never used profanity or raised his voice. In his thirty-four years of coaching, not one technical foul was ever called on Coach McLendon. "Physically he was a small man," declared Clarence "Big House" Gaines. "But to those who

Return to Cleveland State University

McLendon in academic regalia at the Honorary Citizen Award Ceremony, University of Kansas, 1979. (Courtesy Joanna McLendon)

knew him he was a giant." As Dick Barnett said in McLendon's *New York Times* obituary, "You could feel the resolution in his personality." Speaking at McLendon's funeral, Barnett reminded those in attendance of the important legacy his beloved coach had left behind: "He cast a long shadow across the nation and the world as a basketball coach, but his commitment to racial justice wasn't as well known. He was one of the major players in desegregating athletics in America, particularly when it wasn't fashionable."[21]

Those who knew McLendon remember him as a true gentleman, a great humanitarian, and one of the finest human beings they ever met. "His greatness was more than his twelve national championships," his friend Ken Denzel said. "That was overshadowed by his concern for his fellow human beings, to overcoming racial barriers, for helping to make so many of us better persons and this world a better place for all." "His strength was in his love for people and for excellence in

Return to Cleveland State University

his work," Joanna, his wife of thirty-one years, said with understandable pride. "He was also a man of great faith. He was a deacon in our church. But more than just talk about religion, he lived his faith. He really loved people."[22]

John Barnhill, who played for McLendon for seven years at the college, amateur, and professional levels, expressed a sentiment shared by many others: "Coach McLendon was the greatest coach I ever played for at any level. As much as he had accomplished and had been honored in basketball and in life, the most important thing about him was that he was a great human being who had a significant positive effect on me and on so many in so many different walks of life and in so many ways. He was more than a prince among men. He was a king who had been loved by all." Robin Jonathan Deutsch, director of publishing and news media at the Naismith Basketball Hall of Fame, wrote that McLendon "stood for everything that is right and good in basketball," noting that although he wasn't universally famous, he was universally beloved. "Mac was 'Daddy Mac' and he cherished that distinction," wrote Deutsch, adding that McLendon was "a man who graced this earth in such a distinguished and honorable fashion that it's hard to imagine another like him will come around anytime soon."[23]

"John McLendon always represented the best in whatever he did," wrote NBA superstar Julius Erving, remembering the coach who had won his admiration while recruiting him for Cleveland State University. "The Father of Black Basketball, he was also a godfather to the young Black athlete. I saw him as a true caretaker of the sport. His wealth of experience and knowledge allowed for each hour spent with him to be an equivalent to reading an encyclopedia on basketball and on life." "He is probably as respected a basketball analyst and historian as anyone walking the face of the earth," said CBS basketball commentator Billy Packer. "Here's a guy that they ought to just sit down and videotape and put it in the bank. He was a man way ahead of his time."[24]

According to Anthony Coleman, writing in the *Tennessean*, "for Tubby Smith and other African-American coaches, the road to premier coaching positions was cleared of many obstacles by John McLendon." For his part, Smith, award-winning coach of the University of Kentucky Wildcats, remarked: "He helped to smooth the way for guys like me. Guys like him didn't get the opportunities that some of us are getting now. He made it so much easier for me and other coaches. I was the first black coach at the University of Georgia and the first black coach at Kentucky. I can't imagine, though, what he had to go through." Smith pointed out to Coleman that McLendon's death marked the end of a valuable link to the roots of the game: "Coach McLendon was a connection for blacks back to the beginning of the game. Now that connection isn't there any more. But for him to have learned from Phog Allen and James Naismith tells you just how much he meant to basketball."[25]

To honor the man who had worked so assiduously to integrate both college and professional basketball, the NBA's Toronto Raptors established the "Coach Mac" Award in 1999, honoring someone within the Canadian basketball community "who through exemplary character and effort has made a major contribution to the sport of basketball while upholding the principles for which Coach Mac stood—honesty, integrity, competitiveness, and love of the game." Two-time NBA MVP Steve Nash, of the Phoenix Suns, received the "Coach Mac" Award in 2006. On behalf of the Raptors, Isiah Thomas, vice president of basketball operations, wrote that McLendon had not only been his close personal friend and mentor but also an inspirational leader who was always willing to impart the knowledge of basketball and people he had gained through more than six decades in the game.[26]

"The last conversation I had with him was two days before he died," said his longtime friend Clarence "Big House" Gaines. "He could barely talk. But he said that if there is anything he'd like to see done, it's for the record to be set straight about the contributions that blacks made to basketball [before integration]." According to Lut Williams, *Black College Sports Page* editor, on the day of McLendon's passing, he spoke with colleagues about his most recent passion, the Historically Black Colleges and Universities (HBCU) Heritage Museum and Hall of Fame. McLendon's vision went beyond athletics, however; the museum would serve as a lasting memorial to black athletes, coaches, administrators, and others who made significant contributions to the nation. McLendon himself wrote: "We, African-Americans, need a national repository which assembles our HBCU sports and sports-related honored individuals, teams and groups and preserves their records, deeds, and exploits for posterity. . . . We have had an impact that needs historical perpetuation." Williams concluded that McLendon's place in the proposed museum "is secure." Unfortunately, the coach's vision has yet to be realized. As Fred Whitted, author of the *Black College Sports Encyclopedia*, has editorialized, "the time has come for McLendon's dream to be fulfilled."[27]

John Konstantinos, director of athletics at Cleveland State University, also recalled McLendon's special qualities: "The loss of John McLendon is terrible, not just for the school but for everyone. This was a great, great human being, a wonderful man who always stood for what is right." Howard A. Mims, Cleveland State's director of black studies, said that McLendon "was not only one of basketball's greatest coaches, he was one of the finest human beings I ever met, a gentleman at all times and a very kind person. He was probably the most authoritative person about African-American athletes and the socio-political context in which they played. He had a sense of mission."[28]

"What was absolutely astounding was how the media, local and national, overlooked McLendon's death," Ron Chimelis wrote in the *Springfield Republican*. "We probably took him for granted, as if genuine humanitarians and pioneers fall out of trees." Ironically, McLendon and Wilt Chamberlain, enshrined together in the Hall of Fame in 1979, both passed away in October 1999, just four days apart. "Although Chamberlain's death was blared out in the headlines," stated Chimelis, McLendon's was just as significant, if not more so, as it "took from us perhaps the last true link to basketball's origins, but beyond that, a large piece of its soul." "If Wilt the Stilt was larger than life," Chimelis declared, "McLendon celebrated life, enriching everyone he touched."[29]

Russell L. Stockard, writing for the *Black Collegian,* was also incredulous about the dearth of attention given to Coach McLendon and his many accomplishments. "John McLendon is no longer alive, but somehow that does not create a vacuum in the sports world," wrote Stockard. "This is true only if you didn't know this giant of a man, who stood only 5 feet, 6 inches tall and was the best kept 'secret' in the world of basketball, and sports." Describing McLendon as "an unassuming, cheerful, gracious, kind, quiet, helpful, trustworthy, scholarly pioneer, Christian, and coach," Stockard explained that both the man and his approach to dealing with the stain of racism and other social problems were "class acts." "We have already begun to miss him since his death of last October," concluded Stockard. "Yet his quiet presence will never depart from the game of basketball that he touted and taught as a science that he mastered so well."[30]

There is little doubt that McLendon touched many people,

enriching their lives in significant ways. "I spent twenty-four hours on a train for his funeral, because he'd have done the same for me," said Amherst resident Dennis Jackson, whose nonprofit program for high school basketball players embodied the values that McLendon held sacred: education, athletics, respect, responsible manhood, and opportunity. From its inception, McLendon not only endorsed but also promoted Jackson's program, dedicated to providing high school athletes with the academic, athletic, and personal skills necessary to turn a collegiate experience into a college degree. The promotional brochure for Jackson's basketball academy, called P.L.A.Y. (Planned Learning Achievement for Youth), proudly devotes considerable space to remembering John McLendon. "McLendon," Jackson declared, "was one of the great humanitarians and coaches to ever grace the face of the earth. His record was mind-boggling. He broke so many barriers, his list of accomplishments is so long, he was like five great people rolled into one." Jackson blamed the lack of attention to the coach's death not on race but on ignorance. "John McLendon was about America," he argued. "He was like a tree, and everybody else was a root. In his death, we let him down."[31]

Nevertheless, McLendon's legacy will live on thanks to his friend Mike Cleary, executive director of the NACDA, whose foundation endowed a John McLendon Minority Postgraduate Scholarship Fund in 1998 for students intending to pursue a graduate degree in athletics administration. Specifically, five minority college seniors would each receive a ten-thousand-dollar grant. The selection criteria include grade-point average, nomination by a member school, and previous involvement in the university or community. In 2005, thanks largely to Cleary's efforts, the fund reached its one-million-dollar goal, its largest contributors the NACDA Foundation; Sears, Roebuck & Co.; the National Association of Basketball Coaches; the American Football Coaches Association; Major League Baseball; and the NCAA.

Charles Harris, commissioner of the Mid-East Athletic Conference, was the first chair of the awards committee for the John McLendon Minority Postgraduate Scholarship. Said Harris: "The recognition of the contributions of John McLendon in this meaningful way is long overdue, but richly deserved. I am proud to serve as chair of the committee and deeply appreciative of the efforts and vision of the NACDA to insure the name and legacy of John McLendon are perpetuated."[32]

This scholarship is a fitting tribute to McLendon, who was not only a highly successful coach but also an equally able athletic administrator. Indeed, the fund amounts to McLendon's proactive response to the feeble excuse that there is no pool of minority candidates in athletic administration. In announcing the scholarship, sponsored by the Cleveland Cavaliers and the Gund Arena Corporation, Cavs general manager Wayne Embry, who himself broke through racial barriers as the first African American executive of a major sports team in 1972, said that McLendon's contributions went beyond the game. "I always had the utmost regard for him, not just because he was a basketball coach but because he was a humanitarian and historian," Embry said of McLendon. "Given his coaching career and where and how he had to coach in the 1930s, '40s, and '50s, he opened up a lot of doors. He was a great inspiration to all of us who were fortunate to have success in the game. I've always respected him for what he had to persevere through. He crossed all racial lines. He was just a man."[33]

McLendon stated that the establishment of this fund was of special significance to him, since it provides ongoing recognition and opportunity for youth pursuing a graduate degree. "To be in a position to contribute to bringing forward minority candidates of academic achievement prepared to add graduate studies to their development is as honorable an assignment as any ever bestowed upon me," he said. "I eagerly look forward to when the selected young men and women can embark on a career of a valuable and lasting contribution to sports in America. I feel so very fortunate that my name was chosen to be associated with such an educational concept."[34]

On June 9, 2006, Joe Maxse reported in the *Cleveland Plain Dealer* that in honor of John McLendon, Cleveland State University and the NACDA had formally announced that CSU's John McLendon Scholarship Series would commence on December 18, 2007, when the Vikings host Ohio State University. "We need to remember what John did for basketball, but also for humankind beyond basketball," said CSU athletic director Lee Reed." NACDA executive director Mike Cleary stated that some of the game's proceeds will go to the John McLendon Memorial Postgraduate Minority Scholarship Fund. CSU's Athletic Department also established an endowed scholarship in the names of John and Joanna McLendon.[35]

Chicago State University professor Jacqueline Imani Bryant,

introducing an extensive interview with McLendon, wrote: "Coach McLendon taught simply by living a life that was exemplary of action. He cut the cords of racism within institutions while he wove the strength of character in individual lives. In his passion for justice and compassion for humanity, the Coach was relentless in his efforts to go beyond the voice of rhetoric to become a quiet participant of action. Embracing the philosophy passed down through his mentor, Dr. Naismith, Coach McLendon made the sports arena his pulpit and thus changed lives through instruction and example."[36]

Although John McLendon was respected and loved by nearly everyone with whom he came into contact, it is essential to keep in mind that he was also, in Wayne Embry's words, "just a man" tirelessly working to make a positive difference. According to Joanna McLendon, the coach could be overly trusting of people, especially in regards to financial affairs. Too, although he promised to stop traveling so much after his third marriage, he never let up, and his wife and children had to live with the consequences. He also arguably underestimated the passion of young black athletes for personal freedom, and even social revolution, in the late 1960s, faithfully clinging to an idealized view of sports as a noble, society-supporting, character-building endeavor. And when McLendon employed his rigorous training and disciplinary approach with professional athletes, on the 1969 Denver Rockets, he unintentionally divided the team, a factor in his being fired before midseason. Indeed, although he wished to coach in the NBA, his personality and strategies might have been more suited to the college game, where the unique strength of his personal character, in modeling for his student athletes skills they could use both on and off the court, could have maximum results. McLendon's greatest joy came from leading twelve young men, all adhering to strict guidelines, exceeding their abilities, and looking to him for guidance. Like his mentor, Dr. James Naismith, he continued to believe that his players' lives were better because of their involvement in sports and that discipline and respect were the keys to bringing forth powerful personal and social change.

Perhaps McLendon was also overly optimistic about sport's influence in breaking down racial barriers in American society. As numerous scholars have pointed out, although some of the more blatant forms of racial discrimination have been eliminated from sports due to the courageous efforts of John McLendon and a host of others, more subtle forms of discrimination still exist. More important, the power in sports remains largely in white hands.[37]

Richard Lapchick, of the Institute for Diversity and Ethics in Sports, illustrates the progress that has been made in this area since McLendon's first attempt to democratize national athletic competition back in 1948, as well as the challenges that remain. Although he was never hired to coach a NBA team, McLendon certainly helped pave the way for other African Americans. For example, during the 2005–6 NBA season, 73 percent of players were people of color, and eleven head coaching positions out of thirty were held by African Americans. Of equal importance, seven general managers were African Americans, there were four black CEOs or presidents, and 12 percent of team vice presidents were people of color. Robert Johnson, owner of the Charlotte Bobcats, remained pro sports' only African American majority owner. In contrast, the National Football League has only six African American head coaches, and Major League Baseball has just five black or Latino managers.[38]

Still, while some progress is undeniable, racism is too. Authors David Leonhardt and Ford Fesseden point out in the *New York Times* that, although opportunity in the NBA appears to be color-blind, black NBA coaches have lasted an average of just 1.6 seasons over the last decade, compared with 2.4 seasons for white coaches. According to the authors, "that means the typical white coach lasts almost 50 percent longer and has most of an extra season to prove himself."[39]

An equally troubling indictment comes from *New York Times* columnist William C. Rhoden, whose book *Forty Million Dollar Slaves* declares: "Despite their fifty-five-year rise to prominence on the fields of integrated sports, African American athletes—male and female—still find themselves on the periphery of true power in the industry their talent built." Rhoden charges not only the pervasive, institutionalized racism of American life but also the racism of black athletes themselves, calling them "pampered millionaires" who have forgotten or failed to learn and appreciate their own history. Such ignorance, however, can be eliminated, and redemption is still possible. In words that echo many of John McLendon's pronouncements, Rhoden declares, "We have to look backward to see our way forward." We must study how courageous pioneers—athletes and coaches—struggled to overcome the barriers of racism as they "fought dehumanization, an unfair playing field, economic exploitation, and inequalities in power."[40]

The persistence of racism and glaring inequality at all levels in sports would certainly have concerned John McLendon, but he chose to remain an optimist throughout his life. As he learned from Dr. Naismith at the University of Kansas, challenges must be overcome with courage, creativity, and determination. The world will make progress toward social justice if enough good people work together to bring about change.

Countless ordinary individuals make such changes every day, their struggles for equality and justice slowly altering the course of human history. Indeed, it is easy to forget that history is actually made by people much like us, people who commit themselves, their lives, and their energies to obtaining freedom and dignity for all. John B. McLendon Jr. was much more than a highly successful basketball coach, a visionary athletic administrator, and an international ambassador for the game he loved. His remarkable courage, unswerving determination, and moral strength in the pursuit of human rights and social justice brought democracy in America a step closer to reality.

Coach McLendon's Twenty-Five-Year Collegiate Record

North Carolina College, 1940–52: 264 wins, 60 losses (81.2 percent)
Captured CIAA visitation or tournament titles eight times

Hampton Institute, 1952–53: 32 wins, 14 losses (70.0 percent)

Tennessee State A&I University, 1955–59: 149 wins, 20 losses (88.2 percent)
Captured Mid-Western Athletic Conference Tournament title four times
Captured NAIA championship three consecutive times

Kentucky State College, 1964–66: 50 wins, 29 losses (63.8 percent)

Captured Mid-Western Athletic Conference Tournament championship two times

Cleveland State University, 1966–69: 27 wins, 42 losses (39.8 percent)

Total collegiate coaching record: 522 wins, 165 losses (76.0%), as reported in the 1969 *Converse Basketball Yearbook*

AAU and Professional Coaching Record

Cleveland Pipers, 1959–62: 75 wins, 54 losses (58.0%)
Captured National Industrial Basketball League title in 1961
Captured National Amateur Athletic Union Championship in 1961
Captured American Basketball League Eastern Division Championship in 1961

Denver Rockets, 1969: 9 wins, 19 losses (32.0%)

Total NIBL and professional record: 84 wins, 73 losses (54.0%)

Overall

McLendon won over 700 games during his thirty-four-year coaching career, spanning high school, college, university, industrial, AAU, international, and professional basketball.

ODE TO THE VANQUISHED

By John B. McLendon Jr.

Dedicated to one who gives his best

My heart goes out in full embrace
To any man who runs his race
Not almost all, nor just in part,
But wholly from the tensioned start;
And whether of vast or doubtful strength,
Who strides the course its tortured length,
Who will not quit but falters on
Until his entire strength is gone.

Within me there is bursting pride
For one who will not turn aside,
Straining, striving, by others passed,
Outrun, outsped, and often outclassed.
But struggling onward, giving all,
Gaining his prize, refusing to fall,
Such valiance does indeed direct
True inspiration, great respect.

The victor commands the watchful eye
Of the cheering throng as he passes by;
Too often his winning place is stressed
Out of proportion to all the rest,
Though well-deserved his laurel wreath
But as for me, let me bequeath

My praise for an inspiring sight
To him who fights the losing fight.

The stadium's raucous, frenzied shout
Descends to whispers or dies out
As derision's voice and foolish jeers
Grate harshly on the loser's ears.
Rude and thoughtless gestures these;
Giving one's best should always please.
Gold and silver, awards of style;
Effort to win is the thing worthwhile.

Total the sum of life's great test
Find honor is given for only your best.
Regardless of finish, your place in the sun
Is decided by the race you've run.
From birth, as from the starter's blast,
Not whether you win, but whether you last,
Not whether you're beaten by others my friend,
But whether you've run your race to the end.

Appendix

NOTES

Preface

1. Miller andWiggins, *Sport and the Color Line*, x.
2. Gene Menez, "A Night to Remember," *Sports Illustrated*, Jan. 23, 2006, 20. For the pioneering role that McLendon and his Tennessee A&I Tigers played in 1957, see Ed Miller, "Another All-Black Team Was the First on 'Glory Road,'" *Virginian-Pilot*, Jan. 28, 2006; Blair Kerkhoff, "Paving Glory Road: The Path to Integration Began Well before Texas Western's Triumph," *Kansas City Star*, Jan. 29, 2006.

Introduction

1. Alex Rivera, interview with the author, Apr. 5, 2006; Jim Furlong, "NCCU Legend McLendon Dies at 84," *Durham Herald-Sun*, Oct. 9, 1999.
2. "The History of Sports in the United States and the Role of Minorities in Their Development," syllabus, History 393, Cleveland State University, John B. McLendon Collection, Cleveland Heights, Ohio.
3. Lut Williams, "Coach McLendon Ran the Distance," *Carolina Times*, Oct. 16, 1999.

CHAPTER 1
A Kansas Childhood and the Love of the Game

1. John McLendon, interview with the author, Mar. 12, 1987; Arthur McLendon, interview with the author, Oct. 15, 2004.
2. John McLendon, interview, Mar. 12, 1987; John McLendon, "Tales of the Hardwood," McLendon Collection, Cleveland Heights, 1.
3. John McLendon, interview with the author, Mar. 13, 1987.
4. John McLendon, interview, Mar. 13, 1987.
5. John McLendon, interview, Mar. 13, 1987; John McLendon, "Tales of the Hardwood," 2.
6. John McLendon, interview, Mar. 13, 1987; John McLendon, "Tales of the Hardwood," 2.
7. David, "Gospel," 9; Skiff, "John McLendon's Long Road," 8.
8. Greenbaum, *Afro-American Community*, 65.
9. Greenbaum, *Afro-American Community*, 68.
10. John McLendon, interview with the author, Mar. 14, 1987; John McLendon, "Tales of the Hardwood," 3, 4.

CHAPTER 2
The University of Kansas and Dr. James Naismith

1. John McLendon, interview with the author, Mar. 15, 1987; John McLendon, "Tales of the Hardwood," 5.

2. John McLendon, interview, Mar. 15, 1987; John McLendon, "Tales of the Hardwood," 5.

3. John McLendon, interview, Mar. 15, 1987; John McLendon, "Tales of the Hardwood," 5.

4. John McLendon, interview, Mar. 15, 1987; John McLendon, "Tales of the Hardwood," 5.

5. John McLendon, interview, Mar. 15, 1987; Mike Hudson, "Basketball's Quiet Ambassador of Change," *Roanoke Times Extra,* Jan. 3, 1999; George, *Elevating the Game,* 86.

6. Ladd and Mathisen, *Muscular Christianity,* 69.

7. Ladd and Mathisen, *Muscular Christianity,* 70, 71. See also Putney, *Muscular Christianity,* 64–72.

8. John McLendon, interview, Mar. 15, 1987; Bryant, "Basketball Coach John B. McLendon," 730.

9. John McLendon, interview, Mar. 15, 1987; John McLendon, "Tales of the Hardwood," 6.

10. Wolff, *Big Game, Small World,* 140.

11. Mike Walker, "Quietly Blazing Trails," 14.

12. John McLendon, interview, Mar. 15, 1987; John McLendon, "Tales of the Hardwood," 7.

13. Webb, *Basketball Man,* 287; Wolff, *Big Game, Small World,* 140.

14. John McLendon, interview, Mar. 15, 1987; John McLendon, "Tales of the Hardwood," 7.

15. John McLendon, interview, Mar. 15, 1987; John McLendon, "Tales of the Hardwood," 7.

16. John McLendon, interview, Mar. 15, 1987; John McLendon, "Tales of the Hardwood," 7.

17. John McLendon, interview, Mar. 15, 1987; John McLendon, "Tales of the Hardwood," 7.

18. John McLendon, interview, Mar. 15, 1987; John McLendon, "Tales of the Hardwood," 7.

19. John McLendon, interview, Mar. 15, 1987; John McLendon, "Tales of the Hardwood," 7.

20. Wolff, *Big Game, Small World,* 141.

21. John McLendon, interview, Mar. 15, 1987; John McLendon, "Tales of the Hardwood," 7.

22. Ian Naismith, interview with the author, Sept. 15, 2005; John McLendon, interview, Mar. 15, 1987; Mike Walker, "Quietly Blazing Trails," 14.

23. John B. McLendon, "More than Just the Fellow with the Peach Baskets: James Naismith Also Fought against Segregation," *New York Times,* Oct. 27, 1996.

24. John McLendon, interview, Mar. 15, 1987; John McLendon, "Tales of the Hardwood," 8; Robert W. Matthews, "Coach John B. McLendon Jr.," McLendon Collection, Cleveland Heights, 13.

CHAPTER 3
Establishing a Tradition of Excellence

1. John McLendon, interview with the author, Mar. 10, 1988; John McLendon, "Tales of the Hardwood," 9.

2. Packer and Lazenby, *Golden Game,* 237.

3. John McLendon, interview, Mar. 10, 1988; Hudson, "Basketball's Quiet Ambassador."

4. Sam Jones, interview with the author, May 31, 2005; Harold Hunter, interview with the author, July 10, 2005.

5. Richard Miller, interview with the author, May 19, 2005; Hunter, interview, July 10, 2005; Marlon Buckner, interview with the author, July 10, 2005; Ron Hamilton, interview with the author, Feb. 12, 2005; Rivera, interview, Apr. 5, 2005.

6. Thornton Williams, interview with the author, Mar. 15, 2005.

7. Grundy, *Learning to Win,* 182; John B. McLendon, *Fast Break Basketball,* ix, x.

8. John B. McLendon, *Fast Break Basketball,* 15, 16.

9. Grundy, *Learning to Win,* 182; John B. McLendon, *Fast Break Basketball,* 11.

10. Richard Miller, interview, May 19, 2005; Hunter, interview, July 10, 2005; John Brown, interview with the author, Mar. 15, 2006.

11. John B. McLendon, *Fast Break Basketball,* 193, 195.

12. John B. McLendon, *Fast Break Basketball,* 193, 194, 195.

13. John B. McLendon, *Fast Break Basketball,* 193, 194.

14. John McLendon, interview, Mar. 10, 1988; Packer and Lazenby, *Golden Game,* 237.

15. Packer and Lazenby, *Golden Game,* 237; Rivera, interview, Apr. 5, 2005.

16. John McLendon, interview, Mar. 10, 1988; Rivera, interview, Apr. 5, 2005; Hudson, "Basketball's Quiet Ambassador," 4.

17. John McLendon, interview, Mar. 10, 1988.

18. Packer and Lazenby, *Golden Game,* 237, 238; Rivera, interview, Apr. 5, 2005.

19. Packer and Lazenby, *Golden Game,* 238.

20. Packer and Lazenby, *Golden Game,* 238; John McLendon, interview with the author, Mar. 11, 1988.

21. John McLendon, interview, Mar. 11, 1988.

22. Grundy, "Position of Respect," 86.

23. Grundy, "Position of Respect," 87–89.

24. Grundy, "Position of Respect," 89, 90.

25. Grundy, *Learning to Win,* 159; Grundy, "Position of Respect," 86.

26. Grundy, *Learning to Win,* 159; Grundy, "Position of Respect," 91.

27. Pamela Grundy, "Coach, Mentor, Father, Friend: Coaches Taught Many of Their Most Important Lessons Just by Being Who They Are," *Raleigh News & Observer Sunday Journal,* Feb. 24, 2002; Grundy, *Learning to Win,* 159; Grundy, "Position of Respect," 86.

28. Ron Thomas, *They Cleared the Lane,* 167.

29. Grundy, *Learning to Win,* 172.

30. Miller and Wiggins describe "muscular assimilationism" as a deep-seated belief of many African American commentators and coaches, who "have elaborated success in sports as an emblem of race pride and an indicator of accomplishment

that could and should be translated to every domain of human endeavor." See *Sport and the Color Line,* xii. See also Wiggins and Miller, *Unlevel Playing Field,* 3.

31. Grundy, *Learning to Win,* 187, 188.

32. Shaw, "Pivotman," 12, 13; Charles M. Martin, "Jim Crow in the Gymnasium," 247; John McLendon, interview with the author, Mar. 12, 1988.

33. John McLendon, interview, Mar. 12, 1988; John McLendon, "Tales of the Hardwood," 9.

34. George Parks, interview with the author, Mar. 15, 2005; Mike Potter, "The Secret Game," *Durham Herald-Sun,* Nov. 10, 2004.

35. Ellsworth, "Secret Game," 9, 10; Ellsworth, "Secret Game of 1944," 6; John McLendon, interview, Mar. 12, 1988.

36. David Hubbell, interview with the author, May 15, 2005; Ellsworth, "Secret Game of 1944," 6.

37. Querida (McLendon) Banks, interview with the author, Oct. 10, 2004.

38. Hubbell, interview, May 15, 2005; Ellsworth, "Secret Game," 10; "America in Black and White."

39. Ellsworth, "Secret Game," 11; Ellsworth, "Secret Game of 1944," 7; "America in Black and White."

40. John McLendon, interview, Mar. 12, 1988; Parks, interview, Mar. 15, 2005; McLendon, "Tales of the Hardwood," 9.

41. Hubbell, interview, May 15, 2005; Ellsworth, "Secret Game of 1944," 7; John McLendon, interview, Mar. 12, 1988; Potter, "Secret Game."

42. John McLendon, interview, Mar. 12, 1988; Shaw, "Pivotman," 12.

43. "America in Black and White."

44. Strickland, "Friendly Neighborhood Game," *Durham Herald-Sun,* Nov. 11, 2004; Mike Potter, "Perfect Strangers No Longer," *Durham Herald-Sun,* Nov. 12, 2004.

45. Ed Miller, "Basketball's Forgotten Pioneer: John McLendon Learned the Game From Its Founder and Took the Sport to New Levels, Both on and off the Court," *Virginian-Pilot,* Feb. 22, 1995.

46. John McLendon, interview, Mar. 13, 1988; Grundy, *Learning to Win,* 178, 179.

47. Jack Clowser, "McLendon's Pipers Best City Has Ever Seen," *Cleveland Press,* Dec. 22, 1959.

48. John B. McLendon, *First CIAA Championship Basketball Tournament,* 26–28.

49. Earl Lloyd, interview with the author, Oct. 15, 2005; Clarence Gaines, interview with the author, Mar. 15, 1987.

50. Ed Miller, "The History: Forty-Nine Years Later the League Still Hasn't Topped Its Inaugural," *Virginian-Pilot,* Feb. 22, 1995.

51. Richard Miller, interview, May 19, 2005; John McLendon, interview, Mar. 13, 1988; John McLendon, "Tales of the Hardwood," 9.

52. John B. McLendon, "Two in the Corner"; John McLendon, interview, Mar. 13, 1988; Smith, *Dean Smith,* 81; Dean Smith, interview with the author, Sept. 2, 2005.

53. Shaw, "Pivotman," 12.

54. Elson Armstrong Jr., "Small CIAA Trophy Is NCCU's Biggest Prize," *Durham Herald-Sun,* Feb. 29, 1996.

55. John B. McLendon, *First CIAA Championship Basketball Tournament,* 46.

56. John B. McLendon, *First CIAA Championship Basketball Tournament,* 38, 39; John McLendon, interview with the author, Mar. 14, 1988.

57. Richard Miller, interview, May 19, 2005; Thornton Williams, interview, Mar. 15, 2005.

58. John B. McLendon, *First CIAA Championship Basketball Tournament*, 45.

59. John B. McLendon, *Fast Break Basketball*, 10, 11.

60. Fred Whitted, "McLendon Led Central to First CIAA Men's Basketball Title," *Charlotte Post and Triangle Tribune*, special ed., Feb. 2005.

61. John B. McLendon, *First CIAA Championship Basketball Tournament*, 44.

62. John B. McLendon, *First CIAA Championship Basketball Tournament*, 45, 46; Leroy Walker, interview with the author, May 18, 2005.

63. Gaines, interview, Mar. 15, 1987; Furlong, "NCCU Legend McLendon Dies."

64. Packer and Lazenby, *Golden Game*, 238; John McLendon, interview, Mar. 14, 1988.

65. Hunter, interview, July 10, 2005.

66. The most current media guide available from North Carolina Central University, sent to me by sports information director Kyle Serba, lists Coach McLendon's twelve-year record as 239 wins, 68 losses. Although no one at the university can explain this discrepancy, records were sometimes questionable at small schools in the 1940s, and McLendon and his contemporaries most likely counted exhibition games—e.g., against armed forces teams—in their overall record. According to his assistant coach at North Carolina, LeRoy Walker, "McLendon was known by everyone as a man who took record keeping a little more seriously than most of his contemporaries, and his statistics were never in question" (interview with the author, Aug. 9, 2006).

67. "McLendon's Resignation Draws Protest: 200 March on Elder's Home," *Campus Echo*, North Carolina College, May 1952; LeRoy Walker, interview, May 18, 2005. Walker stayed on at the college, bringing it tremendous prestige through his track and field program, as head coach of the U.S. men's Olympic track team, and as president of the U.S. Olympic Committee. He was held in such high regard that from 1983 through 1986, he served as chancellor of North Carolina Central University.

68. "McLendon's Resignation from NCC," *Durham Herald-Sun*, n.d.

69. Querida Banks, interview, Oct. 10, 2004.

70. Ethel Richards (McLendon), interview with the author, Aug. 15, 2005.

CHAPTER 4
A Pioneer for Integration

1. Ron Thomas, *They Cleared the Lane*, 21.

2. Ron Thomas, *They Cleared the Lane*, 24.

3. Ron Thomas, *They Cleared the Lane*, 33, 34; John McLendon, interview with the author, Mar. 15, 1988; John McLendon, "Tales of the Hardwood," 11.

4. Ron Thomas, *They Cleared the Lane*, 32.

5. Ron Thomas, *They Cleared the Lane*, 34; Hunter, interview, July 10, 2005.

6. Lloyd, interview, Oct. 15, 2005.

7. Lloyd, interview, Oct. 15, 2005; Hunter, interview, July 10, 2005; John McLendon, interview, Mar. 15, 1988; Ron Thomas, *They Cleared the Lane*, 34, 35.

8. LeRoy Walker, interview, May 18, 2005; John McLendon, interview, Mar. 15, 1988; Ron Thomas, *They Cleared the Lane*, 35, 36.

9. Ron Thomas, *They Cleared the Lane,* 36, 37; Lloyd, interview, Oct. 15, 2005.

10. Ron Thomas, *They Cleared the Lane,* 37; John McLendon, interview, Mar. 15, 1988.

11. Ron Thomas, *They Cleared the Lane,* 37; Hunter, interview, July 10, 2005; Lloyd, interview, Oct. 15, 2005; John McLendon, interview, Mar. 15, 1988.

12. Walsh, qtd. in Ron Thomas, *They Cleared the Lane,* 37, 38; Lloyd, interview, Oct. 15, 2005.

13. Hunter, interview, July 10, 2005.

14. Lloyd, interview, Oct. 15, 2005.

15. John McLendon, interview, Mar. 15, 1988.

16. T. L. Hill and J. B. McLendon to the National Intercollegiate Basketball Association, Mar. 23, 1948, and John D. Lawther to J. B. McLendon, Mar. 26, 1948, both National Athletic Steering Committee (hereafter NASC) files.

17. J. B. McLendon to Kenneth L. Wilson, Feb. 26, 1949, and Kenneth L. Wilson to J. B. McLendon, Mar. 29, 1949, both NASC files.

18. Kenneth L. Wilson to J. B. McLendon, Mar. 29, 1949, NASC files.

19. J. B. McLendon to Kenneth L. Wilson, May 17, 1949, NASC files.

20. Grundy, *Learning to Win,* 188. See also Walter Byers to J. B. McLendon, June 16, 1949, NASC files.

21. John McLendon, interview, Mar. 15, 1988; John B. McLendon, "Black College Basketball," 7.

22. John McLendon, interview, Mar. 15, 1988; Mack M. Greene to Hugh C. Willet Kenneth L. Wilson, Dec. 5, 1950, NASC files.

23. A. C. Lonborg to J. B. McLendon, Jan. 23, 1951, and Walter Byers to J. B. McLendon, Jan. 23, 1951, both NASC files.

24. J. B. McLendon to National Basketball Committee Members, Jan. 24, 1951, NASC files.

25. Mack M. Greene to Athletic Directors and Administrators in Colleges for Negroes, Feb. 6, 1951, NASC files.

26. John McLendon, interview, Mar. 15, 1988; John B. McLendon, "Black College Basketball," 8.

27. Hoover, *History of the National Association,* 69; A. O. Duer to E. S. Liston, Feb. 4, 1947, and E. S. Liston to A. O. Duer, Feb. 10, 1947, both National Association of Intercollegiate Athletics (hereafter NAIA) files; John R. M. Wilson, *History of the National Association of Intercollegiate Athletics,* 25.

28. Brother B. Thomas to Emil Liston, Mar. 2, 1948, and Louis G. Wilke to E. S. Liston, Mar. 2, 1948, both NAIA files.

29. Blair Kerkhoff, "Paving Glory Road: KC Witnessed Color Barrier Fall," *Kansas City Star,* Jan. 29, 2006.

30. See, e.g., a letter from Carlos Harrison to Liston, dated Mar. 6, 1948 (NAIA files): "Please convey my utter contempt to those who had anything to do with the equal rights' concession in the NAIB. . . . You aren't playing Peewee Truman's politics out there . . . are you? . . . and giving into New York and its lousy Communist trend." For a contrasting view, see John I. Johnson, "NAIB Sees the Light," *Kansas City Call,* Mar. 12, 1948.

31. A. O. Duer to Mack Greene, Oct. 3, 1951, and Mack Greene to A. O. Duer, Nov. 6, 1951, both NASC files; A. O. Duer, interview with the author, Apr. 4, 1980; Mack Greene, interview with the author, May 23, 1980.

32. *National Athletic Steering Committee Newsletter* 2, Apr. 25, 1952, 3, 4.

CHAPTER 5
Groundbreaking Championship Years

1. Dick Mackey, "The NAIA: An Unbelievable Basketball Tournament," *Kansas City Star*, Mar. 14, 1970, NAIA files.

2. Bill Richardson, "Twenty-five Years of NAIA Basketball," *Kansas City Star*, Mar. 15, 1962, NAIA files.

3. John B. McLendon, "Black College Basketball," 8; *National Athletic Steering Committee Newsletter* 2, Apr. 25, 1952, 4, May 17, 1952, 13.

4. *National Athletic Steering Committee Newsletter* 3, Apr. 3, 1953, 1, 2.

5. *National Athletic Steering Committee Newsletter* 3, Apr. 3, 1953, 1, 2.

6. John McLendon, interview, Mar. 12, 1988; John McLendon, "Tales of the Hardwood," 13.

7. John McLendon, interview, Mar. 12, 1988; John McLendon, "Tales of the Hardwood," 13; Sam Lacy, "A to Z with Sam Lacy," *Baltimore African American*, n.d., Kenneth Spencer Research Library, University of Kansas.

8. Lewis and Thomas, *Will to Win*, 210; Hamilton, interview, Feb. 12, 2005.

9. John McLendon, interview, Mar. 12, 1988; John McLendon, "Tales of the Hardwood," 13. Not all the downtown Kansas City hotels refused to house black guests. Each year some enacted changes in policy, but these policies were not clear, and it was never certain just when a coach and team would be turned down because of race. See John I. Johnson, "A Flaw in the Cage Capitol," *Kansas City Call*, Mar. 5, 1954.

10. Govenar, *African American Frontiers*, 305.

11. John B. McLendon, "Black College Basketball, " 11; Duer, interview, Apr. 4, 1980; John McLendon, interview with the author, Mar. 12, 1980.

12. John I. Johnson, "Tip-Off Tourney Triumphs," *Kansas City Call*, Dec. 24, 1954.

13. "Home Debut Is Sweet: Coach McLendon Sees Tigers Oust NAIA Favorite," *Kansas City Star*, Dec. 17, 1954.

14. Wendell Smith, "Sports Beat," *Pittsburgh Courier*, Jan. 22, 1955; "Hawk Bid Falls: Tennessee A&I Races Past Rockhurst to Gain NAIA Cage Title," *Kansas City Star*, Dec. 19, 1954.

15. John McLendon, interview, Mar. 12, 1988; John McLendon, "Tales of the Hardwood," 13.

16. Johnson, "Tip-Off Tourney Triumphs."

17. "Executive Secretary's Annual Report to Executive Committee," 1955, 4, and A. W. Mumford, Chairman, to all District 29 Members, Mar. 2, 1955, both NAIA files.

18. Duer, interview, Apr. 4, 1980; "Shift in NAIA," *Kansas City Star*, Mar. 11, 1956. The following July, Duer received a letter from Luther W. Marlar, chairman of the Louisiana district, stating that "we have been ordered not to participate against any colored personnel at any place or time. As you can see this eliminates us from the NAIA." Although Duer convinced most of the colleges in Louisiana to continue in the organization on an inactive basis, and the majority complied, no team from that district was allowed to play in the 1957–58 tournament. See NAIA files.

19. John I. Johnson, "The NAIA Shows the Way," *Kansas City Call*, Mar. 23, 1956.

20. John Barnhill, interview with the author, Mar. 15, 2005; Bill Richardson, "Pipeline for Talent led to Tennessee State in '50s: McLendon's Teams won 3 Titles," *Kansas City Star*, Mar. 8, 1987.

21. Richard Barnett, interview with the author, Mar. 30, 2005; Richardson, "Pipeline for Talent."

22. John McLendon, interview, Mar. 13, 1988.

23. John McLendon, interview, Mar. 13, 1988.

24. John McLendon, interview, Mar. 13, 1988; Russell L. Stockard, "Coach John McLendon: A Class Act," *Black Collegian Online* (http://www.black-collegian.com/extracurricular/sports/mclendon300.shtml).

25. Barnett, interview, Mar. 30, 2005; "A Celebration of the Life of John B. McLendon," Oct. 13, 1999, Bethany Christ Church, Cleveland, Ohio.

26. William C. Rhoden, "Too Late—Fall Back, Baby," *New York Times,* Feb. 26, 1991.

27. George, *Elevating the Game,* 89, 90.

28. John McLendon, interview, Mar. 13, 1988.

29. Lewis and Thomas, *Will to Win,* 220, 221.

30. David, "Gospel," 10.

31. Lewis and Thomas, *Will to Win,* 214.

32. Ed Garich, "Spivey Rocks Eastern: Tennessee State Is Title Foe," *Kansas City Star,* Mar. 16, 1957.

33. Marv Harshman, interview with the author, Oct. 15, 2005; McLendon, qtd. in John Steen, "A&I's Field Goal Mark in 35 Games: A Sizzling 52 Percent," *Nashville Banner,* Mar. 19, 1957.

34. Ed Garich, "Tennessee State Wins," *Kansas City Star,* Mar. 17, 1957.

35. Lewis and Thomas, *Will to Win,* 214.

36. Steen, "A&I's Field Goal Mark."

37. Hamilton, interview, Feb. 12, 2005; Nurlin Tarrant, interview with the author, Mar. 15, 2005; Barnhill, interview, Mar. 15, 2005; Ed Miller, "Another All-Black Team"; John McLendon, interview, Mar. 13, 1988.

38. Barnhill, interview, Mar. 15, 2005; Joe Buckhalter, interview with the author, Mar. 14, 2005.

39. James Satterwhite, interview with the author, Mar. 14, 2005; Tarrant, interview, Mar. 15, 2005; John McLendon, interview, Mar. 13, 1988.

40. Barnett, interview, Mar. 30, 2005; John McLendon, interview, Mar. 13, 1988.

41. Steen, "A&I's Field Goal Mark"; John McLendon, interview, Mar. 13, 1988; David, "Gospel," 10.

42. Mack Greene, *National Athletic Steering Committee Newsletter* 7, June 6, 1957, 3, 4, NASC files.

43. Nunn, Jacox, and Jackson, qtd. in John B. McLendon, "Black College Basketball," 12.

44. "Tennessee State Tigers Win NAIA Championship," *Kansas City Call,* Mar. 22, 1957; John I. Johnson, "A Great Coach, Period," *Kansas City Call,* Mar. 22, 1957.

45. Johnson, "Great Coach, Period."

46. Duer, interview, Apr. 4, 1980; Duer, qtd. in John B. McLendon, "Black College Basketball," 12.

47. Hudson, "Basketball's Quiet Ambassador," 5.

48. John B. McLendon, "Black College Basketball," 11; John McLendon, interview, Mar. 13, 1988.

49. Henry Carlton, interview with the author, Mar. 16, 2006; John B. McLendon, "Two in the Corner."

50. James C. Brown, "Sport-O-Rama," *Kansas City Call*, Mar. 21, 1958.

51. Earl S. Clanton III, "NAIA Champs Greeted Hilariously on Return Home," *Kansas City Call*, Mar. 28, 1958.

52. John B. McLendon, "Coaching to Win," 2.

53. John B. McLendon, "Coaching to Win," 3.

54. Lewis and Thomas, *Will to Win*, 221.

55. Lewis and Thomas, *Will to Win*, 222.

56. Marion E. Jackson, *Souvenir Program of the 1958 Georgia Invitational Tournament*, John B. McLendon Collection, Spencer Library.

57. Barnett, interview, Mar. 30, 2005.

58. Bill Richardson, "A&I in Again," *Kansas City Star*, Mar. 15, 1959.

59. "Blazing Finish Gives A&I Unprecedented Third Title," *Tennessean*, Mar. 15, 1959; David, "Gospel," 9.

60. Marty Blake, interview with the author, Oct. 5, 2005.

61. Richardson, "Pipeline for Talent."

62. John McLendon, interview, Mar. 14, 1988; Packer and Lazenby, *Golden Game*, 240; Richardson, "A&I in Again"; "Tennessee A&I Caps Third NAIA Championship," *Kansas City Call*, Mar. 20, 1959; Mal Mallete, "Gaines Says Tennessee State on Par with Top Powers," *Winston-Salem Journal and Sentinel*, Mar. 20, 1959.

63. John McLendon, interview, Mar. 14, 1988; John McLendon, "Tales of the Hardwood," 13.

64. Tarrant, interview, Mar. 15, 2005; Ed Miller, "Another All-Black Team."

65. Cal Jacox, "The Amazing Mr. McLendon," *Norfolk Journal and Guide*, Mar. 20, 1959.

66. Bill Nunn, "Give Negro College Teams a Chance to Participate with the Best and We'll Beat the Best," *Pittsburgh Courier*, Mar. 21, 1959.

67. "Tennessee Governor Wires Congrats to Tennessee A&I," *Kansas City Call*, Mar. 20, 1959.

68. John McLendon, interview, Mar. 14, 1988; Wolff, *Big Game, Small World*, 143.

69. A. O. Duer to C. E. McBride, Jan. 19, 1956, Feb. 18, 1956, both NAIA files; John R. M. Wilson, *History of the National Association of Intercollegiate Athletics*, 44, 45. For a perceptive analysis of the dispute, see Ernest Mehl, "Sporting Comment," *Kansas City Star*, Jan. 17, 1956. In Mar. 1957, the North Carolina A&T Aggies, led by Cal Irwin, played as a first-time black-college entrant in the newly formed NCAA College Division Tournament (now NCAA Division 2). A decade later, another black college, Winston-Salem State University, coached by Clarence Gaines and led by Earl "the Pearl" Monroe, captured the NCAA College Division Championship. In 1974, the University of Maryland, Eastern Shore, coached by William Bates, became the first black college to receive an invitation to the National Invitational Tournament (NIT) in New York City. Six years later, Alcorn State University, coached by Dave Whitney, became the first historically black college to participate in the NCAA Division 1 Championship Basketball Tournament.

70. *National Athletic Steering Committee Newsletter* 6, Mar. 3, 1956, 1–17, 7, Sept. 11, 1956, 1–16; Greene, interview, May 23, 1980; John R. M. Wilson, *History of the National Association of Intercollegiate Athletics*, 48.

71. John McLendon, interview, Mar. 14, 1988; David, "Gospel," 8.

72. John McLendon, interview, Mar. 14, 1988. Several decades later, Tennessee

State University joined the NCAA Division 1 Ohio Valley Conference, and in Mar. 1993, the Tigers captured the conference crown, thus earning a berth in the NCAA Championship Basketball Tournament. McLendon was too busy with his duties at Cleveland State to attend this historic game, but he said, "I'd love to be there for the tipoff. I just wish it would have happened earlier." See William C. Rhoden, "Many Miles, and Finally a Finish Line," *New York Times,* Mar. 16, 1993.

73. "TSU's 1957–59 NAIA Champions Salute Coach John B. McLendon Jr.," Bill Bradley, U.S. Senator, to John McLendon, Oct. 16, 1984, McLendon Collection, Cleveland Heights.

CHAPTER 6
Cleveland Pipers

1. Clowser, "McLendon's Pipers."
2. Mike Cleary, interview with the author, Apr. 14, 2004; Chuck Heaton, "McLendon Is Pipers Coach," *Cleveland Plain Dealer,* June 30, 1959.
3. John McLendon, interview with the author, Mar. 13, 1989; John McLendon, "Tales of the Hardwood," 14; Ron Thomas, *They Cleared the Lane,* 167; George Dunmore, "McLendon Aims for 60 Olympics with Cage Team," *Pittsburgh Courier,* July 10, 1959.
4. Clowser, "McLendon's Pipers."
5. Chuck Heaton, "Piper Stars Will 'Run and Shoot'" *Cleveland Plain Dealer,* Apr. 4, 1959.
6. Chuck Heaton, "Truckers Thrashed by Pipers," *Cleveland Plain Dealer,* Apr. 6, 1959; John McLendon, interview, Mar. 13, 1989; Marion E. Jackson, "Sports of the World," *Atlanta Daily World,* Apr. 6, 1959.
7. Cleary, interview, Apr. 14, 2004; Matthews, "Coach John McLendon Jr.," 7.
8. Ron Thomas, *They Cleared the Lane,* 168, 169; Jack Adams, interview with the author, Aug. 29, 2005.
9. Ben Flieger, "McLendon Court Gentleman—He Lets His Record Speak," *Cleveland Press,* Feb. 1, 1961.
10. John McLendon, interview, Mar. 13, 1989; John McLendon, "Tales of the Hardwood," 14.
11. John McLendon, interview, Mar. 13, 1989; John McLendon, "Tales of the Hardwood, 14.
12. Flieger, "McLendon Court Gentleman."
13. John McLendon, interview, Mar. 13, 1989; Ron Thomas, *They Cleared the Lane,* 168; Joe Wise, interview with the author, Aug. 3, 2005.
14. Chuck Heaton, "Pipers Upset Akron, 104–96," *Cleveland Plain Dealer,* Dec. 5, 1959.
15. Chuck Heaton, "Pipers Lose First Game to New York, 110–107," *Cleveland Plain Dealer,* Dec. 22, 1959.
16. Chuck Heaton, "Pipers Are Toppled by Cats, 84–82," *Cleveland Plain Dealer,* Mar. 25, 1960.
17. Clowser, "McLendon's Pipers."
18. Chuck Heaton, "NIBL Okays Cleveland's New Entry," *Cleveland Plain Dealer,* Mar. 27, 1960.

19. Chuck Heaton, "McLendon Free to Look for Job," *Cleveland Plain Dealer,* Apr. 8, 1960.

20. Browning, qtd. in Chuck Heaton, "McLendon Stays as Pipers' Coach," *Cleveland Plain Dealer,* Apr. 22, 1960.

21. Heaton, "McLendon Stays."

22. Charles L. Sanders, "McLendon Gives Terrific Talk," *Cleveland Call & Post,* Apr. 25, 1960.

23. Berea Breezer, "Cheer for a Coach," McLendon Collection, Spencer Library.

24. Don Lightner, "Pipers Trip Olympians 101–96 in Overtime Thriller," *Canton Repository,* Aug. 7, 1960; John McLendon, interview, Mar. 13, 1989.

25. "U.S. Olympic Cagers Show Here Tonight," *Morgantown Post,* Aug. 10, 1960.

26. Marion E. Jackson, "Sports of the World."

27. Chuck Heaton, "Improved Pipers Set to Go," *Cleveland Plain Dealer,* Nov. 24, 1960; poem sent to McLendon by Vicki P., McLendon Collection, Spencer Library.

28. Chuck Heaton, "Pipers Rip 66ers in Opener, 124–96," *Cleveland Plain Dealer,* Dec. 1, 1961; Jack Clowser, "Pipers Basketball Close to Pro's Best," *Cleveland Press,* Jan. 12, 1961.

29. Chuck Heaton, "Russia-Bound Pipers First Ohio Team to Win AAU," *Cleveland Plain Dealer,* Mar. 27, 1961.

30. Cleary, interview, Apr. 14, 2004.

31. John McLendon, interview with the author, Mar. 14, 1989; John McLendon, "Tales of the Hardwood," 14.

32. John McLendon, interview, Mar. 14, 1989; William J. Briordy, "Lucas Says U.S. All-Star Five Will Be Sharp for Soviet Tour," *New York Times,* Apr. 7, 1961.

33. Jack Clowser, "McLendon Perfect to Lead Russian Tour," *Cleveland Press,* Apr. 19, 1961.

34. John McLendon, "AAU Basketball Team Was Eager and Excited over Russian Tour," *Atlanta Daily World,* Apr. 22, 1961.

35. Marion E. Jackson, "The Moscow Basketball Story," *Atlanta Daily World,* May 6, 1961.

36. John McLendon, "AAU Basketball Team."

37. "McLendon in Russia," *Cleveland Press,* May 2, 1961.

38. John B. McLendon, *Fast Break Basketball,* 8.

39. Adams, interview, Aug. 29, 2005; John McLendon, interview, Mar. 14, 1989; John McLendon, "Tales of the Hardwood," 14.

40. Chuck Heaton, "McLendon Returns with Russian Challenge for '64 Olympic Title," *Cleveland Plain Dealer,* May 11, 1961; John McLendon, interview, Mar. 14, 1989.

41. Heaton, "McLendon Returns."

42. *1961–62 Cleveland Pipers Yearbook;* John McLendon, interview, Mar. 14, 1989.

43. Chuck Heaton, "McLendon Signs 2-Year Contract to Coach Pipers," *Cleveland Plain Dealer,* May 16, 1961. William "Pop" Gates was the first African American professional coach, with the National Basketball League's 1948–49 Dayton Rens, but his players were his teammates from the all-black New York Rens.

44. Heaton, "McLendon Signs"; Ben Flieger, "McLendon Leads Pipers to Pros," *Cleveland Press,* May 17, 1961.

45. Jack Clowser, "McLendon First Negro in Pro League," *Cleveland Press,* May 16, 1961.

46. Cleary, interview, Apr. 14, 2004.

47. Cleary, interview, Apr. 14, 2004; Golenbock, *Wild, High, and Tight,* 146, 147.

48. John McLendon, interview, Mar. 14, 1989; John McLendon, "Tales of the Hardwood," 14.

49. Ira Berkow, "Steinbrenner 'Tricks' Are a Familiar Story for First Black Coach," *New York Times,* July 8, 1987.

50. Jack Clowser, "New Piper Setup Still Not Answer," *Cleveland Press,* Feb. 2, 1962; John McLendon, interview, Mar. 14, 1989.

51. Ron Thomas, *They Cleared the Lane,* 169; John McLendon, interview, Mar. 14, 1989.

52. Jack Clowser, "Trouble at Top Endangering Pipers," *Cleveland Press,* Dec. 27, 1961.

53. Berkow, "Steinbrenner 'Tricks'"; Golenbock, *Wild, High, and Tight,* 145, 146; Adams, interview, Aug. 29, 2005.

54. Fritz Kreisler, "Herd Must Stop Pipers' Speed in Big Series," *Kansas City Star,* Jan. 12, 1962.

55. Fritz Kreisler, "Hot Herd Thunders In," *Kansas City Times,* Jan. 13, 1962.

56. Fritz Kreisler, "Pipers Chop Up Steers," *Kansas City Star,* Jan. 14, 1962.

57. Chuck Heaton, "Pipers Fall in Title Game," *Cleveland Plain Dealer,* Jan. 15, 1962.

58. Golenbock," *Wild, High, and Tight,* 148; John McLendon, interview, Mar. 14, 1989.

59. Bob Sudyk, "Pipers Near Revolt over Late Pay," *Cleveland Press,* Jan. 16, 1962.

60. Wayne Coffey, "The Legend of King George," *New York Daily News,* June 21, 2005; Bob Sudyk, "The Birthday Boss Turning 75 on the Fourth: Still Driven, but Minus the Fireworks," *Hartford Courant,* July 3, 2005; Golenbock, *Wild, High, and Tight,* 148.

61. Bob August, "McLendon Resigns in Clash with Piper Prexy: A Statement . . . and a Charge of Coercion," *Cleveland Press,* Jan. 29, 1962; John McLendon, interview, Mar. 14, 1989.

62. August, "McLendon Resigns"; John McLendon, interview, Mar. 14, 1989.

63. August, "McLendon Resigns"; Chuck Heaton, "McLendon Stays as Piper Coach; Adams Is Traded," *Cleveland Plain Dealer,* Jan. 30, 1962.

64. Chuck Heaton, "Sharman, Ex-Celt, New Piper Coach," *Cleveland Plain Dealer,* Jan. 31, 1962; John McLendon, interview, Mar. 14, 1989.

65. Adams, interview, Aug. 29, 2005.

66. Jack Clowser, "New Piper Setup Still Not Answer," *Cleveland Press,* Feb. 2, 1962; Frank K. Gibbons, "Pipers' Boss Put Self on Hot Seat," *Cleveland Press,* Jan. 29, 1962.

67. John McLendon, interview, Mar. 14, 1989; Golenbock, *Wild, High, and Tight,* 150.

68. Golenbock, *Wild, High, and Tight,* 150; Clowser, "New Piper Setup."

69. Cleary, interview, Apr. 14, 2004; John McLendon, interview, Mar. 14, 1989; Golenbock, *Wild, High, and Tight,* 150.

70. Schaap, *Steinbrenner,* 75; Neil Amdur, "John McLendon, 84, Strategist in College and Pro Basketball," *New York Times,* Oct. 9, 1999.

CHAPTER 7
Back to the College Game

1. John McLendon, interview with the author, Mar. 15, 1989; A. O. Duer to John McLendon, Feb. 14, 1962, NAIA files.

2. John R. M. Wilson, *History of the National Association of Intercollegiate Athletics,* 61.

3. John McLendon, interview, Mar. 15, 1989.

4. David Barnes, interview with the author, Aug. 3, 2005.

5. Fritz Kreisler, "Hornets Snuff Last-Half Bid: Defeat Snips John McLendon's Streak," *Kansas City Times,* Mar. 12, 1964.

6. Barnes, interview, Aug. 3, 2005.

7. Fred Whitted, "Coach Mac: The Little Giant," *Charlotte Post and Triangle Tribune,* special ed., Feb. 6, 2005, 9.

8. Charles Scott, interview with the author, Oct. 11, 2005.

9. John R. M. Wilson, *History of the National Association of Intercollegiate Athletics,* 61.

10. John R. M. Wilson, *History of the National Association of Intercollegiate Athletics,* 62.

11. Nicholas Bodis to Dr. Carl M. Hill, *NAIA News* (Spring 1963), NAIA files.

12. John McLendon, "The U.S. Will Become 2d Class in Basketball, Unless," *Cleveland Plain Dealer,* July 2, 1967.

13. "Veteran McLendon Pilots CSU Cagers," *Cleveland Press,* June 19, 1966.

14. Phil Hartman, "Cleveland State Names John McLendon Head Coach," *Cleveland Plain Dealer,* June 18, 1966; John McLendon, interview, Mar. 15, 1989.

15. Hartman, "Cleveland State Names John McLendon"; Merle Levin, interview with the author, Nov. 15, 2005; Ron Roberts, "CSU Has 'Big Time' Basketball Dreams," *Cleveland Press,* Feb. 20, 1967.

16. Bill Nichols, "McLendon's Challenge: A Winner at CSU," *Cleveland Plain Dealer,* Oct. 18, 1966; Bob August, "Bad Night, Good Start for McLendon Era," *Cleveland Press,* Dec. 2, 1966; John McLendon, interview, Mar. 15, 1989.

17. Bill Nichols, "McLendon Starts on 2d 500," *Cleveland Plain Dealer,* Jan. 12, 1967.

18. "CSU Pulls Upset over Central State," *Cleveland Plain Dealer,* Jan. 16, 1969.

19. Sam Thomas, interview with the author, Oct. 20, 2005; Jim Rodriquez, interview with the author, Oct. 17, 2005.

20. Rodriquez, interview, Oct. 17, 2005.

21. Levin, interview, Nov. 15, 2005.

22. Dennis Lustig, "Dr. J. Has Visited Cleveland Before," *Cleveland Plain Dealer,* Nov. 26, 1976; John McLendon, interview, Mar. 15, 1989.

23. Bob August, "The Soiled Side of College Recruiting," *Cleveland Press,* May 16, 1969. Seventeen years after McLendon departed as coach of Cleveland State University, the Vikings realized their dreams, making it all the way to the "Sweet 16" of the NCAA Division 1 Championship Basketball Tournament. See "Winningest Coaches," *Converse Basketball Yearbook,* 1969, 59.

24. Zang, *SportsWars.*

25. Dave Zirin, "The 1968 Olympics Raises the Bar," July 18, 2005 (http://www.haymarketbooks.org/1968.shtml).

26. Bill Nichols, "McLendon Rebukes Olympic Boycott Groups," *Cleveland Plain Dealer,* Aug. 27, 1968.

27. John McLendon, interview, Mar. 15, 1989.

28. Joanna McLendon, interview with the author, Apr. 27, 2005.

29. Joanna McLendon, interview, Apr. 27, 2005.

CHAPTER 8
The First Black Coach in the ABA

1. John McLendon, interview with the author, Mar. 12, 1990; August, "Soiled Side."

2. Skiff, "How John McLendon Came," 23; Ralph Moore, "Black Coach—Vet McLendon at Rockets' Helm," *Sporting News,* June 14, 1969, 55.

3. John McLendon, interview, Mar. 12, 1990; Ralph Moore, "McLendon Off the Hook in 'Heist,'" *Denver Post,* Aug. 6, 1969.

4. Skiff, "How John McLendon Came," 25.

5. Spencer Haywood, interview with the author, Aug. 20, 2005; Skiff, "How John McLendon Came," 25, 26.

6. Irv Moss, "Rockets Sign Olympic Star Haywood," *Denver Post,* Aug. 24, 1969.

7. Moss, "Rockets Sign Olympic Star."

8. Skiff, "How John McLendon Came," 27.

9. Haywood, interview, Aug. 20, 2005; Ron Thomas, *They Cleared the Lane,* 171, 172.

10. Matthews, "Coach John B. McLendon Jr.," 9.

11. Matthews, "Coach John B. McLendon Jr.," 9; Barnhill, interview, Mar. 15, 2005; Haywood, interview, Aug. 20, 2005; Lonnie Lynn, interview with the author, Aug. 20, 2005; Don Ringsby, interview with the author, Aug. 10, 2006.

12. John McLendon, interview, Mar. 12, 1990.

13. Lynn, interview, Aug. 20, 2005; Matthews, "Coach John B. McLendon Jr.," 9.

14. Matthews, "Coach John B. McLendon Jr.," 10; Fred Pietila, "Denver Rockets Fire Coach John McLendon," *Denver Rocky Mountain News,* Dec. 10, 1969. In a recent interview, Ringsby stated that with the addition of All-American Haywood, the Rockets ownership was under tremendous pressure to win. When McLendon's team failed to do so, he had no choice but to fire the coach. He told me how painful this was, for "McLendon was a charming, wonderful man and a fine gentleman. There is no one I respected more" (Ringsby, interview, Aug. 10, 2006).

15. John McLendon, interview, Mar. 12, 1990; Ralph Moore, "Secret Timetable Surprised Coach," *Denver Post,* Dec. 10, 1969.

16. Moore, "Secret Timetable Surprised Coach."

17. Charlie Dreux, "Players Express Mixed Emotions," *Denver Rocky Mountain News,* Dec. 10, 1969; Matthews, "Coach John B. McLendon Jr.," 10.

18. Haywood, interview, Aug. 20, 2005; Lynn, interview, Aug. 20, 2005.

19. Chet Nelson, "Too Nice a Guy," *Denver Rocky Mountain News,* Dec. 10, 1969.

20. John McLendon, interview, Mar. 12, 1990; Joanna McLendon, interview, Apr. 27, 2005; Burt Graeff, "Firing Not the End," *Cleveland Press,* Dec. 12, 1969.

21. Burt Graeff, "John McLendon Seeks Post with City's New NBA Team," *Cleveland Press,* Feb. 7, 1970; Ron Thomas, *They Cleared the Lane,* 164.

22. David, "Gospel," 11.

CHAPTER 9
National and International Ambassador of Basketball

1. John McLendon, interview with the author, Mar. 13, 1990.

2. Grady Lewis, interview with the author, July 15, 2005.

3. Roger Morningstar, interview with the author, May 15, 2005; Howie Evans, "Record-Setting Coach McLendon Passes Away," *Cleveland Call & Post*, Oct. 14–20, 1999.

4. Matthews, "Coach John McLendon Jr.," 11; John McLendon, interview, Mar. 13, 1990.

5. Gregory Huskisson, "Athletics Is a Vehicle to Scholastic Goals, McLendon Tells Players," *Atlanta Daily World*, Jan. 29, 1980.

6. John McLendon, interview, Mar. 13, 1990; Jack Beary, "Basketball Great Tours China," *Footwear News*, Nov. 24, 1980.

7. Marv Harshman, interview, Oct. 15, 2005.

8. Collie Nicholson, "African Basketball On Brink of a New Era," *Black College Basketball Yearbook, 1980*, 9, 10.

9. Ken Denzel, interview with the author, July 30, 2005. Dorothy Gaters, interview with the author, July 2, 2005.

10. Norm Sonju, interview with the author, Aug. 20, 2005.

11. Howie Evans, "Basketball Hall of Fame Ignoring Black Coaches," *New York Amsterdam News*, Mar. 12, 1977.

12. Lee Williams to John McLendon, Jan. 26, 1979. McLendon was first nominated for the Hall of Fame by Roy D. Moore, chairman of the Department of Health, Physical Education, and Recreation at Tennessee State University on May 8, 1970. Subsequent letters for his nomination were submitted by Richard Mack, basketball coach at Tennessee State; Clarence Gaines, basketball coach at Winston-Salem State University; Charles D. Henry, assistant commissioner of the Big Ten Conference; Leroy T. Walker, track and field coach at North Carolina Central University; A. O. Duer, executive secretary of the NAIA; and, as a group, the National Athletic Steering Committee. See the John B. McLendon Collection, Naismith Memorial Basketball Hall of Fame; McLendon Collection, Spencer Library; John McLendon, interview, Mar. 13, 1990.

13. Gerry Finn, "Spiritual Reunion at 'Hall,'" *Springfield Union*, May 1, 1979.

14. Finn, "Spiritual Reunion at 'Hall.'"

15. Bill Jauss, "Winding Road to Hall Ends for Black Coach," *Chicago Tribune*, Apr. 30, 1979.

16. Howie Evans, "Wilt Chamberlain . . . John McLendon: All Time Greats Inducted as Hall of Famers," *New York Amsterdam News*, May 12, 1979; Lee Williams to John McLendon, May 4, 1979. See the McLendon Collection, Spencer Library.

17. Evans, "Record-Setting Coach"; Howie Evans, interview with the author, Mar. 15, 2006.

18. John McLendon to Joe O'Brien, Nov. 18, 1996, McLendon Collection, Naismith Hall of Fame. Most likely, O'Brien chose to respond to McLendon with a telephone call since no letter of reply has been found.

19. Denzel, interview, July 30, 2005; Jones, interview, May 31, 2005; LeRoy Walker, interview, May 18, 2005.

20. Jones, interview, May 31, 2005.

21. *League of His Own.*

22. Lacy J. Banks, "Hardcourt Tributes: McLendon Made Huge Contributions," *Chicago Sun-Times,* Oct. 12, 1999.

23. Taylor Bell, "Basketball Still Feels McLendon's Touch," *Chicago Sun-Times,* Oct. 17, 1999.

24. Gaters, interview, July 2, 2005; Tina A. Kouris, "Gater's Milestone Truly Amazing," *Chicago Sun-Times,* Dec. 10, 2004.

25. Luther Bedford, "Tribute to Coach McLendon," Chicago Public League Basketball Coaches Association, Apr. 5, 1991.

26. Denzel, interview, July 30, 2005; Lacy J. Banks, "Hardcourt Tributes."

27. Gaines, interview, Mar. 15, 1987; John McLendon, interview, Mar. 12, 1988; Querida Banks, interview, Oct. 10, 2004.

28. John McLendon, "Code of Conduct for Coaches before the Players and Fans," McLendon Collection, Cleveland Heights; John McLendon, interview, Mar. 13, 1990.

29. Katz and McLendon, *Breaking Through.*

CHAPTER 10
Return to Cleveland State

1. John McLendon, interview with the author, Mar. 14, 1990.

2. "History of Sports and the Role of Minorities" (syllabus).

3. Merle Levin, "McLendon Named Special Assistant to Athletic Director at Cleveland State University," press release, Oct. 8, 1991, McLendon Collection, Cleveland Heights.

4. "NACDA Announces the John McLendon Minority Postgraduate Scholarship Awards," *Athletics Administration,* Dec. 1998, 16.

5. Alice Khol, interview with the author, Apr. 30, 2005.

6. "The Father of Black Basketball," *CIAA Tournament Program,* 2005.

7. Gene Beck, "A Special Tribute to a Living Legend—John B. McLendon," Tennessee Secondary School Athletic Association, 1992, McLendon Collection, Cleveland Heights.

8. Isaacs, *All the Moves,* 164; Rhoden, "Many Miles."

9. *Inside the NBA; A League of His Own;* Cleary, interview, Apr. 14, 2004.

10. Blake, interview, Oct. 5, 2005.

11. See the appendix for the entire poem.

12. Rev. Robin Hedgeman, interview with the author, Mar. 20, 2006; Sam Thomas, interview, Oct. 20, 2005.

13. Leslie Scanlon, "Coach's Leadership Was Rooted in His Faith," *Louisville Courier-Journal,* Oct. 16, 1999.

14. Shaw, "Pivotman," 14; John McLendon, interview, Mar. 14, 1990.

15. Packer and Lazenby, *Golden Game,* 241; Blair Kerkhoff, "A Groundbreaker: McLendon Was a Pioneer in Basketball, Racial Relations," *Kansas City Star,* Oct. 10, 1999; John McLendon, interview, Mar. 14, 1990.

16. "NACDA Announces," 22; Mary Schmitt, "Basketball Coach Blazed Trails for Blacks," *Kansas City Star,* Mar. 15, 1995; Hudson, "Basketball's Quiet Ambassador."

17. Hudson, "Basketball's Quiet Ambassador."

18. Denzel, interview, July 30, 2005.

19. MacGregor, "Birth of Basketball," 5; Debora Dekok and Theresa Fritz, "John McLendon Embodied All that James Naismith Stood For," *Almonte Gazette,* Oct. 13, 1999.

20. Rick Dean, "McLendon an Overlooked Basketball Pioneer," *Topeka Capital-Journal,* Feb. 7, 1998.

21. John McLendon, interview, Mar. 14, 1990; Gaines, interview, Mar. 15, 1987; Barnett, interview, Mar. 30, 2005; Amdur, "John McLendon."

22. Denzel, interview, July 30, 2005; Joanna McLendon, interview, Apr. 27, 2005.

23. "A Celebration of the Life of John B. McLendon"; Barnhill, interview, Mar. 15, 2005; Deutsch, "Remembering Johnny Mac."

24. "In Memory of John McLendon," press release, Oct. 21, 1999, National Association of Collegiate Directors of Athletics (NACDA hereafter) files; Billy Packer, interview with the author, Apr. 20, 2005.

25. Anthony Coleman, "Black Coaches Laud McLendon," *Tennessean,* Oct. 9, 1999.

26. Other recipients of the Coach Mac Award include Leo Rautins, Al Quance, Jay Triano, Bernie Offstein, and Jack Donohue. Thomas, qtd. in Lacy J. Banks, "Hardcourt Tributes."

27. Lacy J. Banks, "Hardcourt Tributes"; Lut Williams, "Coach John McLendon Ran the Distance"; John McLendon to HBCU Coaches and Athletic Directors, Oct. 15, 1990, McLendon Collection, Cleveland Heights; Fred Whitted, *A View from the Shadow: For the Good of the Game—Part 2,* Black Athlete Sports Network, Feb. 15, 2005 (http://www.blackathlete.net/artman/publish/article_0419.shtml).

28. Richard M. Perry, "John McLendon, Basketball Coach, Innovator, Dies," *Cleveland Plain Dealer,* Oct. 9, 1999.

29. Ron Chimelis, "McLendon Broke Basketball Barrier," *Springfield Republican,* Oct. 20, 1999.

30. Stockard, "Coach John McLendon."

31. Dennis Jackson, interview with the author, Sept. 30, 2005; Chimelis, "McLendon Broke Basketball Barrier."

32. "NACDA Announces the John McLendon Minority Postgraduate Scholarship Awards," press release, Dec. 15, 1988, NACDA files.

33. Mary Schmitt Boyer, "Scholarship Will Honor Former CSU Coach McLendon," *Cleveland Plain Dealer,* Dec. 5, 1999; Wayne Embry, interview with the author, Apr. 14, 2005.

34. "NACDA Announces," 23.

35. Joe Maxse, "Tourney Series to Honor McLendon," *Cleveland Plain Dealer,* June 9, 2006.

36. Bryant, "Basketball Coach John B. McLendon," 720.

37. See, e.g., the introductions to Miller and Wiggins, *Sport and the Color Line,* and Wiggins and Miller, *Unlevel Playing Field.*

38. Richard Lapchick with Stacy Martin, "The 2005–06 Season Racial and Gender Report Card: National Basketball Association," Institute for Diversity and Ethics in Sport, Feb. 9, 2006.

39. David Leonhardt and Ford Fessenden, "Black Coaches in NBA Have Shorter Tenures," *New York Times,* Mar. 22, 2005. For a more sanguine view of the racial climate in professional basketball, see David Aldridge, "On the NBA: In Coaching Ranks, Color Now a Nonissue," *Philadelphia Inquirer,* Jan. 16, 2006.

40. Rhoden, *Forty Million Dollar Slaves,* 2, 6–8.

BIBLIOGRAPHY

Manuscript Collections

John B. McLendon Collection, Cleveland Heights, Ohio.

John B. McLendon Collection, Kenneth Spencer Research Library, University of Kansas.

John B. McLendon Collection, Naismith Memorial Basketball Hall of Fame, Springfield, Mass.

Files of the National Association of Collegiate Directors of Athletics (NACDA), Cleveland, Ohio.

Files of the National Association of Intercollegiate Athletics (NAIA), Kansas City, Mo., and Olathe, Kans.

Files of the National Athletic Steering Committee (NASC), Chicago, Ill.

Interview Subjects

Jack Adams	Mack Greene	Ian Naismith
George Altman	Ron Hamilton	Billy Packer
Querida Banks	Marv Harshman	George Parks
David Barnes	Spencer Haywood	Ethel Richards
Richard Barnett	Robin Hedgeman	Bill Richardson
John Barnhill	C. D. Henry	Don Ringsby
Margaret Black	David Hubbell	Alex Rivera
Marty Blake	Harold Hunter	Jim Rodriquez
John Brown	Dennis Jackson	James Satterwhite
Joe Buckhalter	Sam Jones	Charles Scott (Mass.)
Marland Buckner	Alice Khol	Charles Scott (N.C.)
Henry Carlton	Merle Levin	Bud Shaw
Mike Cleary	Grady Lewis	Dean Smith
William Coker	Earl Lloyd	Norm Sonju
Ken Denzel	Lonnie Lynn	Nurlin Tarrant
Roscoe Dickerson	Arthur McLendon	Sam Thomas
A. O. Duer	Joanna McLendon	Leroy Walker
Wayne Embry	John McLendon Jr.	Troy Weaver
Howie Evans	Vernon McNeal	Eugene Werts
Clarence Gaines	Richard Miller	Thornton Williams
Dorothy Gaters	Roger Morningstar	Joe Wise

Newspapers

Almonte Gazette

Atlanta Daily World

Baltimore Afro-American

Black College Sports Page

Campus Echo (North Carolina College)

Canton Repository

Carolina Times

Charlotte Post

Chicago Sun-Times

Chicago Tribune

Cleveland Call and Post

Cleveland Plain Dealer

Cleveland Press

Denver Post

Denver Rocky Mountain News

Durham Herald-Sun

Hartford Courant

Kansas City Call

Kansas City Star

Kansas City Times

Louisville Courier-Journal

Morgantown Post

Nashville Banner

New York Amsterdam News

New York Times

Norfolk Journal and Guide

Philadelphia Inquirer

Pittsburgh Courier

Raleigh News & Observer

Roanoke Times

Springfield Republican

Springfield Union

The Tennessean

Topeka Capital-Journal

Virginian-Pilot

Videography

A League of His Own: The John McLendon Story. Cleveland: Tom Sweeney
Productions, 1995.

Inside the NBA: John McLendon. TNT, 1999.

"America in Black and White: The Secret Game." *Nightline,* April 1, 1997.

Articles and Books

Asante, Molefi K., and Mark Mattson. *Historical and Cultural Atlas of African-
Americans.* New York: MacMillan, 1991.

Bryant, Jacqueline Imani. "Basketball Coach John B. McLendon, the Noble
Revolutionary of U.S. Sport." *Journal of Black Studies* 30, no. 5 (2000): 720–34.

David, Darin. "The Gospel according to John . . . McLendon." *NAIA News,*
February 1997, 8–11.

Deutsch, Robin. "Remembering Johnny Mac." Naismith Memorial Basketball Hall
of Fame, October 1999.

Ellsworth, Scott. "Jim Crow Loses: The Secret Game." *New York Times Magazine,* March 31, 1996, 19–20.

———. "The Secret Game: Defying the Color Line." *Duke University Alumni Magazine,* September–October 1996, 8–11, 40.

———. "The Secret Game of 1944." *Duke University Medical Alumni News* (Spring 1998): 6, 7.

Embry, Wayne, with Mary Schmitt Boyer. *The Inside Game: Race, Power, and Politics in the NBA.* Akron: University of Akron Press, 2004.

Gaddy, Charles. *An Olympic Journey: The Saga of an American Hero: Leroy T. Walker.* Glendale, Calif.: Griffin Publishing Group, 1998.

Gaines, Clarence E., with Clint Johnson. *They Call Me Big House.* Winston-Salem: John F. Blair, 2004.

George, Nelson. *Elevating the Game: Black Men and Basketball.* Lincoln: University of Nebraska Press, 1999.

Golenbock, Peter. *Wild, High and Tight: The Life and Death of Billy Martin.* New York: St. Martin's Press, 1994.

Govenar, Alan. *African American Frontiers: Slave Narratives and Oral Histories.* Santa Barbara: ABC Clio, 2000.

Greenbaum, Susan. *The Afro-American Community in Kansas City, Kansas: A History.* Kansas City, Kans.: n.p., 1982.

Grundy, Pamela. *Learning to Win: Sports, Education, and Social Change in Twentieth-Century North Carolina.* Chapel Hill: University of North Carolina Press, 2001.

Grundy, Pamela, and John B. McLendon Jr. "'A Position of Respect': A Basketball Coach Who Resisted Segregation." *Southern Cultures* 7 (Summer 2001): 84–91.

Hoover, Francis Lentz. "A History of the National Association of Intercollegiate Athletics." Ph.D. diss., Indiana University, 1958.

Isaacs, Neil. *All the Moves: A History of College Basketball.* Philadelphia: J. B. Lippincott Co., 1975.

Katz, Milton S. "Coach John B. McLendon Jr. and the Integration of Intercollegiate and Professional Athletics in Post World War II America." *Journal of American Culture* 13, no. 4 (1990): 35–42.

Katz, Milton S., and John B. McLendon Jr. *Breaking Through: The NAIA and the Integration of Collegiate Athletics in Post–World War II America.* Downers Grove, IL: Maxaid, 1988.

Ladd, Tony, and James A. Mathisen. *Muscular Christianity: Evangelical Protestants and the Development of American Sport.* Grand Rapids: Baker Books, 1999.

Lazenby, Roland. "Breaking Down the Walls: Little-Known John McLendon Did Much More Than Revolutionize the Game of Basketball." *Black History Month Commemorative Issue,* 2001, 24–31.

———. "A Living Legend." *CIAA Tournament Bulletin,* n.d.

Lewis, Dwight, and Susan Thomas. *A Will to Win.* Mt. Juliet, Tenn.: Cumberland Press, 1983.

MacGregor, Roy. "The Birth of Basketball." *Legion Magazine,* May–June 1997, 5.

Martin, Charles M. "Jim Crow in the Gymnasium: The Integration of College Basketball in the American South." In *Sport and the Color Line: Black Athletes and Race Relations in Twentieth-Century America,* ed. Patrick B. Miller and David K. Wiggins, 233–50. New York: Routledge, 2003.

McLendon, John B. "Black College Basketball: A Historical Chronology, 1891–1978." *Black College Basketball Yearbook,* 1979, 6–16.

———. "Coaching to Win." *Journal of Health–Physical Education–Recreation* (October 1958): 1–3.

———. *Fast Break Basketball: Fine Points and Fundamentals.* West Nyack, N.Y.: Parker, 1965.

———. *The Fast Break Game.* Stone Park, Ill.: Offset Graphics, 1974.

———. *The First CIAA Championship Basketball Tournament.* Downers Grove, IL: Maxaid, 1988.

———. *McBasket: A Three on Three Full Court Basketball Game.* Downers Grove, IL: Maxaid, 1987.

———. "'Two in the Corner': An Offense for Freezing the Ball." *Converse Basketball Yearbook,* 1957.

Miller, Patrick B., and David K. Wiggins, eds. *Sport and the Color Line: Black Athletes and Race Relations in Twentieth-Century America.* New York: Routledge, 2003.

Moore, Ralph. "Black Coach—Vet McLendon at Rockets' Helm." *Sporting News,* June 14, 1969, 55.

Nicholson, Collie. "African Basketball on Brink of a New Era." *Black College Basketball Yearbook,* 1980, 9–23.

Packer, Billy, and Roland Lazenby. *The Golden Game.* Springfield, Mass.: Naismith Memorial Basketball Hall of Fame, 1991.

Putney, Clifford. *Muscular Christianity: Manhood and Sports in Protestant America, 1880–1920.* Cambridge: Harvard University Press, 2000.

Rhoden, William C. "The Father of Black Basketball." *Code,* February 2000, 42, 44–45.

———. *Forty Million Dollar Slaves: The Rise, Fall, and Redemption of the Black Athlete.* New York: Crown, 2006.

Schaap, Dick. *Steinbrenner.* New York: G. P. Putnam's Sons. 1982.

Shaw, Bud. "The Pivotman." *Cleveland Plain Dealer Sunday Magazine,* May 11, 1997, 10–14.

Skiff, Carl. "How John McLendon Came to Denver." *Denver Post Empire Magazine,* October 26, 1969, 21–27.

———. "John McLendon's Long Road to the Rockets." *Denver Post Empire Magazine,* October 19, 1969, 7–11.

Smith, Dean. *A Coach's Life.* New York: Random House, 1999.

Thomas, Ron. *They Cleared the Lane: The NBA's Black Pioneers.* Lincoln: University of Nebraska Press, 2002.

Walker, Mike. "Quietly Blazing Trails." *Kansas Alumni Magazine* (Fall 1979): 13–16.

Webb, Bernice Larson. *Basketball Man: James Naismith.* Lawrence: University of Kansas Press, 1994.

Wiggins, David K., and Patrick B. Miller. *The Unlevel Playing Field: A Documentary History of the African American Experience in Sport.* Urbana: University of Illinois Press, 2005.

Wilson, John R. M. *The History of the National Association of Intercollegiate Athletics.* Monterey: Coaches Choice, 2005.

Wolff, Alexander. *Big Game, Small World: A Basketball Adventure.* New York: Warner Books, 2002.

Zang, David. *SportsWars: Athletes in the Age of Aquarius.* Fayetteville: University of Arkansas Press, 2001.

INDEX

Index

Index

MILTON S. KATZ is professor of American studies, School of Liberal Arts, Kansas City Art Institute. He is the author of *Ban the Bomb: A History of SANE, the Committee for a Sane Nuclear Policy* and over two dozen book chapters, articles, and essays on peace and social justice movements in contemporary American history. Katz met John McLendon in 1980 and became close friends with him after spending untold hours interviewing the legendary Coach Mac and researching his life.

BILLY PACKER, a basketball analyst for CBS, has been a color commentator for college basketball since 1974. He is the author of a number of books, most recently, *Why We Win*.

IAN NAISMITH is the grandson of the inventor of basketball, Dr. James A. Naismith. He is the founder and director of the Naismith International Basketball Foundation, headquartered in Chicago.